Corporate Cultures

The Rites and Rituals of Corporate Life

Terrence E. Deal and Allen A. Kennedy

Corporate Cultures

The Rites and Rituals of Corporate Life

Terrence E. Deal and Allan A. Kennedy

ADDISON-WESLEY PUBLISHING COMPANY, INC.
Reading, Massachusetts • Menlo Park, California • Don Mills, Ontario
Wokingham, England • Amsterdam • Sydney • Singapore • Tokyo
Mexico City • Bogotá • Santiago • San Juan

To Tom Peters, Willie Nelson, and others like them.

Library of Congress Cataloging in Publication Data

Deal, Terrence E.
  Corporate cultures.

  Bibliography: p.
  Includes index.
  1. Organization.   2. Culture.   3. Corporations.
I. Kennedy, Allan A.   II. Title.
HD38.D397   1982   658.4   82-71753
ISBN 0-201-10277-3   AACR2
ISBN 0-201-10287-0 (pbk.)

Cover design by Marshall Henrichs

FGHIJ-DO-85

Sixth Printing, May 1985

Acknowledgements

Two greenhorn writers weaned on memos, academic treatises, and consulting reports need all the editorial assistance they can get. Eliza Collins of the *Harvard Business Review* introduced us to Addison-Wesley and provided material, suggestions, and spirit as the book moved along. Roland Mann of McKinsey got us set on the right track and was there when we needed him. We got help from Doug Dickson of the *Harvard Business Review* and a lot from our editor Harriet Rubin of Addison-Wesley's New York Office and from Ann Dilworth, publisher.

Tom Peters is the intellectual and spiritual godfather of this book. Tom rejoined McKinsey several years ago after having spent time in a variety of places—Palo Alto, Washington, Southeast Asia, and Candlestick Park—learning about the whys and wherefores of organizational behavior. His official stated charter when he rejoined the firm was to improve McKinsey's technology for addressing the organizational problems of its clients.

In pursuing this charter for several years, Tom wrote notes, memos, articles; traveled thousands of miles, usually under extreme time pressures; gave literally hundreds of speeches, offered thousands of ideas to any who cared, and formed some very close friendships—one of them with Allan Kennedy. We will not catalogue the specifics of Tom's influence on the book; suffice to say his influence is pervasive throughout. Without Tom's relentless pushing, encouraging, cajoling, and just plain emotional support, the ideas contained in this book would not have evolved nearly as far as we hope they have.

Along with Tom, many others at McKinsey contributed to this book. Julien Phillips, who did the original work on the ideas in the values chapter, had even more influence on the rest of the book because of his comprehension of the full scope of issues related to culture and his unfailing willingness to contribute fresh perspectives whenever asked. Next, Bob Waterman, who kept us all going through a near magical capacity for the right kind of nudge—intellectual, emotional, or managerial—at precisely the right time. For all the interference Bob has run as well as the continual input of ideas, we are grateful. Finally, and by no means definitively, there is the long list of McKinsey colleagues who have made input at one stage or another: Dave Anderson, Jim Balloun, Ron Bancroft, Steve Brandon, Dick Cavanagh, Fons Driessen, Alan Gayer, Fred Gluck, Don Gogel, Nancy Kaible, Jon Katzenbach, Peter Kraljic, Paul Krauss, Linda Levinson, Bill Meehan, David Meen, George Norsig, Bob O'Block, Hugh Parker, Bob Paulson, Bill Seelbach, and Lee Walton.

Jeannette Robinson, a recent graduate of Harvard College, was a painstaking researcher whose ability to ferret out fresh facts from old dusty volumes and keen anthropological insight were much appreciated.

Sara Roy, a graduate student at Harvard's Graduate School of Education, stalked biographies and research studies in the dusty corridors of Baker and Widener libraries. Her early efforts to bring historical accounts to our attention provided a link between our contemporary experience and the rich legacy of corporate heroes and values—old fashioned but still sound. Her wise counsel was always welcomed.

Bill Epifanio of McKinsey and Harvard College chased the most obscure facts, found many interesting stories and examples, and contributed throughout the whole experience.

Stone Wiske and Cynthia Ingols, graduate students at Harvard, made many suggestions on earlier drafts which we found very helpful.

Gloria Bronsema, Sue Lowe, and Mary Amsler provided case information which is salted throughout the manuscript.

Sharon McDade, first-year doctoral student at the Harvard Graduate School of Education and a former drama teacher, provided consultation in the area of theater and dramatics.

Chris Argyris, Jerome T. Murphy, Lee Bolman, and other colleagues at Harvard's Graduate School of Education provided insights and criticism that we always welcomed and occasionally followed. Conversations with Sara Lawrence Lightfoot, John Shlien, Dick Katz, David Cohen—all at the Harvard Graduate School of Education—stimulated ideas that undergird the book. Earlier talks with Liz Cohen, Vic Baldridge, Jim March, John Meyer, Sandy Dornbusch, Dick Scott, and Ed Bridges at Stanford started the early gravitation toward these ideas. Brooke Derr, University of Utah, was also helpful. The rich conversations and discussions in the academy stimulate many thoughts and ideas. We can see the imprints of a thousand interchanges between the covers of this book. We hope people will publicly claim what they like and silently disown what they don't. The parade of other thoughtful scholars whose ideas have influenced our own can be witnessed by skimming the bibliography.

Claudine Wilder, formerly of Prime Computer, now one of Mary Kay's field representatives, made numerous suggestions about ideas and provided first-hand material from her corporate experience.

Lee Regal, Polaroid's former director of corporate education, provided us with first-hand observations about Land and Polaroid.

Jerry Mechling—with able assistance from Gerry Brehm—did all of the original research and thinking on cultures of the future. Little did Jerry or we realize that what started out as research on the impact of technology on organizations would end up as a chapter in a book on corporate cultures.

Students who enrolled in Symbolism in Organizations for the past three years provided stimulation, ideas, and examples that have been incorporated throughout the book.

Betty Barnes, Linda Pollet, and Beverly Parker provided important secretarial and administrative support throughout.

Sandra Deal and Alison Kennedy—women with important careers of their own—put up with the agony and ecstasy that writing a book always produces in the authors. Their stinging and insightful criticism was always welcome and without their support we would never have made it to the end. We'll be repaying the debt for many years.

Finally, we are grateful to a legion of past clients, current friends, and the ghosts of corporate heroes who have taught us all we know about the real world of corporate cultures. We will not name them here; they know who they are.

Needless to say, all the fuzzy thinking, faulty logic, poor grammar, and just plain mistakes are our fault.

Conten

Part I

CULTURES

1

Strong Cultures:
The New "Old Rule"
for Business Success

S. C. Allyn, a retired chairman of the board, likes to tell a story about his company—the National Cash Register Corporation. It was August 1945, and Allyn was among the first allied civilians to enter Germany at the end of the war. He had gone to find out what had happened to an NCR factory built just before the war but promptly confiscated by the German military command and put to work on the war effort. He arrived via military plane and traveled through burned-out buildings, rubble, and utter desolation until he reached what was left of the factory. Picking his way through bricks, cement, and old timbers, Allyn came upon two NCR employees whom he hadn't seen for six years. Their clothes were torn and their faces grimy and blackened by smoke, but they were busy clearing out the rubble. As he came closer, one of the men looked up and said, "We knew you'd come!" Allyn joined them in their work and together the three men began cleaning out the debris and rebuilding the factory from the devastation of war. The company had even survived the ravages of a world war.

A few days later, as the clearing continued, Allyn and his co-workers were startled as an American tank rumbled up to the site. A grinning GI was at its helm. "Hi," he said, "I'm NCR, Omaha. Did you guys make your quota this month?" Allyn and the GI embraced each other. The war may have devastated everything around them, but NCR's hard driving, sales-oriented culture was still intact.

This story may sound unbelievable, but there are hundreds like it at NCR and every other company. Together they make up the myths and legends of American business. What do they mean? To us these stories mean that businesses are human institutions, not plush buildings, bottom lines, strategic analysis, or five-year plans. NCR was never just a factory to the three men who dug it out of the rubble. Nor was it to others like them. Rather it was a living organization. The company's real existence lay in the hearts and minds of its employees. NCR was, and still is, a corporate culture, a cohesion of values, myths, heroes, and symbols that has come to mean a great deal to the people who work there.

Culture, as *Webster's New Collegiate Dictionary* defines it, is "the integrated pattern of human behavior that includes thought, speech, action, and artifacts and depends on man's capacity for learning and transmitting knowledge to succeeding generations." Marvin Bower, for years managing director of McKinsey & Company and author of *The Will to Manage*, offered a more informal definition—he described the informal cultural elements of a business as "the way we do things around here."

Every business—in fact every organization—has a culture. Sometimes it is fragmented and difficult to read from the outside— some people are loyal to their bosses, others are loyal to the union, still others care only about their colleagues who work in the sales territories of the Northeast. If you ask employees why they work, they will answer "because we need the money." On the other hand, sometimes the culture of an organization is very strong and cohesive; everyone knows the goals of the corporation, and they are working for them. Whether weak or strong, culture has a powerful influence throughout an organization; it affects practically everything—from who gets promoted and what decisions are made, to how employees dress and what sports they play. Because of this impact, we think that culture also has a major effect on the success of the business.

Today, everyone seems to complain about the decline in American productivity. The examples of industries in trouble are numerous and depressing. Books proclaim that Japanese management practices are the solution to America's industrial malaise.

But we disagree. We don't think the answer is to mimic the Japanese. Nor do we think the solution lies with the tools of "scientific" management: MBAs' analyses, portfolio theories, cost curves, or econometric models. Instead we think the answer is as American as apple pie. American business needs to return to the original concepts and ideas that made institutions like NCR, General Electric, International Business Machines (IBM), Procter & Gamble, 3M, and others great. We need to remember that people make businesses work. And we need to relearn old lessons about how culture ties people together and gives meaning and purpose to their day-to-day lives.

The early leaders of American business such as Thomas Watson of IBM, Harley Procter of Procter & Gamble, and General Johnson of Johnson & Johnson believed that strong culture brought success. They believed that the lives and productivity of their employees were shaped by where they worked. These builders saw their role as creating an environment—in effect, a culture—in their companies in which employees could be secure and thereby do the work necessary to make the business a success. They had no magic formulas. In fact, they discovered how to shape their company's culture by trial and error. But all along the way, they paid almost fanatical attention to the culture of their companies. The lessons of these early leaders have been passed down in their own companies from generation to generation of managers; the cultures they were so careful to build and nourish have sustained their organizations through both fat and lean times. Today these corporations still have strong cultures and still are leaders in the marketplace.

We think that anyone in business can learn a lot from these examples. A major reason the Japanese have been so successful, we think, is their continuing ability to maintain a very strong and cohesive culture throughout the entire country. Not only do individual businesses have strong cultures, but the links among business, the banking industry, and the government are also cultural and also very powerful. Japan, Inc., is actually an expansion of the corporate culture idea on a national scale. Although this homogenization of values would not fit American culture on a national scale, we do think that it has been very effective for individual companies. In fact, a strong culture has almost always been the driving force behind continuing success in American business.

We came to this conclusion through our work and study—Kennedy at McKinsey & Company and Deal at Harvard's Graduate School of Education. The idea had several origins. One was at a meeting at Stanford. A group of sociologists was puzzling over the absence of relationships among variables that organizational theory said should be related. If the structure of an organization doesn't control work activities, what does it do? These questions led to new theories and views: structure and strategy may be more symbolic than substantive. The other was a McKinsey meeting. We were talking about the problems of organizations, and someone asked, "What makes for consistently outstanding company performance?" Another person offered the hypothesis that the companies that did best over the long haul were those that believed in something. The example was, "IBM means service." Others chimed in, and soon the table was full of examples:

- GE: "Progress is our most important product."

- DuPont: "Better things for better living through chemistry."

- Chubb Insurance: "Excellence in underwriting."

While the focus at that point was on slogan-like evidence of a paramount belief—which we later called a "superordinate goal"—we were struck by the fact that each of the companies named had an impressive track record in the marketplace.

Intrigued by this initial evidence of support for our somewhat unconventional hypothesis, we conducted an informal survey over the next several months by interviewing McKinsey consultants about companies or organizations* they knew on a firsthand basis. The questions we asked were:

- Does Company X have one or more visible beliefs?

- If so, what are they?

- Do people in the organization know these beliefs? If so, who? And how many?

*Our survey covered both profit-making companies and a few non-profit organizations we found particularly intriguing. For simplicity we refer in the text to all of these as "companies."

- How do these beliefs affect day-to-day business?
- How are the beliefs communicated to the organization?
- Are the beliefs reinforced—by formal personnel processes, recognition, rewards?
- How would you characterize the performance of the company?

In total, over a period of about six months, we developed profiles of nearly eighty companies. Here's what we found out:

- Of all the companies surveyed, only about one third (twenty-five to be precise) had clearly articulated beliefs.

- Of this third, a surprising two-thirds had qualitative beliefs, or values, such as "IBM means service." The other third had financially oriented goals that were widely understood.

- Of the eighteen companies with qualitative beliefs, all were uniformly outstanding performers; we could find no correlations of any relevance among the other companies—some did okay, some poorly, most had their ups and downs. We characterized the consistently high performers as strong culture companies.*

These strong culture companies, we thought, were on to something. And so were we. Although this was far from a scientific survey, we did have evidence that the impact of values and beliefs on company performance was indeed real. We decided to follow up this "finding" by trying to figure out how these values got there and how they were transmitted throughout the corporation. We wanted to see what had made America's great companies not merely organizations, but successful, human institutions.

*These were: Caterpillar Tractor, General Electric, DuPont, Chubb Insurance, Price Waterhouse & Co., 3M, Jefferson-Smurfit, The Training Services Administration Agency of the British government, Digital Equipment Corporation, International Business Machines, Dana Corporation, Procter & Gamble, Hewlett-Packard, Leo Burnett Advertising Agency, Johnson & Johnson, Tandem Computer, Continental Bank, and the Rouse Corporation.

Here we stumbled onto a goldmine of evidence. Biographies, speeches, and documents from such giants of business as Thomas Watson of IBM, John Patterson (the founder of NCR), Will Durant of General Motors, William Kellogg of Kellogg's, and a host of others show a remarkable intuitive understanding of the importance of a strong culture in the affairs of their companies.

We read about Edwin Land, who built Polaroid into a successful $1 billion company (before losing control and having the company fall on hard times) and who developed a whole theory for Polaroid's culture; he called it "Semi-Topia" after the theories of Utopia. We also learned about Alfred Sloan, the manager who built General Motors into a monolith, who spent three full days every quarter reviewing person-by-person the career progression of his top 1,000 managers. And about Charles Steinmetz, the crippled Austrian dwarf who brought alternating current into electrical systems of the world while at GE, but who also adopted his lab assistant and the man's entire family. These, and many more stories, led us to one unmistakable conclusion: the people who built the companies for which America is famous all worked obsessively to create strong cultures within their organizations.

In our own research and consulting, we also found that many of the exciting, new, high-tech businesses springing up around Route 128 in Boston and Silicon Valley in California seem obsessed with culture. Consider the case of Tandem.

The Business of Culture

The Tandem Corporation, one of Silicon Valley's most highly publicized companies, is a company whose president deliberately manages the "informal," human side of the business. Founded by four former Hewlett-Packard employees, Tandem has built a highly successful company by solving a simple problem: the tendency of computers to break down. By yoking two computers together in one mainframe, Tandem offers customers the assurance that they will always have computer power available. If one of the processors breaks down, the other will carry on.

"Tandem is saying something about the product and people working together. Everything here works together. People with people; product with product; even processor with processor, within the product. Everything works together to keep us where we are." The quotation is not from Jim Treybig, Tandem's chief executive officer. It came from one of Tandem's managers, and the same sentiment is echoed through the ranks of the employees:

"I feel like putting a lot of time in. There is a real kind of loyalty here. We are all working in this together—working a process together. I'm not a workaholic—it's just the place. I love the place."

"I don't want anything in the world that would hurt Tandem. I feel totally divorced from my old company, but not Tandem."

These employees seem to be describing an ideal corporation, one most managers would give their eyeteeth to create. And by most standards, Tandem is enormously successful. It is growing at the rate of 25 percent per quarter, with annual revenues over $100 million. The turnover rate is nearly three times below the national average for the computer industry. Tandem's loyal employees like their jobs and the company's product. They are led by a talented group of experienced managers, a group which so far has been able to handle the phenomenal growth of the company.

Only time will tell whether Tandem can maintain its pattern of high performance. While it is easy to attribute the success of the company to fast growth and lack of competition, other things at work internally at Tandem suggest an interesting rival explanation—that the strong culture of Tandem produces its success. Here is how.

A Widely Shared Philosophy. Tandem is founded on a well-ordered set of management beliefs and practices. The philosophy of the company emphasizes the importance of people: "that's Tandem's greatest resource—its people, creative action, and fun." This ethic is widely shared and exemplified by slogans that everyone knows and believes in:

"It's so nice, it's so nice, we do it twice."

"It takes two to Tandem."

"Get the job done no matter what it takes."

"Tandemize it—means make it work."

The slogans are broadcast by T-shirts, bulletin boards, and word of mouth.

Top management spends about half of its time in training and in communicating the management philosophy and the essence of the company. Work is underway on a book that will codify the philosophy for future generations of workers at Tandem. "The philosophy is our future," one senior manager notes:

> "It mostly tells the 'whats' and 'hows' for selecting people and growing managers. Even though everything else around here changes, I don't want what we believe in and what we want to change."

At Tandem the management philosophy is not an afterthought, it's a principle preoccupation.

The Importance of People. Tandem has no formal organizational chart and few formal rules. Its meetings and memos are almost non-existent. Jobs are flexible in terms of duties and hours. The absence of name tags and reserved parking spaces suggests a less well-defined hierarchy than is typical in the corporate world. Despite this, the organization works and people get their jobs done.

What keeps employees off each other's toes and working in the same direction? One possibility is the unwritten rules and shared understandings. As one person put it: "There are a lot of unwritten rules. But there is also a lot of freedom to make a jerk out of yourself. Most of the rules are philosophical rules." Another is dispersed authority:

> "The open door policy gives me access to anyone—even the president."

> "Everyone here, managers, vice-presidents, and even janitors, communicate on the same level. No one feels better than anyone else."

Tandem seems to maintain a balance between autonomy and control without relying heavily on centralized or formalized procedures, or rigid status hierarchies.

Heroes: The President and the Product. Jim Treybig is a hero at Tandem, and his employees confirm it:

> "Jimmy is really a symbol here. He's a sign that every person here is a human being. He tries to make you feel part of the organization from the first day you are here. That's something people talk about."

> "The one thing you have to understand about the company— Treybig's bigger than life."

Treybig shares the hero's limelight with the Tandem Continuous 10 Computer—the backbone product of the company. The computer design is the company's logo and provides the metaphor for the "working together" philosophy.

> "The product is phenomenal, everyone is proud to be part of it."

> "When a big order was shipped, everyone in the plant was taking pictures. There were 'oh's' and 'ah's'. People were applauding. Can you believe it? For a computer."

Treybig and the computer share the main spotlight. But there are countless other heroes at Tandem—people whose achievements are regularly recognized on bulletin boards as "Our Latest Greatests."

Ritual and Ceremony. Tandem is renowned for its Friday afternoon "beer-busts" which everyone attends. But the ritual does more than help people wind down after a busy work week. It serves as an important vehicle for informal communication and mingling across groups.

Tandem's emphasis on ritual, ceremony, and play is not confined to beer-busts, however. There is a golf course, exercise room, and swimming pool. Company-wide celebrations are staged on important holidays. These provide opportunities for employees to develop a spirit of "oneness" and symbolize that Tandem cares about employees.

Tandem's attention to ritual and ceremony begins in its personnel selection interviews. During the hiring process, potential employees are called back two or three times for interviews and must accept the position before salary negotiations take place. The interviews have been likened to an "inquisition." The message conveyed to prospective employees is "we take longer, and take care of people we hire—because we really care." The impact of this process is significant.

> "They had me here for four interviews. That's about four hours, for a position of stock clerk. It was clear that they were choosy about the people they hired. That said something about what they thought I was. They thought I was good."

Treybig personally appears at each orientation to welcome new employees and to explain the company's motivation and commitment philosophy. His appearance reinforces the honor of being accepted to work at Tandem. It's no surprise that people at Tandem feel special—after all, they were made to feel that way before they were hired. Moreover, they feel special because the company and its product are special. And their feelings are expressed in an unusual display of loyalty and commitment to the company.

> "My goals follow the company's. It's the company and I. I think that's pretty true of everyone. We all want to see it work. You have to have it all or don't have any of it."

Employees see their work as linked to Tandem's success:

> "My job is important, and if I don't do it, Tandem doesn't make a buck."

Tandem is a unique company. And much of its success appears as intimately tied to its culture as to its product and marketplace position. The company has explicit values and beliefs which its employees share. It has heroes. It has storytellers and stories. It has rituals and ceremonies on key occasions. Tandem appears to have a strong culture which creates a bond between the company and employees, and inspires levels of productivity unlike most

other corporations. Established heroes, values, and rituals are crucial to a culture's continued strength, and Tandem has kept them.
The trick is in sustaining the culture so that it in turn drives the
company.

Will Tandem's culture last? Although Tandem is neither big
enough nor old enough to judge whether or not it will ultimately
take a place in the annals of great American business, we think it
is off to a good start. Indeed, other companies like IBM and P&G
have already succeeded in sustaining and evolving culture over
generations. These strong culture companies truly are the giants of
American industry. Yet, their cultures began taking shape in a way
that was very similar to Tandem.

The Elements of Culture

What is it about Tandem's organization that exerts such a grip
on its employees? Why do other strong culture companies seem to
inspire such loyalty? As we continued our research, we delved
into the organizational literature to understand better the elements that make up a strong culture. What is it that determines
the kind of culture a company will have in the first place? And
how will that culture work in the day-to-day life of a company?
Although we examine each one in depth later in the book, let's
summarize the elements now:

Business Environment. Each company faces a different
reality in the marketplace depending on its products, competitors,
customers, technologies, government influences, and so on. To
succeed in its marketplace, each company must carry out certain
kinds of activities very well. In some markets that means selling;
in others, invention; in still others, management of costs. In short,
the environment in which a company operates determines what it
must do to be a success. This business environment is the single
greatest influence in shaping a corporate culture. Thus, companies
that depend for success on their ability to sell an undifferentiated
product tend to develop one type of culture—what we call a work
hard/play hard culture—that keeps its sales force selling. Companies that spend a great deal of research and development money

before they even know if the final product will be successful or not tend to develop a different culture—one that we call a bet-your-company culture—designed to make sure decisions are thought through before actions are taken.

Values. These are the basic concepts and beliefs of an organization; as such they form the heart of the corporate culture. Values define "success" in concrete terms for employees—"if you do this, you too will be a success"—and establish standards of achievement within the organization. The strong culture companies that we investigated all had a rich and complex system of values that were shared by the employees. Managers in these companies talked about these beliefs openly and without embarrassment, and they didn't tolerate deviance from the company standards.

Heroes. These people personify the culture's values and as such provide tangible role models for employees to follow. Some heroes are born—the visionary institution builders of American business—and some are "made" by memorable moments that occur in day-to-day corporate life. Smart companies take a direct hand in choosing people to play these heroic roles, knowing full well that others will try to emulate their behavior. Strong culture companies have many heroes. At General Electric, for instance, the heroes include Thomas Edison, the inventor; Charles Steinmetz, the compleat engineer; Gerald Swope and now Jack Welch, the CEO entrepreneurs; and a legion of lesser-known but equally important internal figures: the inventor of the high-torque motor that powered the electric toothbrush; the chief engineer of the turbine works; the export salesman who survived two overseas revolutions; the international manager who had ghosts exorcised from a factory in Singapore; and many others. These achievers are known to virtually every employee with more than a few months' tenure in the company. And they show every employee "here's what you have to do to succeed around here."

The Rites and Rituals. These are the systematic and programmed routines of day-to-day life in the company. In their mundane manifestations—which we call rituals—they show employees the kind of behavior that is expected of them. In their extravaganzas—which we call ceremonies—they provide visible and potent examples of what the company stands for. Strong culture companies go to the trouble of spelling out, often in copious detail, the routine behavioral rituals they expect their employees to follow.

The Cultural Network. As the primary (but informal) means of communication within an organization, the cultural network is the "carrier" of the corporate values and heroic mythology. Storytellers, spies, priests, cabals, and whisperers form a hidden hierarchy of power within the company. Working the network effectively is the only way to get things done or to understand what's really going on.

The Importance of Understanding Culture

Companies that have cultivated their individual identities by shaping values, making heroes, spelling out rites and rituals, and acknowledging the cultural network have an edge. These corporations have values and beliefs to pass along—not just products. They have stories to tell—not just profits to make. They have heroes whom managers and workers can emulate—not just faceless bureaucrats. In short, they are human institutions that provide practical meaning for people, both on and off the job.

We think that people are a company's greatest resource, and the way to manage them is not directly by computer reports, but by the subtle cues of a culture. A strong culture is a powerful lever for guiding behavior; it helps employees do their jobs a little better, especially in two ways:

A strong culture is a system of informal rules that spells out how people are to behave most of the time. By knowing what exactly is expected of them, employees will waste little time in deciding how to act in a given situation. In a weak culture, on the other hand, employees waste a good deal of time just trying to figure out what they should do and how they should do it. The impact of a strong culture on productivity is amazing. In the extreme, we estimate that a company can gain as much as one or two hours of productive work per employee per day.

A strong culture enables people to feel better about what they do, so they are more likely to work harder. When a sales representative can say "I'm with IBM," rather than "I peddle typewriters for a living," he will probably hear in response, "Oh, IBM is a great company, isn't it?" He quickly figures out that he belongs to an outstanding company with a strong identity. For most people, that means a great deal. The next time they have the choice of working an extra half hour or sloughing off, they'll probably work. Overall, this has an impact on productivity too.

Unlike workers ten or twenty years ago, employees today are confused. According to psychologist Frederick Herzberg, they feel cheated by their jobs; they allow special interests to take up their time; their life values are uncertain; they are blameful and cynical; they confuse morality with ethics. Uncertainty is at the core of it all. Yet strong culture companies remove a great degree of that uncertainty because they provide structure and standards and a value system in which to operate. In fact, corporations may be among the last institutions in America that can effectively take on the role of shaping values. We think that workers, managers, and chief executive officers should recognize this and act on it.

People at all stages of their careers need to understand culture and how it works because it will likely have a powerful effect on their work lives. People just starting their careers may think a job is just a job. But when they choose a company, they often choose a way of life. The culture shapes their responses in a strong, but subtle way. Culture can make them fast or slow workers, tough or friendly managers, team players or individuals. By the time they've worked for several years, they may be so well conditioned by the culture they may not even recognize it. But when they change jobs, they may be in for a big surprise.

Take an up-and-coming executive at General Electric who is being wooed by Xerox—more money, a bigger office, greater responsibility. If his first reaction is to grab it, he's probably going to be disappointed. Xerox has a totally different culture than GE. Success (and even survival) at Xerox is closely tied to an ability to maintain a near frenetic pace, the ability to work and play hard, Xerox-style.

By contrast, GE has a more thoughtful and slow-moving culture. The GE culture treats each business activity seriously—

almost as though each activity will have an enormous impact on the company. Success at GE is a function of being able to take work seriously, a strong sense of peer group respect, considerable deference for authority, and a sense of deliberateness. A person of proven success at GE will bring these values to Xerox because past experience in GE's culture has reinforced them. But these same values may not be held in high esteem elsewhere.

Bright young comers at GE could, for example, quickly fizzle out at Xerox—and not even understand why. They'll be doing exactly what they did to succeed at GE—maybe even working harder at it—but their deliberate approach to issues large and small will be seen by insiders at Xerox as a sign that they "lack smarts." Their loss of confidence, self-esteem, and ability will be confusing to them and could significantly derail their careers. For Xerox, the loss of productivity could be appreciable.

This is no imaginary scenario. It happens again and again at Xerox, General Electric, and many other companies when managers ignore the influence of culture on individual approaches to work. Culture shock may be one of the major reasons why people supposedly "fail" when they leave one organization for another. Where they fail, however, is not necessarily in doing the job, but in not reading the culture correctly.

People who want to get ahead within their own companies also need to understand—at least intuitively—what makes their culture tick. If product quality is the guiding value of your company, then you'd better be thinking about getting into manufacturing where you can contribute to the work on quality control teams. If you're a marketing whiz in a company where all of the heroes are number crunchers, then you may have a problem. You can start taking accounting courses, or you can start trying to find a more compatible environment. Unless the culture itself is in a state of change—shifting, say, from a financial emphasis to a marketing orientation—then the chances are very slim for any single person who is out of step with the culture to make it to the very top.

Aside from considerations of personal success, managers must understand very clearly how the culture works if they want to accomplish what they set out to do. If you're trying to institute a competitive, tough approach to marketing in a company that is full of hail-fellow-well-met salesmen, then you have your work cut out for you. Even if everyone agrees with what you want to do, you must know how to manage the culture—for instance, create new role model heroes—in order to teach your legion of easy-going salesmen the new rules of the game.

Finally, senior executives and especially chief executive officers may be missing out on one of the key ingredients for their companies' eventual success by ignoring either the influence of culture on corporate success or their own central role in shaping it. Their culture may be rich with lore or starved for shared values and stories. It may be coherent and cohesive, or fragmented and poorly understood. It may create meaning or contribute to blind confusion. It may be rich, fiery, focused, and strong; or weak, cold, and diffuse. Understanding the culture can help senior executives pinpoint why their company is succeeding or failing. Understanding how to build and manage the culture can help the same executives make a mark on their company that lasts for decades.

Can every company have a strong culture? We think it can. But to do that, top management first has to recognize what kind of culture the company already has, even if it is weak. The ultimate success of a chief executive officer depends to a large degree on an accurate reading of the corporate culture and the ability to hone it and shape it to fit the shifting needs of the marketplace.

In reading this book, we can imagine that many managers will ask themselves, is culture too "soft"? Can serious managers actually take the time to deal with it? Indeed, we believe that managers must. Management scientists sometimes argue that corporations are so complex and vulnerable to diverse external and internal forces that managers' freedom to act and lead is limited. Their argument is plausible, but our experience does not support it. By and large, the most successful managers we know are precisely those who strive to make a mark through creating a guiding vision, shaping shared values, and otherwise providing leadership for the people with whom they work.

It all comes down to understanding the importance of working with people in any organization. The institution builders of old knew the value of a strong culture and they worked hard at it. They saw themselves as symbolic players-actors in their corporations. They knew how to orchestrate, even dramatize events to drive their lessons home. They understood how corporations shape personal lives and were not shy about suggesting the standards that people should live by. If we are to have such great institutions tomorrow, the managers of today will have to take up this challenge again.

Our goal in this book is to provide business leaders with a primer on cultural management. In showing how several excellent companies* manage their cultures, this book is meant to be suggestive only, not hard and fast or prescriptive. Our aim is to heighten the awareness of our readers, to jog them into thinking about the workplace in its role as a mediator of behavior, and to show the positive effects of culture-building. Along the way, we hope to instill in our readers a new law of business life: In Culture There is Strength.

---

*You may see several companies—such as General Electric—and several individuals—such as Thomas Watson—named again and again throughout the book. This is because we consider them the absolutely best examples we could find to illustrate our ideas. Managers could do worse than to emulate these examples.

2
Values: The Core of the Culture

Values are the bedrock of any corporate culture.* As the essence of a company's philosophy for achieving success, values provide a sense of common direction for all employees and guidelines for their day-to-day behavior. These formulas for success determine (and occasionally arise from) the types of corporate heroes, and the myths, rituals, and ceremonies of the culture. In fact, we think that often companies succeed because their employees can identify, embrace, and act on the values of the organization.

These values may be grand in scope ("Progress is our most important product"), or narrowly focused ("Underwriting excellence"). They can capture the imagination ("The first Irish multinational"). They can tell people how to work together ("It takes two to Tandem"). Or they can simply drive ("15 percent period-to-period sales and earnings growth"). If they are strong, they command everyone's attention: "What people really care about around here is quality." If they are weak, they may often be ignored: "It's not the same company since the old man stepped down. Nowadays everyone around here is just more or less doing his own thing."

"Rational" managers rarely pay much attention to the value system of an organization. Values are not "hard," like organizational structures, policies and procedures, strategies, or budgets. Often they are not even written down. And when someone does try to set them down in a formal statement of corporate philosophy, the product often bears an uncomfortable resemblance to the Biblical beatitudes—good and true and broadly constructive, but not all that relevant to Monday morning.

*Much of the original work on the ideas expressed in this chapter was done by McKinsey consultant Julien Phillips.

We think that society today suffers from a pervasive uncertainty about values, a relativism that undermines leadership and commitment alike. After all, in this fast-paced world, who really *does* know what's right? On the philosophical level, we find ourselves without convincing responses. But the everyday business environment is quite different. Even if ultimate values are chimerical, particular values clearly make sense for specific organizations operating in specific economic circumstances. Perhaps because ultimate values seem so elusive, people respond positively to practical ones. Choices must be made, and values are an indispensable guide in making them.

Moreover, it is clear that organizations have, in fact, gained great strength from shared values—with emphasis on the "shared." If employees know what their company stands for, if they know what standards they are to uphold, then they are much more likely to make decisions that will support those standards. They are also more likely to feel as if they are an important part of the organization. They are motivated because life in the company has meaning for them.

Since organizational values can powerfully influence what people actually do, we think that values ought to be a matter of great concern to managers. In fact, shaping and enhancing values can become the most important job a manager can do. In our work and study, we have found that successful companies place a great deal of emphasis on values. In general, these companies shared three characteristics:

- They stand for something—that is, they have a clear and explicit philosophy about how they aim to conduct their business.

- Management pays a great deal of attention to shaping and fine-tuning these values to conform to the economic and business environment of the company and to communicating them to the organization.

- These values are known and shared by all the people who work for the company—from the lowliest production worker right through to the ranks of senior management.

What are these values that hold a company and its workforce together? Where do they come from? And more important, how do they influence the successful operation of an organization?

The Corporate Character

For those who hold them, shared values define the fundamental character of their organization, the attitude that distinguishes it from all others. In this way, they create a sense of identity for those in the organization, making employees feel special. Moreover, values are a reality in the minds of most people throughout the company, not just the senior executives. It is this sense of pulling together that makes shared values so effective. Let's look at a few:

- *Caterpillar*: "24-hour parts service anywhere in the world"—symbolizing an extraordinary commitment to meeting customers' needs.

- *Leo Burnett Advertising Agency*: "Make great ads"—commitment to a particular concept of excellence.

- *American Telephone & Telegraph*: "Universal service"—an historical orientation toward standardized, highly reliable service to all possible users, now being reshaped into values more relevant to a newly competitive marketplace.

- *DuPont*: "Better things for better living through chemistry"—a belief that product innovation, arising out of chemical engineering, is DuPont's most distinctive value.

- *Sears, Roebuck*: "Quality at a good price"—the mass merchandiser for middle America.

- *Rouse Company*: "Create the best environment for people"—a dominating concern to develop healthy and pleasant residential communities, not just to build subdivisions.

- *Continental Bank*: "We'll find a way" (to meet customer needs).

- *Dana Corporation*: "Productivity through people"—enlisting the ideas and commitment of employees at every level in support of Dana's strategy of competing largely on cost and dependability rather than product differentiation.

- *Chubb Insurance Company*: "Underwriting excellence"—an overriding commitment to excellence in a critical function.

- *Price Waterhouse & Company*: "Strive for technical perfection" (in accounting).

Most of these phrases sound utterly platitudinous to the out-sider. Indeed, many of them are little more than slogans that might be (and often were) used in advertising campaigns. What makes them more than slogans is the degree to which these phrases cap-ture something people in the organization deeply believe in. Within each of these corporations, these words take on rich and concrete meaning.

We call these phrases "core values" because they become the essence of the organization's philosophy. These slogan-like themes are only the most visible parts of a complex system that includes a whole range of beliefs about how the organization should achieve success. These values and beliefs are closely linked to the basic concept of the business and provide guidelines for employees to follow in their work.

For example, if you are in the business of selling cars—as is Joe Girard, the world's most successful car salesman—and if your experience in the marketplace leads you to think that taking care of your customers is *the key way* to get them to come back again, then you will put this philosophy to work. Girard's core value is "customer service." From this basic concept, Girard has devel-oped a number of beliefs—that you should studiously respond to all customer complaints, make sure their service problems are handled, even send them cards at Christmas and on their birth-days. In some months Girard sends out more than 13,000 cards to customers. He puts his values and beliefs into action, and he sells more automobiles every year than any single car salesman in the world.

In the case of one person, it is easy to see how one basic value backed by enormous energy can make for success. What is harder to understand is how this same principle applies in a larger corpo-ration. Companies are, after all, only collections of individuals. If they all believe and behave as Joe Girard does, they will un-doubtedly succeed at what they set out to do. And that is the real challenge for management: to make thousands and thousands of people Joe Girard-like figures who have a strongly ingrained sense of the company's value.

The Pepsi-Cola Company seems to have met this challenge by fostering the values of competition. As *Business Week* recently reported, "Once the company was content in its No. 2 spot, offer-ing Pepsi as a cheaper alternative to Coca-Cola. But today, a new employee at PepsiCo quickly learns that beating the competition, whether outside or inside the company, is the surest path to success. . . . Because winning is the key value at Pepsi, losing has its penalties. Consistent runners-up find their jobs gone. Employees know that they must win merely to stay in place—and must devastate the competition to get ahead."

Dana Corporation, on the other hand, has a very different, but still successful, set of values. As a competitor in the long-established automobile-parts manufacturing business, it has virtually doubled its productivity over the past seven years, a period when the overall growth of American productivity has been slowing. Dana did not accomplish this record with massive capital investment, with sophisticated industrial-engineering studies, or with management-imposed speed-up measures. Instead, it relied on its people, right down to the shop-floor level. Management continually stressed the value of productivity to company success. It put this value into action by creating a multitude of task forces and other special activities; by giving its people practical opportunities to generate productivity; by listening to ideas and then implementing them; and by consistently, visibly, and frequently rewarding success. "Productivity through people" is no mere advertising phrase to the employees of Dana Corporation.

Procter & Gamble: Forging a Value System

Although a value system may be most visible in the few words that make up an advertising slogan, many successful companies have a very rich tradition of values, beliefs, and themes that have developed over the years. Where do these values come from? They mostly come from experience, from testing what does and doesn't work in the economic environment. But individual people within an organization also have strong influence in shaping the standards and beliefs of the organization.

In Chapter 1 we looked briefly at the values of Tandem, a relatively new, fast-growth company. Now let's look at a different kind of corporation, one that has been able to sustain its strong philosophy—and its success—over 150 years of growth.

By almost any measure, the Procter & Gamble Company of Cincinnati, Ohio, is one of the best models of persistent long-term attention to building a strong culture company, particularly in its emphasis on values. First, let's look at a brief history:

In 1837, upon the suggestion of their father-in-law, William Procter and James Gamble joined forces in a partnership. The candle and soap industry they entered that year was a highly competitive one; there were eighteen direct competitors in the Cincinnati market alone and many more across the burgeoning country. In P&G's early years, candles were the company's principle source of income, and the company enjoyed a modest success. By the 1870s, however, the growing popularity of oil lamps for illumination left Procter and Gamble justifiably worried about the future of their candle-making business. To protect their future, they redoubled their efforts to become a leader in the soap market. In 1878, James N. Gamble, son of the founder and a chemist by education, perfected the formula for a new, white soap.

It was cousin Harley Procter's job to sell the soap. He sensed it could be a good product, so he spent weeks trying to come up with the right name. In church one Sunday it came to him while reciting Psalms 45:8—"All thy garments smell of myrrh and aloe, and cassia, out of the ivory palaces whereby they have made thee glad." Ivory soap was born.

Realizing the opportunity this invention offered the company, Harley employed the creative use of the new medium of display advertising to turn Ivory into the first nationally branded soap product. The company's major growth had begun.

The initial success with Ivory soap was followed up some thirty-three years later by the introduction of Crisco shortening; as a substitute for lard, it was a radically new product at the time. Then came Camay (1923), Tide and Prell (1946), Joy (1949), Cheer (1950), then Crest and Comet (1956), Head & Shoulders (1960), Pampers (1961), Safeguard (1963), and, more recently, Downy, Mr. Clean, and Top Job. As any consumer can attest, to this day these products are leaders in the market segments they serve.

What was it that made this company so strong in the field of consumer packaged goods? What is it about P&G that has allowed it to sustain its enviable track record so long and so consistently through good economic times and bad? Was it being first to the market with a new product? Perhaps true in the early days but certainly not relevant for products like Tide and Charmin. Was it an absence of competition in its main markets? Certainly never true in any of the markets P&G served. Was it a better strategy than Colgate or others? We doubt there are that many degrees of strategic freedom available to allow P&G to differentiate itself in all the diverse markets it serves.

We believe P&G's success can be traced most directly back to a very strong culture, founded on a set of beliefs and values. The first and most basic of these values is "do what is right." As William Cooper Procter said at the time he handed the reins of management to Richard R. Deupree, the first non-Procter or Gamble to run the company: "Always try to do what's right. If you do that, nobody can really find fault." This rule has lived to this day, being passed on to every head of P&G since Cooper—and every new employee as well.

Where did this and other beliefs and values come from? There was no visionary among the early Procters and Gambles to codify the value system and drum it into the heads of employees. Rather these values evolved over years and years of trial and error as many people worked to figure out just how such a business should be run. Let's see how a few of these key values evolved.

"THE CONSUMER IS IMPORTANT"

From the earliest days of P&G, its founding fathers always had an eye clearly fixed on what might be important to customers. One morning in 1851, William Procter noticed that a wharfhand was painting black crosses on P&G's candle boxes. Asking why this was done, Procter learned that the crosses allowed illiterate wharfhands to distinguish the candle boxes from the soap boxes. Another artistic wharfhand soon changed the black cross to a circled star. Another replaced the single star with a cluster of stars. And then a quarter moon was added with a human profile. Finally, P&G painted the moon and stars emblem on all boxes of their candles.

At some later date, P&G decided that the "man in the moon" was unnecessary so they dropped it from their boxes. Immediately P&G received a message from New Orleans that a jobber had refused delivery of an entire shipment of P&G candles. Since these boxes lacked the full "moon and stars" design, the jobber thought they were imitations. P&G quickly recognized the value of the "moon and stars" emblem and brought it back into use by registering it as a trademark. It was the beginning of brand name identification for P&G and the first of many times that P&G listened to its customers.

P&G paid attention to customers because over the years they learned that the more they did so, the greater the payback to the company. Certainly, the customers discovered and launched Ivory soap. Soon after it was introduced, P&G learned from its customers that Ivory floated. Initially, P&G managers were so surprised by this they assumed it was an accident in the mixing of the soap. So it was, but customers kept asking for the "floating soap" so P&G incorporated the "mistake" into their regular production.

P&G continued listening to customers, who helped them develop all of their major products. Their experience through the years has taught them step-by-step that such attention always pays off. P&G calls this mania "consumerism: a response, after comprehensive market research, to what consumers need and want." Over the company's history, consumerism has taken many forms, from testing kitchens for Crisco in 1912; to hiring housewives to provide consumer feedback on liquid dish detergents in 1922; to large-scale, door-to-door sampling efforts for Camay in the 1920s. Today, P&G conducts over 1.5 million telephone interviews annually. That's the equivalent of 1,000 Gallup polls each year.

In short, P&G is a culture that glories in listening and listening well to consumers. Furthermore, they have developed more ways to listen to customers than anyone else. And why wouldn't they, they've spent years learning how.

"THINGS DON'T JUST HAPPEN, YOU HAVE TO MAKE THEM HAPPEN"

P&G is the largest consistent advertiser among the giant consumer-products companies. For the last century, managers at P&G have believed that advertising works and they bet their company's future on it. How did they develop this trust in the media's efficacy? Again the answer did not come easily, but through years and years of hard work.

It all started with Harley Procter and his Ivory soap. For several years, Harley had been arguing with his relatives-colleagues in the company to convince them that media advertising could sell more soap. Finally, he convinced them to take the first step and allocate $11,000 to this new and unproven medium.

Harley decided to emphasize the purity of Ivory in his first advertising effort. To do this he hired a science consultant from New York who both defined purity and went on to determine that, given this definition, Ivory was 99.44 percent pure. Armed with this statistic, Harley began advertising Ivory. The results of this brilliant innovation were twofold: booming sales for P&G and the birth of modern advertising. Like listening to consumers, it worked.

But getting hooked on advertising in a company like P&G does not mean standing still. When P&G begins to believe in something like advertising, given such bedrock cultural values as "make it happen," they keep testing, keep trying new ideas, keep evolving the basic idea year by year. In 1923, P&G was first to capitalize on the use of what was then a brand-new advertising medium—radio. Starting with informational radio spots, P&G went on to invent the daytime soap opera. Thirty years later, P&G did the same for television.

"WE WANT TO MAKE EMPLOYEE INTERESTS OUR OWN"

Even as early as the late 1880s, and with a hot, new product in Ivory, William Cooper Procter had a problem: how to keep P&Gers not just productive but loyal, too, and how to express the company's sense of responsibility to its people.

In 1883, Procter started working for P&G at the lowest level of menial factory labor—loading the soap mixers, a job that wasn't just for show. At work, Procter lived the life of a laborer to its fullest, even eating lunch with the other workers while sitting on the factory floor. During this early work, Procter developed a first-hand understanding of the perspectives and concerns of the P&G workers. This understanding was to serve as a foundation for his insistence on improved labor relations.

In 1884, Procter finally persuaded his father and uncle to give workers Saturday afternoons off without loss of pay, a radical proposal at the time. However, growing labor unrest across the country quickly proved Procter's plan to be grossly inadequate. He wrestled with this problem for two years, then suggested that profit-sharing might develop greater loyalty and respect among P&G workers. Again failure—Procter's profit-sharing plan realized no gains in productivity and loyalty; workers simply viewed the payments they received as extra salary. Undaunted, he tinkered with it over several years, and in 1903 devised a scheme to couple profit-sharing with the purchase of P&G stock—the company would add $1 for every $1 invested by a worker up to an amount equal to the worker's annual salary. Its success emboldened Procter to establish ongoing two-way communications between management and workers by instituting the Employee Conference Plan (1918) and creating one seat for a worker representative from each domestic plant on P&G's board of directors (1919). Then he shortened the workday from ten to eight hours. Still not content in his efforts to improve worker relations and realizing his action would benefit all involved, Procter singlehandedly abolished job uncertainty at P&G by guaranteeing employment for workers. To do this he took the enormous risk of developing direct distribution (in other words, a sales force), thus bypassing the distributors who previously had created highly uneven demand. The risk succeeded and, even during the Depression, P&G was able to keep its workers on the payrolls.

So Procter & Gamble has a long history of working hard on the "right" things: James Gamble perfecting his soap, Harley Procter forging a new field of advertising, and William Cooper Procter establishing the principle that the interests of the company and those of its employees were inseparable. All along, P&G paid scrupulous attention to its customers. These values were formed and refined by years of experience in the marketplace. They didn't just appear overnight. Although P&G is a highly successful company, it has had its share of problems; Rely tampons are only the most recent example. Still, its continuing experiences in the marketplace have evolved into a rich and varied culture that has sustained it through difficult times.

The evolution of a value structure like P&G's is the core element in all the strong culture companies we studied. The stronger the culture, the richer and more complex the value system, the longer the chain of evidence that these values really do produce results.

The Influence of Corporate Values

As we've seen with P&G, a corporation's values will affect all aspects of the company—from what products get manufactured to how workers are treated. Companies that are guided by strong shared values tend to reflect those values in the design of their formal organization. The most readily recognizable case is the company that believes that the way to put its values to work is to control costs tightly. Generally, its financial vice president and controller will be leading members of the top-management group, and very frequently the divisional controllers will report directly to the corporate controller rather than to the division head. Almost always, its dominant management systems will be those for budget development and operation control, and even its longer-range planning will be geared to the needs of financial control.

A company with values geared primarily to the external marketplace, like P&G, will probably have several very senior marketing vice presidents in its top-management structure, and it is likely to rely on some version of product managers or brand managers to handle product marketing. It will surely have rather elaborate systems for gathering and shifting data on customer tastes, customer response to its products, and initiatives by its competitors.

The values and beliefs of an organization indicate what matters are to be attended to most assiduously—for instance, current operations in one company, external relations in a second, longer-term strategy in a third. They suggest what kind of information is taken most seriously for decision-making purposes—experienced judgment of "old hands" in one organization, detailed "number-crunching" in another. They define what kind of people are most respected—engineers versus marketing men versus financial types.

Values also play a very important role in determining how far one can rise within an organization. If product development is the company's overriding ethic, the best people will want to work in the company's research and development laboratories. If customer service is the important value, the go-getters won't want to be in finance but in a sales or field service function. The company will tend to reinforce the primacy of that value by promoting a disproportionate share of the people in these jobs.

Shared values and beliefs also play an important role in communicating to the outside world what to expect of a company. The philosophy at Sears, for instance, marks its corporate personality consistently to suppliers and customers alike: the Sears value—"Quality at a good price"—encourages buyers to become crusaders in driving down the cost of products. Many companies depend on Sears for most of their business, yet these companies often live in fear of the giant retailer. "That price isn't good enough," Sears buyers will say. "We want to sell a muffler for $19.95 and buy it from you for $9.95 and that's it." The producer can argue that the steel costs $7.14 and that something in addition must be charged to manufacture the muffler, but then Sears will only threaten to take their business someplace else. After all, Sears sells more mufflers than anyone in the world. So the producer huffs and puffs and figures how to make a muffler for $9.95. That's the way Sears does its purchasing and it's infamous for it. Yet that's part of its image for its customers: Sears gets the lowest prices for quality products.

Delta Airlines' value as "the people company" is expressed in its slogan, "The Delta Family Feeling." As only a caring family would, Delta pays higher salaries than the industry average and thus attracts the best employees—people whom the company works very hard to get and to whom it gives significant responsibilities for delivering quality service. It was only natural, therefore, that when Delta braced itself for the last recession, senior management, in effect, told shareholders and the financial community, "Now that times are tough, you'll have to pay. We're not going to earn what we could over the long term if we let go of people now; our people are very important to our long-term performance; they're what makes this place work. So, shareholders, it's your time to give a pint of blood; until this recession is over, our earnings and maybe even our dividends are going to be down because we are not going to lay our people off." Such a move was acceptable only because Delta had communicated the sanctity of this value of "family" over a long period of time. Shared values are what has made Delta great.

In 1982, while other carriers made cutbacks of 15,000 workers, Delta held firm. As a result, the company gained considerable loyalty from its employees. In the past, non-unionized employees have carried luggage and handled the ticket counters to help the airline get through the slumps so that regular employees would not be laid off.

Delta points up the importance of a company's living by its values, even in a difficult situation. Yet the example also underlines the all-or-nothing stakes involved. Once a company tries to shape values, the company is often locked in—the actions of management must be consistent, because the inconsistencies will be noticed and magnified out of proportion. In creating values that will work, managers are forced to live life as they say they would . . . whatever the circumstances.

How do shared values affect organizational performance? In broad terms, they act as an informal control system that tells people what is expected of them. More specifically, shared values affect performance in three main ways:

Managers and others throughout the organization give extraordinary attention to whatever matters are stressed in the corporate value system—and this in turn tends to produce extraordinary results. An oil company produces crude and petroleum products much more efficiently than others because efficient operation is what it values and what its managers concentrate on. One of this company's principal competitors values trading and financial management most highly. Accordingly, its managers worry less about production operations and concentrate instead on squeezing every cent of potential revenues from their sales.

Down-the-line managers make marginally better decisions, on average, because they are guided by their perception of the shared values. When a manager at Dana is confronted by a close question—like making a particular investment in increased productivity versus one in new product development—the manager is likely to opt for productivity.

People simply work a little harder because they are dedicated to the cause. "I'm sorry I'm so late getting home, but the customer had a problem and we never leave a customer with a problem."

Risks and Pitfalls of Strong Values

The power of values is that people care about them. This power can be a problem as well as a source of strength. If managers choose to build or reinforce the shared values of the group of people they work with, they had better recognize the risks they are assuming:

The risk of obsolescence. What if the environment changes? One of the most serious risks of a potent system of shared values is that economic circumstances can change while shared values continue to guide behavior in ways no longer helpful to the organization's success. When a company with strongly held values finds that it has lost marketplace or economic relevance, it generally has great difficulty adjusting successfully. Witness AT&T's current difficulty in adapting to a newly competitive marketplace.

"Universal Service" is AT&T's slogan, which Theodore Vail, a former chairman of the company, first articulated. For a long time, that label served AT&T well because it was, until recently, a regulated entity that only needed to make its regulators happy to receive rate increases. As elected or appointed officials, regulators were naturally influenced by their constituencies; given AT&T's phenomenally good strategy to get a phone to everyone who wanted it ("Universal Service"), the company could consistently ask governmental regulators for rate increases and get them. After all, the mass of voters were well served and treated equally, even if equality meant the inefficiency of installing one telephone at the dead end of a desolate country road. Wherever the unconnected in America wanted a telephone, a line would be installed shortly thereafter.

Yet in clinging to this value, AT&T has had tremendous difficulty in adapting to a newly competitive, deregulated environment. Week in, week out over the past several years, newspapers have announced yet another element of the proposed realignment of the company. In the business press, especially, there have been repeated stories about the Bell system's "new marketing thrust." A different reality is apparent, however, when a repairman who visited one of our homes spent two full hours regaling us with his version of the demise of the company. His diatribe concluded with a recommendation that we buy a non-Bell answering device. And indeed, while AT&T continues to struggle to adapt, companies like MCI and Rolm have started to move in on its market, particularly in switchboard systems especially tailored for use in small offices and commercial long-distance phone calls.

With a monopoly franchise, a paramount goal of universal service made sense and worked. (The United States does have the best telephone system in the world, in case you hadn't noticed.) But it also fostered a preoccupation with total system integrity that has inhibited AT&T's ability to identify and meet the needs of particular market segments—a serious limitation now that competitors have been allowed to enter the marketplace. Senior management perceives the threat very clearly and understands what must be done, but the mentality and work practices of down-the-line employees are so strongly tied to the obsolete value system that it will take years for the company to adapt itself fully to the new circumstances.

The consequences of obsolescence are serious enough to give some managers pause in their pursuit of shared values. But they should look at the other side of the coin as well: would AT&T have been as successful in the past had it lacked such strongly held values? Almost certainly not.

The risk of resistance to change. Barring an environmental upheaval that forces everyone to adapt or perish, can an institution of true believers ever change? Look at Sears, Roebuck. It faced no fundamental transformation in its environment like that in telecommunications, but its management nonetheless saw an opportunity to become an up-scale merchandiser on the department store model. The market was large and growing rapidly, and margins were undoubtedly fatter.

Yet no sooner had Sears set out on this road than it faltered. Its army of loyal employees, who had cut their eyeteeth on delivering value to middle-American consumers, simply did not know how to run a Macy's-style operation. As a result, performance lagged, and the appealing strategy had to be abandoned.

Sears is by no means an isolated example. In a glamour growth company, one of the authors spent two years trying to help the CEO in a determined effort to cut out excessive overhead in the face of increasingly strong cost competition. Overall, fewer than 1,000 overhead positions were eliminated, and many of those were soon added back. Because of the powerful growth mentality that persisted in the company, cost reduction simply would not fly.

The risk of inconsistency. What if managerial behavior contradicts professed values? In one company we know, the CEO speaks frequently and eloquently about the value of serving customers better. But when the year-end approaches, he demands financial performance—the customer be hanged. Given the demonstrated primacy of clearly articulated financial objectives, it is no wonder that very few people in the organization buy into the customer-service rhetoric.

In a second company, a large bank, top management talks constantly about the need to become more entrepreneurial in response to the changing regulatory and competitive environment. When budget time comes around, however, new ventures are held to the same targets of financial return and cost growth as established divisions. Not surprisingly, evidence of real entrepreneurship is very hard to find.

In order to build a strong culture top management must be convinced that it can adhere faithfully and visibly to the values it intends to promote. Any inconsistency in adhering to or failing to promote the company's enunciated values will begin to undermine the strength of the culture.

In Part II of the book, we discuss in more detail how companies can avoid the risks and pitfalls of stong values by constantly tuning them to the business environment. But the point we want to make here is that values do their share of day-to-day business. What brings values to life is the awareness of everyone in the organization about these values and why they are important. It's not just values, it is the extensive sharing of them that makes a difference.

How do values come to be shared in a company? Through the reinforcement provided by all the other elements of the company's culture, but primarily by the culture's lead players—its heroes.

3
Heroes: The Corporate Right Stuff

If values are the soul of the culture, then heroes personify those values and epitomize the strength of the organization. Heroes are pivotal figures in a strong culture. Like a John Wayne or a Burt Reynolds in pinstripes, they create the role models for employees to follow. The hero is the great motivator, the magician, the person everyone will count on when things get tough. They have unshakable character and style. They do things everyone else wants to do but is afraid to try. Heroes are symbolic figures whose deeds are out of the ordinary, but not too far out. They show—often dramatically—that the ideal of success lies within human capacity.

America's boardrooms need heroes more than Hollywood's box offices need them. Heroism is a leadership component that is all but forgotten by modern management. Since the 1920s, the corporate world has been powered by managers who are rationalists, who do strategic planning, write memos, and devise flow charts. But we are not talking about good "scientific" managers here. Managers run institutions; heroes create them.

The one quality that more than anything else marks a manager is decisiveness, but heroes are often not decisive; they're intuitive; they have a vision. They don't make any decisions, except one: does it fit the vision or not? Managers are busy; heroes have all the time in the world because they make time. Managers are routinizers; heroes are experimenters. Managers are disciplined; heroes are playful and appreciate the value of "hoopla,"—ceremonies and rewards to honor top performance. Both managers and heroes fuss about details, but managers will spend hours refining their numbers, while heroes will plant a garden so that it will look just right.

37

The management ethic has to do with order, procedure, and fitting square pegs into square holes. Heroes defy order in pursuing their vision. And this violates the management canon: you don't do anything unless you can figure out whether it makes sense. So, while business certainly needs managers to make the trains run on time, it more desperately needs heroes to get the engine going.

If heroes are so important in company life, why do we hear so little about them? Management may have grown amnesiac about heroes, but within a company employees look up to certain people who personify their aspirations. People can't aspire to be "good" or "successful" or "smart" or "productive"—no matter how much management encourages them in these directions. They can, however, aspire to be like someone: "He's just an ordinary person, but look how successful he is. I can be successful like that too." Thus heroes are anointed day in and day out at the slightest sign of successful behavior as employees try to find a realistic match between their personal aspirations and corporate goals. Nowadays, only the most culturally aware managers recognize this phenomenon and take advantage of it.

Some heroes are "born" and have become part of the folklore of American industry: Tom Watson and IBM; Will Durant and General Motors; John D. Rockefeller and Standard Oil; Helena Rubenstein and her namesake company; Henry Ford and Ford Motor Company; Pierre DuPont and DuPont; Mary Kay Ash and Mary Kay Cosmetics; Ken Olsen and DEC; Dave Packard and Hewlett-Packard; Jim Treybig and Tandem.

Of course "born" heroes are in short supply. The vast majority of the heroes in American business life are what we call "situational" heroes: ordinary people anointed by their peers in recognition of some aspect of their behavior. Companies with strong cultures take advantage of this natural phenomenon by making their own: the supersalesperson of the month, the elder statesman corporate president, the maverick scientist tinkering away in the R & D lab.

Recently one of us witnessed the anointing of just such a hero at a brand-new high-tech company still in the blueprint stage. The company has hundreds of tasks to accomplish in order to begin operations, but the founders have first and foremost chosen a hero. After some discussion, they named a superior inventor as chairman of their new company. He was selected over a high-finance whiz or a marketing dynamo to convey the fact that in this new business, invention is the key. The company showcased the new hero by giving him a private laboratory and inviting workers and friends in for a celebration. The inventor presided, and after fiddling with his personal computer for a bit, he made a robot suddenly appear, walk across the room, and turn on the air conditioner. What would seem to some outsiders as a joke was in fact a demonstration of faith in the technology to come and, more important, in the new hero who symbolizes the company's inventiveness and ambitions. The founders explained that they are thinking ahead to the 700th employee, not the seven they now have. They expect every new worker to discover the inventor-hero puttering in the lab and, with that, understand perfectly the company's goals.

The Impact of Heroes

Whether "born" like Henry Ford or "made" like the young inventor, heroes reinforce the basic values of the culture by:

Making Success Attainable and Human.   A recent edition of "Think," IBM's house organ, profiled Joe McClosky, a veteran typewriter salesman in the Seattle branch, after he had logged thirty straight years in the Hundred Percent Club. By extolling the virtues of a veteran salesperson like McClosky, IBM told its young salespersons: here's a hero to follow. As motivation, McClosky was clearly superior to a memo on a new increase in sales quotas.

Providing Role Models.   Richard A. Drew, a banjo-playing college dropout working in 3M's research lab in the 1920s, promised to help some colleagues solve a problem they had with masking tape. Soon thereafter, DuPont came out with cellophane. Drew decided he could go DuPont one better and coated the cellophane with a colorless adhesive to bind things together—and Scotch tape was born. In the 3M tradition, Drew carried the ball himself by managing the development and initial production of his invention.

Moving up through the ranks, he went on to become technical director of the company and showed other employees just how they could succeed in similar fashion at 3M.

Mary Kay Ash, founder of Mary Kay Cosmetics, believes in offering herself as a visible role model to her employees. She trains saleswomen not simply to represent her but to believe that they *are* Mary Kay. To inspire them with her own confidence, she awards diamond bumblebee pins and explains that, according to aerodynamic engineers, the wings of the bumblebee are too weak and the body is too heavy for the insect to fly. But bumblebees don't know this, and so they fly anyway. The message is clear: anyone can be a hero if they have the confidence and persistence to try.

Symbolizing the Company to the Outside World. Lee Iacocca conveys the hope that Chrysler may yet produce another Mustang. Frank Borman strives mightily to tell the world and the employees of Eastern Airlines that service is what really counts. Frank Perdue has tried to brand chickens the way that Procter & Gamble brands soap. We haven't done the comparison testing to know personally if Perdue chickens are more tender, but Perdue himself has done a good job convincing consumers that they are.

Preserving What Makes the Company Special. What better heroes for GE engineers to identify with than Thomas Edison or Charles Steinmetz—both giant contributors to progress. By keeping the memory of these giants alive, GE provides inspiration to a whole new generation of engineers and scientists.

Setting a Standard of Performance. When Ed Carlson took over troubled United Airlines, it was heavily bureaucratized and simply did not work. Carlson knew he had to motivate *everyone*—right down to the baggage handlers—so he hit the road and logged 186,000 miles touring United facilities in his first year. At each stop, Carlson told his people what was going on in United management and encouraged them to do what they thought was best for the company within the scope of their own jobs.

Adolph Ochs, founder of *The New York Times*, sat glaringly

quiet in a meeting of *Times* editors who congratulated themselves for reporting a big story very well, according to author Gay Talese, a former *Times* reporter. "Suddenly Ochs silenced them by saying he had read in another paper a fact that seemed to be missing from the *Times'* coverage. 'I want it *all*,' he told them."

Motivating Employees. When Jack Welch, recently appointed CEO of General Electric, was an up-and-coming group executive, he had a special telephone installed in his office with a private number which was made available to all the purchasing agents in his group. If the agents ever got a price concession from a vendor, they could phone Welch and the call would come in on his telephone. Whether he was making a million-dollar deal or chatting with his secretary, Welch would interrupt what he was doing, take the call and say: "That's wonderful news; you just knocked a nickel per ton off the price of steel." Then, straightaway, he'd sit down and scribble out a congratulatory note to the agent—a profoundly messy, and ambiguous, motivational procedure. But Welch not only made himself a hero by this symbolic act, he also transformed each and every purchasing agent into a hero too.

Perhaps most importantly, heroes provide a *lasting influence within the organization*. The values of Thomas Watson, Charles Steinmetz, General Johnson, and William Cooper Procter still provide the glue that bonds the great organizations they built. A favorite story of Ochs's at *The New York Times*—still told today—illustrates the point. The story concerns a traveler who in medieval times meets three stonecutters along a road and asks each of them what he's doing. The first says, "I am cutting stone." The second says, "I am shaping a cornerstone." But the third answers, "I am building a cathedral." The strength of *The New York Times* lies in the fact that its staff are cathedral builders, as Ochs encouraged them to be, not stonecutters.

Managers, But Not Heroes

In contrast to Ochs, Harold Geneen who ruled the "sovereign state of ITT" was the epitome of the hard-driving, rational manager. When Geneen took over ITT it was a sleepy little company going nowhere. Geneen, widely regarded as a brilliant man, set out to revitalize ITT by setting up a competitive system of management designed to root out "the unshakable facts" around which sound business plans could be made. To do this, Geneen first decentralized the company into a series of free-standing divisions; then, to act as a crosscheck on the judgments of division managers, Geneen established elaborate, financially oriented reporting systems and a strong, aggressive central staff.

The cornerstone of Geneen's management process was the monthly division-review meetings. In these mandatory meetings—held around a block-long conference table set up with microphones for about 150 people—division managers would report their results and then be subjected to intense, rapid-fire questioning from the sharp-eyed staffers around the table. Throughout the questioning, Geneen would sit quietly at the head of the table waiting for a sign of uncertainty or weakness on the part of the manager. At the first such sign, Geneen—in complete command of the facts because of his hard work and infallible memory—would take over the questioning and more often than not tear the manager's presentation to shreds. The search for the unshakable fact was such a grueling experience that grown men were known to break down and cry under the pressure.

Geneen's own ability to achieve results with his unique system of management is undeniable. Under his tenure, ITT was transformed into one of the fastest-growing and most profitable companies on the American business scene. Yet, as soon as Geneen stepped down, a story swept the business world that his successor, Lyman Hamilton, immediately sawed off one end of the infamous conference room table to use for his own, more intimate meetings. As legend has it, he left the rest of the table intact as a symbol of times gone by. We called Hamilton (who was removed from his post by Geneen and other board members nine months after taking over) to verify the story. His response: "It never happened." The fact that such a story circulated—even though it was not true—tells a great deal about the culture that Geneen built at ITT.

Years later, the story of ITT is a different one. Geneen's well-publicized success has eluded his successors. Results are down. The press now focuses more on management blunders than successes. The public reads stories of overseas bribery—during

Geneen's reign—by ITT officials trying to survive the stress of the Geneen system.

Managers like Geneen are guided by an *ethic of competition,* of winning the game. Geneen was a brilliant manager—but surely no hero. Heroes, by contrast, are driven by an *ethic of creation.* They inspire employees by distributing a sense of responsibility throughout the organization. Everybody performs with tangible goals in sight. There is more tolerance for risk taking, thus greater innovation; more acceptance of the value of long-term success, thus greater persistence; more personal responsibility for how the company performs—thus a work force that identifies personal achievement with the success of its firm. Geneen's ethic of competition has not survived as well as Thomas Watson's ethic of creation. Geneen tore his people apart; Watson tore them down only so he could build them back up. Watson's heroism still drives IBM today, decades after his death.

Born Heroes

Some heroes are made, Hollywood-style, in the back lots of corporations. But other heroes are born. These are what we call the visionary heroes, the people whose influence lasts for generations. Visionary heroes like Henry Ford, John D. Rockefeller, William Kellogg, Harley Procter, and others established the major businesses of America. The entrepreneurial spirit of the country fostered them, and they in turn became symbols of that spirit.

The success of these visionaries lies not only in having built an organization but also in having established an institution that survived them and added their personal sense of values to the world. Their visions changed the way we do business, and their influence is still pervasive. By working at institutions like GE, P&G, or IBM, employees share the values of Thomas Edison, the Procters and Gambles, or Thomas Watson—heroes who have been dead for many years but whose ghosts still roam the halls of their companies. These heroes have great symbolic and mythic value within the cultures of their companies. In fact, as leadership symbols today, they are, in an odd way, perfect heroic figures; since they are dead, everyday reality cannot intrude to muddy their exalted images.

In the oral tradition, stories recounting the histories of these visionary heroes pass from generation to generation of managers. Consider Thomas Watson, the builder of IBM. Watson had reached the top of NCR when he was suddenly fired at the age of thirty-nine. He was newly married and out of work for eight or nine long, lean months, when he finally landed a job with a fledgling concern, the Computer Tabulatory Record Company. For his first six years there, Watson had to play second fiddle to the chairman of the board—a financial man who had founded the company—carrying out his decisions, catering to his whims. But he never lost sight of what the company could be. Only when his boss had grown old and Watson had won his trust was Watson able to gain a free hand in managing the organization and to proceed with turning the company into IBM.

His persistence and belief in himself and his vision served him well once again, years later. When the United States was deep into the Depression and countless people were losing their jobs, Watson began hiring salespeople wherever he stumbled upon them. When asked why, he responded, "It's my hobby." In fact, he was convinced that more salespeople would lead to more sales, despite the Depression. He was right, even though all the signs then indicated otherwise.

William Kellogg was another visionary hero who turned out to be right. Few people realize that the cereal we eat today had its origins in the kitchen of a sanitarium. Kellogg was hired by his big brother, Dr. John Harvey Kellogg, to help run his Battle Creek Sanitarium. The doctor kept his thirty-five-year-old brother working twenty hours a day at humiliating chores. He would go to a meeting and tell Will to wait outside the door until he finished his business, and then Will would drive him home late at night even though he would have to be back at the sanitarium at 5 A.M. the next day.

Will labored for two decades in this routine. Finally, he and his brother John had a falling out. John, a vegetarian and a health food fiend, had long experimented—with his brother—with special foods to improve the care given sanitarium inmates. Along the way, their experiments led them to discover a process for making first wheat and then corn flakes as a cereal breakfast. Will, recognizing the potential commercial significance of these discoveries, wanted to set up a company to serve the broader consumer market; John was not in favor. Finally, after years of arguing, Will set out on his own and established the Battle Creek Toasted Corn Flake Company against his older brother's wishes. (One of Will's fiercest competitors turned out to be C.W. Post, a former patient at the sanitarium.) Six months into production, the factory burned down and Will rebuilt it; but twelve months after that, John's sanitarium burned down and Will returned to help him, working at the Battle Creek Corn Flake Company at night only. Despite all of this, William Kellogg continued to turn out his cornflakes, laying the foundation for one of America's largest businesses today.

Charles Steinmetz is one of the greatest heroes of the bet-your-company culture of General Electric. A crippled Austrian immigrant, Steinmetz came as a young man to America and worked in Thomas Edison's lab, which he ran after Edison left. He was responsible for dozens of inventions still used by GE and other companies. But Steinmetz is revered for other reasons. Whenever young engineers joined GE, Steinmetz would invite them home for the weekend in order to learn, sincerely and without political intent, what kind of people they were. Once he adopted one of GE's leading engineers as his own son—and the man's whole family. They all moved into Steinmetz's house and lived with him for twenty years.

These stories have everything to do with GE's supportive, sane culture that demands people treat one another fairly. Steinmetz once remarked that he read fairy tales because he found them packed with more wisdom than scientific tomes. From anyone else, the statement would appear ludicrous; but from Steinmetz, the example is accepted and probably followed.

Stories like those of Watson, Kellogg, and Steinmetz serve a definite purpose in a rich culture. They embody the values of the culture and pass along important lessons in business success and motivation. Visionary heroes share several characteristics that guarantee their survival as legends within their institutions and that become standards of behavior for others to follow. The first and most obvious characteristic is that they were right—about a new product, a new way of doing business, a different organization, whatever. Moreover, they were right in a big way. In most instances, their ideas and visions carved out totally new institutions in America. These heroes have proved the old saying "nothing succeeds like success."

Second, these heroes were persistent; indeed, they were virtually obsessed with seeing their visions become reality. In 1908, the country was in a deep recession, but Will Durant continued to manufacture Buicks even though no buyers could be found. This risk-taking drove the fledgling General Motors to the brink of bankruptcy. But when the recession lifted in 1909, Buick's inventory of unsold cars positioned it for a sales drive that led it to the number one spot in the car market. Often the ideas of heroes run counter to conventional wisdom, and like the heroes in classical literature, each one had dragons to slay and obstacles to overcome. The tales of these heroic efforts add dash to their characters and a mythic quality to their accomplishments.

The third characteristic of the visionary hero is a sense of personal responsibility for the continuing success of the business. Watson once said, "You have to put your heart in the business and the business in your heart." This is more than the testimony of an obsessive workaholic. It's the counsel of a heroic individual who strove to build a business that was as important in what it stood for as it was for its success.

John Patterson, Watson's mentor at NCR, epitomized the sense of personal responsibility visionary heroes bring to their companies. Patterson started NCR when he bought the rights to sell a newfangled contraption—the mechanical cash register—for $5,000 from a group of investors. Shortly after he bought these rights, he tried to sell them back, but the original owners refused— if Patterson wanted his cash back, he would have to make the business a success.

In the 1880s, when Patterson started, goods were most commonly sold by traveling drummers. These colorful characters used to roam the countryside by horse and wagon selling whatever products had been assigned to them on a commission basis.* The only problem from Patterson's point of view was that they were not too successful with the cash register—except for one drummer who for some unknown reason kept sending in orders.

To find out how this one succeeded while the others failed, Patterson traveled along with him, watching, writing notes, and learning the secret of his sales pitch. Then he set up a school and

---

*Few people today realize that Tom Watson, Sr., got his start in business as one of these traveling drummers.

trained the other salesmen, forcing them to memorize the pitch. He kept statistics on their performance, invented sales contests, the 100 Percent Club, and sales meetings. Patterson worked over four decades to learn what selling was all about and then drummed the lessons into his work force. His most famous disciple, Tom Watson, took the lessons further than Patterson could have imagined at IBM.

Patterson was also one of the early businessmen to recognize the importance of the people who worked for him. Again, he took the matter into his own hands. In the early days of NCR, the company exported $50,000 worth of cash registers to Great Britain, which didn't seem to work when they arrived. To find out why, Patterson moved his own desk down to the factory floor. For several weeks he observed the poor working conditions that demotivated the work force. To correct the problem, he thoroughly cleaned the plant, installed special washroom facilities and indoor restrooms, and opened a subsidized employee cafeteria. Few others would have even considered such actions in the period of the 1890s when Patterson took them.

It is this commitment to making the business strong by treating people well and instilling in them a lasting sense of values— even after the hero is gone—that distinguishes visionaries from other dynamic managers. The values and deeds of these heroes live on in the companies they founded and touch each worker in a very personal way. When one of us was working with General Electric, we drove by the General Electric Research Lab where— in an earlier era and building—Charles Steinmetz had conducted his experiments. The driver of the car motioned to the building and said, "Sometimes I get the feeling I can still see the lights on in there and Steinmetz working away." For the driver, and for other employees of GE *who never knew Steinmetz,* he still was a strong influence and serves as an unshakable reminder of the inventiveness that GE holds as a core value of its corporate culture.

Even in today's sophisticated, tabulated world, visionary heroes still spring up, often with the same characteristics as the heroes of earlier times. Visionaries today continue to build institutions and occasionally even new industries—particularly in the world of high-tech. Ken Olsen and a few colleagues conceived of computers that were smaller, cheaper, and hence more useful than the larger mainframes then available. The result was that he founded Digital Equipment Corporation and virtually single-handedly established the minicomputer industry. We've already talked about Jim Treybig and Tandem Computer. And then there is Mary Kay Ash, the housewife, who overcame debilitating arthritis to establish one of the most successful door-to-door sales operations ever. "You can do it" is an ethic that pervades her cosmetic firm, now one of the largest companies in the world headed by a woman. Do Olsen, Treybig, and Ash have the lasting power of a Watson? Only time will tell.

Modern industry needs visionary heroes more than ever before, not only to build new worlds but also to invent better mousetraps. Detroit is desperately in need of a visionary hero to succeed at a seemingly simple task—to build a cheaper and better car. Perhaps the only way such a hero will appear is when one of GM's or Ford's senior managers, literally or figuratively, moves his desk down—John Patterson-style—onto the factory floor.

Visionary heroes in business—as in every other part of life—are a rare breed. Like the heroic generals and political figures of history, they often seem to appear when they are most needed. Yet the function of the hero within an organization is so important that companies with strong cultures often decide to leave little to chance. If a hero hasn't been born, one must be made.

Heroes Who Are Made

Some of the most successful companies in America believe so strongly in heroes that they regularly, and subtly, make them. We call these people "situational heroes," because they tend to arise from particular situations within the business; they are heroes of that moment or day, although they can last for years given the right environment. Watson was a visionary hero for IBM; his supersalesperson of the month is a situational hero. Corporations need both. Visionary heroes light the way for all employees, but their influence is broad and philosophical. Situational heroes, on the other hand, inspire employees with the example of their day-to-day success.

Corporate heroes are like heroes in a war. Time and time again, the people who think they're heroes and charge out of the foxhole before everyone else are not heroes; they're casualties.

The real heroes are those who get medals by doing extraordinary things under the circumstances and who embody the culture's ethic of success. Companies award these heroes with Purple Hearts by naming them "editor of the year," or star regional manager, or by rewarding the person who lands a big contract, or by tolerating the renegade whose outrageous deeds can be counted on to break tense deadlocks. The employee who wants to gain power and responsibility often looks to these heroes. A new worker will ask an old hand, What am I supposed to do? The old hand replies, Look to Charlie, he's on the fast track. Charlie is that employee's hero of the moment.

Companies with strong cultures are quite adept at recognizing and creating situational heroes. Many place their potential candidates in bellwether jobs—certain critical positions that epitomize what the core of the culture is all about. When people know what the hero-making jobs are, they're energized. They know what's expected of them; they're free to be innovative. And over a period of time, the company becomes more innovative; it performs better. Creating such jobs and increasing their visibility is a prime requisite for hero-making.

Unfortunately, not many companies have such a keen sense of influence; too many today are promoting the wrong people and sending conflicting signals through the corporate culture. The 1960s was the age of conglomerates, and sharp-pencil financial types got ahead. The 1970s was the decade of strategic planning, and MBAs armed with cats, dogs, cash cows, and stars ascended the corporate heights. The danger here is obvious—industry needs to stop promoting by fad and, instead, must promote people who embody key values of the business if it is to be successful.

At Procter & Gamble, the brand manager job is as prestigious as a Ph.D from Harvard; it's the premier young turk job. IBM, that paragon of effective culture-building singles out the fast-track newcomers from its thousands of new employees and then assigns them, for a year at a time, as "assistants to" senior managers. Each of them is clearly a nominee for the hero role. For the year of their assignment, these heroes-to-be are given the task of answering customer complaint letters. A dubious reward? Indeed not. This seemingly ho-hum function ensures an increased sensitivity on their part to the importance that IBM attaches to customer service. Service is of major importance at IBM, a lesson the young heroes never forget. Similarly, at GE, being a general manger is what's celebrated; the ethic that goes with the turf is that the general manager can handle anything.

Employees don't have to be leaders or young turks to win the rewards of heroism. Strong-culture companies create heroes throughout the corporation. The following line from IBM's house organ, "Think," is a case in point: "All those happy faces, you'd think he was the Prince carrying the glass slipper to Cinderella, when in fact he's dropping off a Selectric that the customer recently ordered." Yet this line anoints salesman Don McCroskey a hero for being a thirty-year member of the company's highly honored Hundred Percent Club. Only those IBMers who have consistently met sales quotas are eligible to join. The trick? IBM deliberately sets their sales quotas so that roughly 80 percent of the force makes the club.

Outsiders may question the value of such an easy reward. The value is that there are more heroes, and IBM can thus rave about how a McCroskey first got to join the club when he received an unexpected order for eight typewriters at the last minute. If you're having a hard time at IBM, you'll measure yourself against McCroskey. If he can do it, so can you. Think of the effectiveness of McCroskey as a hero versus a corporate policy memo on the virtues of perseverance. There's no question which will serve to motivate salespeople to sell one more typewriter every day.

Not only do strong culture companies recognize and reward certain positions within the organization, they also foster the development of certain types of people as heroes. Perhaps no other situational hero fires the imagination of employees more than the outlaw or maverick: Billy the Kid, Patton, bad boys with a heart of gold. This hero is necessary when the company needs some degree of creativity for a challenge to existing values. Outlaws can symbolize the darker side of an organization, yet their bizarre behavior will release the pent-up tension everyone feels, and, for savvy companies, help identify areas where change is necessary.

Twenty years ago, an outlaw at IBM was famous for driving his big Harley-Davidson motorcycle inside the research center, which is normally quieter than a morgue. While the scientists were working busily, he would come roaring down the corridors. Yet IBM didn't fire him, and not just because he was extremely good at what he did. More important, he was useful to the corporation because he was a lightening rod for releasing people's tension—not at the corporation but at himself. Yet on the whole, the scientists liked him *because* he was a lunatic. They admired his ability to do things they would like to do themselves, if only they could get away with them.

Outlaws are eccentric but highly competent. They are deliberate violators of cultural norms, but at the same time they have enough talent to meet the main requirements that ensure their survival within the culture. All those who don't have the ability or possibly the talent to violate those demands identify with the person who does. Robert Townsend, when he ran Avis, was an outlaw. As CEO he took a six-month sabbatical, which is bizarre behavior. Later, he reported to the press that CEOs had nothing to do; they *had* to play golf. Townsend, of course, knew exactly what he was doing; he had thousands of people out there "trying harder" while he ostensibly relaxed.

Another outlaw, a young inventor who didn't like working in a big, impersonal office, got himself moved to a smaller unit elsewhere within his office equipment company. But he wasn't content to stay there. At night, he and his buddies would sneak back into the main factory and "steal" parts because they weren't supposed to be producing new products, yet that's what they wanted to do. They soon built an entire series of new products for the company. What's more incredible, more than half of the new products that the company introduced over the next four years were produced by this engineer and his buddies. And he's a big hero for having actually pulled that off—albeit a hero despised by mainstream engineering managers of the corporation.

As outlandish as it may sound, smart managers actually cultivate certain of these mutineers. At IBM, top management created the IBM Fellows Program to free outstanding technical personnel from organizational constraints. Deciding that the company was too straitlaced, that maybe there were too many white shirts around, this bastion of conservatism through this program encouraged its outlaw heroes—just as they do most things in that highly structured company, systematically. Ads in *Newsweek* described the program by speaking about IBM's affection for "Dreamer's, Heretics, Gadflies . . ."

One of the outlaws IBM finally hired was a man who owned two California wineries, ran war-game simulations as a hobby, held a Ph.D. in microelectronics, and wore open shirts and gold chains down to his waist. IBM gave him a $10 million budget to spend in any way he wanted and access to four thousand engineers. In all, about fifty such outlaw heroes were consciously and deliberately created as countercultural to the rest of the organization but crucial for instilling the ethic that ideas are really important, that a creative personal style can make an important difference. There are comparable programs at Texas Instruments and at other strong culture companies.

Outlaws are highly valued in a strong culture company; they keep the company evolving. Knowing this, corporate directors commonly place them in creative jobs or appoint them to head R & D divisions—skunk works. In a strong culture company, outlaws—despite their maverick bent—can still identify with the company's values. In a weak culture, however, mavericks can't identify with the culture's vague or contradictory values, and so they turn against those values and become whistle blowers. Whistle blowers are forced out of the mainstream and into a subculture that competes with the main culture. This was John Z. DeLorean's predicament at GM. As an outlaw, he was tolerated and performed successfully while the GM culture maintained its strength in the 1950s and 1960s. But later, as the culture faltered, DeLorean resigned and got involved in a book criticizing the company's practices.

A second type of "made" hero is the compass-hero. If a company is in a situation where things have to change and there are no role models for the change, it is good management practice to find role models, plant them inside the company, and make them heroes. By doing so, top management communicates that, in the future, business will be done either more aggressively or more courteously; in any case, less as it was done and more as the new hero's style conveys.

For years, AT&T had developed an organization of almost consciously average, low-key, likeable people called "Bell-shaped men." All of them, even those high in the executive ranks, were exemplified by the repairmen who traditionally took their sweet time installing telephones and making sure they worked, even though many of these accounts were not profitable for AT&T. But when phone service was deregulated, AT&T employees suddenly needed to learn marketing in their newly competitive business environment. Thus Archie McGill, a former IBM executive, was made vice president of business marketing, and he became a compass hero. He had cut his teeth in a much more competitive environment, and as a result, his approach to business is very different from traditional AT&T norms. McGill and his people challenge traditional practices, and, according to the *Wall Street Journal*, step across organizational lines. Thus, at AT&T, McGill stands out. In hiring McGill, management brought in not only important new skills but a symbol of the new direction.

The hunker-down hero is the direct opposite of the compass hero. Persistence is a highly valued characteristic in most companies, and most of them honor their persisters by deifying them. For instance, 3M is a very innovative company. Lew Lehr, the current CEO, tells a story about a now-retired vice president who at one point in his career was fired because he persisted in working on a new product idea even though his boss was hounding him: "That's a stupid idea. Stop! We gave you a year to try it and it isn't working, so go do something else." The worker refused, so they fired him.

But he wouldn't leave. He stayed on in an unused office working without salary on his idea. In due course, he was rehired and worked out the idea. Years later he became a vice president of the company. He finally did perfect his idea, and his invention earned windfalls for 3M. What 3M people remember is his persistence in doing the right thing—which was to keep working on the new product. A major element in the 3M culture, therefore, concerns doing what you believe in—and persisting at it. As Raymond Herzog, a retired CEO, said, "If a guy has a really good success pattern, I'll go along with him if he says he can go to the moon on Scotch tape."

L. L. Bean's Maine Hunting Shoe spawned a multimillion dollar mail-order business which now has a real hero to protect it. L. L. Bean's grandson, Leon Gorman, refused to remove a Maine Warden Jacket from the Bean catalog even though none had been sold for many years. Why? Gorman understands that, in the face of a throwaway culture, long-lasting, even permanent, products have built the corporate reputation. And so he is reluctant to drop old items or add new ones. Unlike his unfortunate competitor,

Abercrombie & Fitch, Gorman never moves far from the Maine Hunting Shoe, or the Warden Jacket. Employees and customers can depend on the culture of L. L. Bean.

Sacred-cow heroes have a minor niche of their own. Every company, every industry has its objects of reverence. Scholars are pale, disheveled, and disorganized; bankers are solid; high-tech people are roll-up-the-sleeves types. In all these cultures you find heroes who are heroes simply because they epitomize the norms of the culture. They dress like it, look like it, and are liked by everyone. They're not quite heroes, but are sacrosanct people because though they may or may not be competent, they do personify what the organization thinks it is about.

Take as an example one of the survivors in one of the toughest businesses we know—a manufacturer of large complicated equipment. In a business like this—where machines are years in the making and where it takes up to five years to find out if the team made the right decision—managers tend to be tough, macho, and well into their sixties.

One of the leading engineers at one of these firms was called on to examine a machine that was making suspicious noises. As the expert, he put his ear to the machine to find out what the noises were when suddenly it exploded and burned him horribly down one side of his face. He spent months recovering, but when he finally did, he wore his disfigurement proudly as though to show it off. And instead of feeling repulsed, everybody revered him for it. The most savvy engineers would almost tiptoe into his office to ask if he would check their calculations. They assumed that "any man who had been through all that would know whether you were doing it right. He knew how bad it was to make a bad calculation," as one engineer said. He is a good manager but an even greater hero, regardless of what he may accomplish from now on. The myth of him does his real work in the company. He is a hero.

In general, sacred cows tend either to be precociously young or old and statesmanlike. For a brief, sweet period of time, the corporation's young will be revered as its hope for the future. And the same is true with "the old man" to whom more is attributed than is really there.

A word of caution: beware the company with a sacred cow at its helm. Sacred cows rarely make anything happen; they want things to work as they've always worked and thus can be blind-sided in a crisis. Only when a company's historic vision is perfectly compatible with its environment is it better off having a sacred cow at the helm to continue the time-honored traditions.

Heroism—Not Charisma

In our pop society, the excesses of the media often suggest that heroes—born or made—are charismatic individuals, leaders who will deliver a speech, a request, an edict, and in the end inspire everyone to rise in absolute agreement and trust. This is not the picture in corporate America (nor according to James MacGregor Burns's *Leadership* is it generally the case elsewhere). On the contrary, heroes—such as General Woods at Sears, Watson, Ford, Rockefeller, and others—tend not to be charismatic. They're hard, insensitive, often unlikable sorts—not the John Kennedys of the world but the Lyndon B. Johnsons.

Whatever else he was, LBJ was tremendously effective at getting things done. He established the Great Society and passed an incredible barrage of legislation that changed the face of this country. John Kennedy, the exemplar of the charismatic leader, had nowhere near the record of accomplishment in his sadly shortened term as president. Because Johnson saw himself cast in a symbolic role, he could pretend to be difficult and angry—for a purpose. When Johnson was trying to swing around a male senator, he would call the man into his office, verbally assault him, and then put his arm around him and take him into the men's room. Once there, he would regale his guest and former antagonist with a story about life on the ranch—only minutes after he had swarmed all over his target.

In recent times, this behavior could be encapsulated in one single infamous sentence of doom: "I just don't like you very much." Thus, according to *The Wall Street Journal*, did Henry Ford II bluntly explain to a startled Lee Iacocca—a thirty-year veteran at Ford Motor Company who had worked his way right up to the presidency—why he was being summarily fired. If nothing else,

Ford knew what he wanted done and did it—honestly and directly, without carping.

In contrast to the warm, humane managers promoted by business publications today, what businesses need are individuals concerned about building something of value and sensitive mostly to the needs of the organization they are trying to establish. Call it bastardly, but also call it heroic. The point is this: modern managers who try to be humane may at the same time undermine the values upon which the culture of the institution rests. Modern heroes may need to be hard and "insensitive" to keep a company consistent with its goals and vision—the very elements that made it strong in the first place.

Thomas Watson himself confessed to learning leadership under NCR's Patterson, whom he described as "an amalgam of St. Paul, Poor Richard, and Adolf Hitler." Watson could be a benevolent boss, but even IBMers who worshipped him never considered Watson a friend or, given his obsessiveness, a very pleasant person to be around.

Heroes are concerned with the set of beliefs and values they hold and in making sure these beliefs and values are inculcated in the people around them. On the one hand, this means protecting the people in one's organization—taking care of them in times of sickness, giving them full employment, and being otherwise responsible for the lives of those over whom you have stewardship. On the other hand, this means not permitting them to fail in any way. When this happens, heroes tend to overreact, sometimes in a dramatic way.

NCR's John Patterson was unique in his tortures. One of his executives once returned from lunch to find his desk and chair parked outside on the curb in front of the factory. He emerged from the cab to watch his furniture get soaked in kerosene, then set afire. He got back in the cab and drove off, lest he too should be torched. This was not a humane way of being told you're through; but whatever the executive had done to deserve this, the deed was probably never repeated by others.

In more recent time, a visionary who didn't quite succeed in institution-building is Dr. Edwin Land of Polaroid, inventor of the Polaroid-Land Camera. He wanted desperately to convey the essence of his social vision of what Polaroid should be to the rest of the people in his employ. Land worked to create an environment in which good scientific work could be done, and he wanted to give others the freedom to do it. Thus, he invented programs at Polaroid wherein if employees in Job A thought they might like Job B better, they could sample Job B on a half-day basis for three months. If the trial worked out, they could change jobs. If it didn't work out, they were guaranteed a return to Job A at no cost to their career. Land insisted on this policy. The whole reason for making new products that would make money was to create an environment in which people could be free to pursue their own interests.

As soon as Land stepped down from the stewardship of Polaroid, the policy disappeared. Managers complained that it ruined production lines because everybody wanted to go work in the lab. Land had the vision but not the hardness to communicate it forcefully to the rest of the organization or to the new generation of managers.

Powerful leaders traditionally consider the company first. Like Watson, they "put the business in their heart" and thus crowd out softer sentiments. It's a lesson today's managers should learn as an antidote to the hype on business humaneness. Humaneness is important, but the goals of the culture are paramount.

It is time that American industry recognized the potential of heroes. If companies would treat people like heroes even for a short time, they might end up being heroes. Employee motivation is a complex science, but its foundations rest on the simple recognition that we all need to feel important in some phase of our lives. Heroes, as they epitomize the best that people can be, are the stuff and hope of culture. Quality circles, management by objectives (MBO), organizational charts, and concepts are useful, but they cannot influence behavior the way a hero can. When companies make heroes out of bosses and workers—that is, when we all accept the responsibility of playing to a world stage—will we banish the sterility of modern organization.

Heroes are the leading actors in a strong corporate culture, yet they are only part of a rich set of behavioral procedures that define how work gets done day by day. These procedures—the rites and rituals of corporate life—provide the fabric in which heroes can be showcased. Let's look at them next.

4

Rites and Rituals:
Culture in Action

When critics lambasted Napoleon for reinstituting the merely symbolic and practically worthless Legion of Honor medal, he replied, "You lead men by baubles, not words." This sounds cynical, but actually it's a realistic view of human nature. Achievements deserve recognition, and recognition in turn motivates even greater accomplishments. Like Napoleon's army, a corporate culture—and the values it embodies—must be ritualized and celebrated if it's going to thrive.

But celebration and hoopla, as we all know, are only a small part of corporate life—albeit a larger part of the life of strong culture companies. What about the day-to-day activities in a corporate culture?

Marvin Bower in *The Will To Manage* describes a manager's responsibility to spell out for his or her employees "the way we do things around here." Bower's implicit assumption was that unless you tell people what you want them to do and how you want them to do it, you have no right to expect them to infer, by some mysterious alchemic process, just what you had in mind. Therefore, you have no real right to expect them to do what you want them to do.

Strong culture companies understand this dilemma very well. They communicate exactly how they want their people to behave. They spell out standards of acceptable decorum—so people who visit or work in any of their places of business can know what to expect. They call attention to the way in which procedures—for example, strategic planning and budgeting—are to be carried out, so the fault if the procedures fail is substantive, not just a failure to follow prescribed process. Often they also establish ways, or at least the settings, in which their people can play and have fun—so that people will know they belong to a functioning and complete society. In short, strong culture companies create the rites and rituals of behavior in their corporate life—the rites and rituals that exercise the most visible and pervasive influence on, as Bower says it, "the way we do things around here."

The old heroes of corporate culture were attentive to the orchestration of all rituals of work life—from hirings and firings, to rewards and meeting formats, to writing styles, modes of speech, and the way to conduct a retirement dinner. They knew how significant these rituals were because they gave the culture a tangible, cohesive form. Today most managers will recognize formal procedures like budgeting or strategic planning as being important and manageable; but they miss or ignore all the rest of what goes on around them: the life of the culture.

In strong culture companies, *nothing is too trivial.* Any event that occurs in a work context is an event to be managed. These companies take pride in the way they do things and work hard to make sure that way is right. They regard the carrying out of activities in the correct way as tangible examples of the strength of the culture. Consider breakfast, for instance. You'll never see IBM salespeople along with the hordes of others congregating at Howard Johnson's every morning, because IBMers are encouraged to see their time as too valuable to waste in a roadside diner. When IBMers want coffee they will share it with a client or colleague. The point is for IBMers to begin the day not discussing baseball or the price of steak but to get a head start by focusing on the company, the industry, and their habits as professionals. In its early days, Holiday Inns had similar intentions via prayer breakfasts. In another company, everyone gathers for a regular Friday lunch, during which the entire staff mingles as equals in a camaraderie the otherwise busy work routine doesn't permit. Only in this benign atmosphere can serious things be discussed—and not be taken too seriously.

At Vector, the ritualized lunch serves a different purpose. According to president and founder Lore Harp, "I started something a year ago called the Friendship Lunch, where every week we post a sign throughout the company and nine people can sign up to be taken to a restaurant for lunch with a different vice president or myself. My turn is every fifth week.

"What prompted me to do that was that one day I was walking through the manufacturing floor and I just stood there and looked at all those people working and I thought, 'you really don't know any of them.' I don't know what they think, what makes them tick. And I looked at that age group and they were something between 18 and 30, and I thought, 'my God they are really much more representative of the United States than I am. They are the people who will be voting for the next president. They are the people who will make major decisions and make a great impact on the economy. I really would like to hear what they have to say.'

"It was important for them to know me, but I wanted to hear more about how they felt. It's vital to know how people function in the office during the day. And to assure them that they're not considered 'kitchen help.' "

Many rituals or ceremonies seem like just a lot of hoopla. Yet the underlying purpose is very serious, as in the case of one large company we know: the company recognizes many successful efforts by transforming an old Navy back-patting ritual into the presentation of a plaque called the "Attaboy." When someone receives five "Attaboys" at this company, they are eligible for one "Gotcha," which is a still higher tribute, personally signed by the head of the company's U.S. operations.

The presentation of each Attaboy plaque is accompanied by a big ceremony. All work comes to a halt as a manager marches out into the hallway and rings a bell. Everyone files down from the executive suite and other offices, interrupting whatever they were doing to gather around. With a great flourish, the manager announces that another "Attaboy" is to be awarded. He reads its contents:

"I hereby announce, by the power vested in me, the award of one big Attaboy to _____ in return for his/her exemplary service in _____ program." There are congratulations all around, and when the winner goes back to his/her office, he/she probably tacks the Attaboy to the office wall.

Managers earning $150,000 a year or more earnestly compete for these plaques. "Attaboys" are a symbol of recognition, and there is enough humor in the process to make it more fun than competitive. In awarding the "Attaboy," the company laughs at itself in a gentle way. Employees can't take the ceremony seriously—but it's a very serious ceremony. People care so much about these awards that when they complete a successful project, they automatically joke "Do I get an 'Attaboy' for that?" The "Attaboy" ritual acknowledges achievement, and thus makes the corporate do's and don'ts clear to everyone in the culture. The bottom line gets a boost along with morale.

Awards such as "Attaboy" are serious and important because they are signs of belonging to the culture. For instance, one of our colleagues visited a friend to celebrate with him his promotion to vice president in his company. As our colleague entered his office, he was in the process of nailing a "Jack-in-the-Box" award plaque to the wall of his new office. Seeing our colleague, he said in a slightly embarrassed voice, "This is the fifth time I've tacked this silly damned plaque up in a new office. I've had it for so long, it just wouldn't seem right to be without it."

The Impact of Symbolic Actions

The practical payoffs of "Attaboy" plaques and other forms of play, ritual, and ceremony are obvious to culture builders:

Play.   This creative side of corporate life releases tension and encourages innovation. Despite the fact that it has no real purpose and no rules, play in its various forms (jokes, teasing, brainstorming, and strategizing) bonds people together, reduces conflict, and creates new visions and cultural values. By encouraging experimentation, it can help regenerate the culture. Tandem, IBM, and DEC all provide opportunities for play on company time, whether through workshops, exercise facilities, beer busts, retreats, or strategy sessions.

Ritual.   These rules guide behavior in corporate life and are, in effect, dramatizations of the company's basic cultural values. Behind each ritual is a myth that symbolizes a belief central to the culture. Without this connection, rituals are just habits and do nothing but give people a false sense of security and certainty. Rituals provide the place and script with which employees can experience meaning; they bring order to chaos. IBM, Dana, Mary Kay Cosmetics, NCR, Holiday Inns, and P&G all make ritual a serious part of day-to-day operations, not simply an afterthought.

Ceremony.   Whether they are cultural extravaganzas or simple events when employees pass particular milestones, ceremonies help the company celebrate heroes, myths, and sacred symbols. Like habits, rituals are commonplace and taken for granted. Ceremonies, meanwhile, are extraordinary; the full corporate spotlight shines on them. Ceremonies place the culture on display and provide experiences that are remembered by employees. Anyone who has been to or read about the Polaroid annual meeting or Mary Kay's conventions feels the power of these events. Properly done, ceremonies keep values, beliefs, and heroes uppermost in employees' minds and hearts.

The Necessity of Rituals

Without expressive events, any culture will die. In the absence of ceremony or ritual, important values have no impact. Ceremonies are to the culture what the movie is to the script, the concert is to the score, or the dance is to values that are difficult to express in any other way.

Let's look at a manager who hasn't learned this lesson: as a young executive, he had just taken over the helm of a company. Imbued with idealism, he wanted to end the bickering he had seen take place in negotiations with labor. To do this, he was ready to give workers as much as his company could afford. Consequently, he asked some members of his staff to study his firm's own wage structure and decide how it compared with other companies, as well as a host of other related matters. He approached the collective bargaining with a halo of goodness surrounding him. Asking for the floor, he proceeded to describe what he had done and with a big smile on his face, he made an offer.

Throughout the entire presentation, the union officials simply stared at him in amazement. The executive had offered more than the union could have reasonably expected. But that didn't matter. When he finished, the officials lambasted and denounced him for trying to destroy the collective bargaining process and for attempting to buy off labor. They announced that they would not stand for unethical maneuvering and immediately asked for five cents more than the idealistic executive had offered.

Like many others of his breed, the modern executive was missing an essential point. Collective bargaining is a ritual that helps parties reach an agreement, and the form is just as important as the results. Without these forms—whether play, ceremony, or ritual—the unique characteristics of the culture are lost.

People, such as the young executive described above, often miss the point or overlook the benefits of focusing on the ritualistic aspect of day-to-day corporate life. Like this young executive, they say "Let's skirt the process and get right to the substantive heart of the matter." But by doing this they cut other people—like the union reps in the story—out of the process and thus not only alienate them but also lose the value of their contributions. Some react negatively to spelling out rituals in such copious detail by saying that they are too authoritarian. What these critics miss is the tremendously liberating influence of an agreed-upon set of ground rules. If employees live within these ground rules—ground rules which facilitate communication and commerce with others in the culture—then they are free to exercise all manner of creativity in ways that don't foul up everyone else. As the chief financial officer of a fast-growing computer company said to his managers after taking them through their first budgeting exercise, "Trust the budget; the budget will make you free." Every good company and its managers need to know the full range of opportunities available in creating an array of ceremonies and rituals that exemplify the culture; savvy top managers will take advantage of all options.

Communications and Social Rituals

The unwritten rules of personal communication (let's call them "howdy" rituals) occupy an amazing amount of company time. But take them away and no one would know how to behave. They let people know where they stand, reinforce an individual's identity within the company, and set the tone for the way in which people relate to one another.

When Thomas Watson insisted that everyone in IBM address each other as Mr., Mrs., or Miss, he wasn't arbitrarily exercising personal power. He was signaling instead that everyone who worked at IBM was a professional worthy of respect. This kind of recognition at companies from IBM to P&G to GE shows up in the way employees think about their companies and their work.

These rituals of social exchange govern relationships between bosses and workers, old and young, professionals and support staff, men and women, insiders and outsiders. They specify how formally or informally individuals are addressed, the long-standing customs that govern conversation, how much emotion or public controversy is permitted, who speaks first in meetings, and even who is permitted to end a conversation.

How do people learn them? In part through hazing rites that are often staged to tear people down before accepting them into a culture. Such was the experience of a young engineer, fresh from college, who survived his first days at General Electric. As he told us:

"When I graduated from MIT, my first job was with GE in Venezuela, and it was terrible. I walked in with my brand-new slide rule, wearing my newly bought suit and college ring, when I was greeted by some gruff old supervisor who immediately handed me a broom and told me to go sweep the floor. Needless to say, I stood there for a while with my mouth hanging open.

"With all my engineering credentials and my new suit, I couldn't believe this jerk expected me to sweep the floor. But since I was new to the job, I did as he asked. It was the best lesson I ever learned in my life."

GE makes their trainees learn about the real world before they are allowed to enter it. The message of the hazing rite is clear: you may know a lot, but here your vast knowledge of ideas needs to be matched with an intimate knowledge of this place—from the ground up.

Hazing is a common rite in business. Managers often transform new hotshots into sacrificial lambs by sending them to consult with the well-known bastard who can't stand young kids. The manager knows the bastard will knock the hotshots off their feet every time; they'll learn the importance of experience within the culture. To succeed, it is necessary to recognize the contribution and wisdom of those who have been with the company for a long time.

This hazing rite also communicates a culture's values. Henry Kissinger, then secretary of state, asked a young Rhodes scholar on his staff to write a paper on a rather esoteric topic. Because the young man was new to this very prestigious job, he sweated over it for two weeks. Two days after he submitted it, Kissinger returned it with a note scrawled across the top: "This is awful, do it again."

The young man was shattered. But, he thought hard about the paper and decided he could do a better job. Slaving away on it for another week, he sent a new version to Kissinger, which was again returned with a note: "This is worse that the first version; can't you do better?"

He did a third rewrite and this time attached a note that said: "It may not be good enough and I'm sorry for wasting your time. But this is the best I can possibly do on this subject. I'm sorry it took so long." In response came Kissinger's note: "I'll read it now." The hazing conveyed the message that you never give anything to a superior in that culture unless it represents your best effort.

Just as the hazing ritual sets up a conflict, so other bonding and healing rituals help mediate the conflicts and misunderstandings that threaten cultural harmony. Consider an example from a high-tech firm. A company division manager was dominating a meeting to the consternation of the marketing manager. After the first day, the marketing manager exploded with the complaint that no one ever listened to him. He believed the company should move in new directions to seize new market opportunities. As an example, he noted that the company could produce liquid soap for a nickel and sell it for five times that amount. His colleagues, genetic engineers, coldly dismissed the idea; they weren't about to stoop to making liquid soap. Although the marketer was only using soap as a metaphor, the meeting ended with bad feelings.

Toward the end of the second day, however, the marketing manager received an award from his colleagues: a bottle of liquid soap. This healing process converted a tantrum into some fun that everyone could appreciate. The ritual rebuilt cohesion among the different divisions and provided a story that would long be remembered in the culture.

Strong cultures also have rituals that mediate differences before conflict takes place. Dee Hock, president of Visa International, carefully staged such a ritual in 1974 when the International Organizing Committee, composed of members throughout the world, was experiencing a particularly difficult time. The differences among the committee members, who represented divergent parts of the Visa organization, seemed irreconcilable.

Before abandoning the effort, a final meeting was held. Hock explains: "A gift for those who had labored so hard on an apparently futile task seemed appropriate. A unique set of cuff links was designed. On one was a relief map of one-half of the world. Around it in Latin was inscribed the phrase, 'Studium Ad Prosperandum,' or 'The Will to Succeed.' On the other, in relief, was the other half of the world surrounded by the phrase, 'Voluntas in Conveniendum,' or 'The Grace to Compromise.' They were cast in gold and the die stored in a vault—to be broken if the effort was abandoned, or kept for the production of future sets for directors should it succeed.

"At a welcoming dinner, they were presented to each member of the organizing committee with the request that they be worn throughout the meeting—on their right arm 'The Will to Succeed,' and on their left, 'The Grace to Compromise' as a reminder that if the world of bank cards was to be united, it could only be through their efforts." The ritual dissipated tension between the disparate committee members *and* reinforced the values of Visa's culture.

These cuff links, says Hock, are now treasured possessions, and their slogans have become the Visa International motto. Without these rules of social exchange, which Hock's ritual made plain, no one would know what to do and nothing would ever get done.

Work Rituals

Most of us can see that social amenities are ritualized. But we'd like to suggest that much of what managers and workers do seriously each day is also ritual. Unlike the social exchanges, work rituals do not produce direct results, but they are just as valuable because they provide a sense of security and common identity and assign meaning to mundane activities.

Prevailing ideas about the importance of tangible results in business obscure the ritualistic part of work. Employees value procedures, not as rituals but because they "get the job done." Most managers can provide elaborate justifications for just how important their individual strategies are to productivity. Salespeople point out the importance of a certain pitch; bureaucrats swear by their memos; surgeons substantiate precisely how an operation saved a patient's life; an oil company executive can describe in great detail how computerized management brought the project in on time without cost overruns.

Consider the ritual of surgeons. They "scrub down" for about seven minutes before an operation (in fact automatic timers shut off the water after seven minutes in some hospitals). Now most doctors will argue that germs are destroyed in thirty seconds—but the tradition is faithfully upheld. To do otherwise is to "break scrub"—a signal that the surgeon is ill-prepared. By following this and other rituals, the surgeon stays within cultural boundaries that provide security during a high-risk operation. If the operation is not a success, it is not the fault of the culture. Such procedures also maintain our belief in the value of medical science.

The importance of work rituals is easily proved if we take them away. For example, many companies are now computerizing work at the technical level. On paper, the change appears liberating; employees will no longer have to do repetitive work. But managers all over the country are finding that these employees are *resisting* the change. This reluctance to change makes sense if we look at technical work as a cultural ritual that contributes to the stability of the company. The employees are signaling that they are comfortable with the work the way it used to be done. They know it produces results; for example, they get paid for doing it each month. Therefore, in enacting the old ritual, they enhance their own sense of self-worth. To enter figures on a balance sheet is doing the job. To enter numbers on a computer is something else all together. It's more productive, but it's also different, unproven, and therefore also far less satisfying. To these employees, it is like substituting a Cheezit cracker for a communion wafer.

In a way, of course, it is the business of culture: it provides a way for people to justify a belief in their own self-worth and that of their work. But work rituals are important to the company as a whole. They signal to the outside world just how effective the culture is, especially if the product is intangible. By recognizing this importance, companies can use work rituals to help build a strong culture that will produce even better results.

Management Rituals

In the same way that much of the work of a company is carried out in the form of prescribed work rituals, managers are engaged in rituals in their day-to-day life as well. We acknowledge that most managers today would be very reluctant to admit that their cherished procedures are no more nor less than rituals.

What do we mean when we talk of managerial rituals? Let's start by exploring some popular ideas about what a manager's job consists of. First there is coordination. But what is coordination other than performance of one or more commonly accepted rituals, such as "touching base," writing memos, or holding meetings. No one we know of really knows what coordination means; so what a manager does is to carry out these rituals *in the hope* that the desired end product—better coordination—will be achieved.

Let's look at another common managerial activity—decision-making, and even more important, strategic decision-making. The literature on management is full of treatises on optimization and conceptual strategic frameworks such as portfolio analysis and cost curves. But are these tools really involved in decision-making? They are—we believe—as rituals that give individual managers a comfortable feeling that they are bringing the best available managerial technology to bear on carrying out this key responsibility: decision-making. How managers really make decisions is to gather people in a room, review *available* information and data, and if pressed, "decide" as best they can. And, as Alfred Sloan of GM reportedly said, "If you do it right 51 percent of the time you will end up a hero. Everything else involved in the process is simply ritual."

The literature provides direct evidence of this ritualistic side of managerial life. The Navy began construction of the Polaris nuclear submarine in the 1950s using three innovative management techniques: a management center, PERT, and a weekly management meeting presided over by the project's CEO, Admiral Raborn. These techniques were credited with the initial success of the submarine, although later research studies found few connections between these procedures and the project's progress.

This is an indication, we think, that the techniques were more important as rituals. The weekly meetings provided an opportunity for the admiral to criticize members of the staff in front of an audience of officers and civilians. In later years, the meetings were "like going to church"; they bonded everyone together. On the other hand, the management center and PERT (performance, evaluation, and review technique) created a good image for the project. PERT, after all, was then a brand-new management concept. Outsiders who came to observe the project were led straight-away to the management center to be dazzled by a display of charts and related jargon. Even the most worldly visitor would leave saying "Polaris has a lot of pizazz. These people must really know what they're doing." Insiders, of course, knew that the PERT business had nothing to do with running the actual Polaris project. PERT's real value was in convincing the outside world that this project was important. As one insider said years later: "These procedures were valuable in selling the importance of the mission. More importantly, the PERT charts and the rest of the gibberish let us build a fence to keep the rest of the Navy out and get across the message that *we* were the top managers."

In the Navy—or anywhere else—the most important manage-ment ritual continues to be the formal meeting. All companies have them, but their form varies widely in terms of:

The number held.   Some companies require many; in oth-ers it is a real breakthrough to get everyone to sit down to one meeting a month.

The setting.   Formal conference rooms are favored most often, but others relegate meetings to desks or tables crammed into offices.

The table's shape.   Round tables help create good peer rela-tions among meeting participants; tables with distinct heads rein-force hierarchies.

Who sits where.   In high-tech firms, the seats are up for grabs; in more structured companies, the boss sits at the head, with the next most important person beside him or her.

Number and composition of attendees.   In very formal cultures, only peers attend meetings; junior people wait to be sum-moned by the court. In less formal companies, attendees represent a hodgepodge of levels.

The conduct.   Give-and-take predominates in some com-panies; others favor theater-like settings in which the attendees are mesmerized by dazzling slide presentations.

Unlike some aspects of company culture, no one meeting form seems better than any other. The form of the meeting is simply a reflection of the culture. Bennett Cerf, co-founder of Random House,would bolt out of any room the instant he sensed that a meeting might start. In the publishing world, where individual initiative is crucial, Cerf felt that meetings were the worst possible way to get work done.

A successful high-tech company took the opposite approach to meetings. Some years ago, we acted as consultants to this company because top management wanted to reduce overhead costs. Our initial effort fell on deaf ears. To help, a senior vice-president suggested, "You don't understand the culture. Live the way I live and you'll get it."

One of our colleagues, Tom Peters, lived with the manager for a week. He slept in the senior vice-president's house, played with the kids and the dog, went to work with him in the morning, spent the day, and returned at night. At the end of the week, Peters drew up an accurate picture of their ritualistic meetings that pointed up flaws in the larger management structure:

- Ninety-seven percent of all working hours were spent in meetings.

- Most meetings were prescheduled.

- The meetings were attended by an average of thirty-five people usually drawn from three or four different staff levels.

- The meetings featured lengthy, complex slide shows filled with facts and figures, and presented by junior staff people.

- The purpose of the meetings was to facilitate decision-making.

- But few decisions were actually made because of time pressures and confusion over real options.

We showed the presentation to the senior vice-president who said that indeed it reflected their culture perfectly. They believed in facts and a meritocracy—but the rituals that buttressed these beliefs (the long recitation of facts at the meetings and the large numbers of people invited) prevented them from accomplishing their goals and only added to company overhead. Over a period of time, the company changed the rituals to bring them into line with other values.

Those unproductive meetings were stifling a culture that needed good results to succeed. But in other cultures, meetings without specific results *reinforce* success. In a capital-goods company we know, meetings are held during lunch and practically everyone is involved. The company head sits in the head chair, and next to him sits whichever privileged guest is invited. Everyone else takes the same chairs each week, and everyone knows who can speak and who cannot. This fully scripted luncheon format has endured for decades; as a ritual, it reaffirms the deliberateness and experience that have made this company highly successful. The meetings don't always, or even often, produce decisions, but they provide occasions for expression, growth, and celebration of a culture that works.

This is the point: meetings don't necessarily always have to be occasions where things get done. As rituals, they can provide opportunities for managers to stage events that dramatize cultural beliefs and values. What managers do with them depends on their corporate culture. Whatever they do, however, good management rituals provide collective cohesion and solidarity, all the while conveying a solid image to the outside.

Recognition Rituals

Strong culture companies create a great deal of hoopla when someone does well and exemplifies the values the company seeks to preserve. And the best-run firms always make certain that everyone understands why someone gets a reward, whether it's trivial or grand ceremony.

At Intel, when someone does something well, the founder calls him or her in, reaches in his desk, and produces a handful of M&Ms as a sign of recognition. The ceremony began years ago, and now everyone keeps a supply of these candies ready. The giving and receiving makes everyone feel good.

At Addison-Wesley Publishing Company, a bronze star is passed from one achiever to the next. At the same time, a "Martyr of the Week" award consoles the person having the roughest time. The point here is the recognition that even a good worker can have a bad time.

More significant occasions deserve special treatment and companies often stage the well-known rites of passage when someone gets promoted or retired. At the corporate headquarters of a major insurance company, a promotion means a new office or furnishings to create an environment equal to the new station. The company carefully manages the size and arrangement of the offices of each executive grade. On the day of a promotion, cigars and candy are provided for well-wishers who drop by to pay their respects. The ritual is a ceremony that publicly recognizes the executive's transition from one status to another.

Retirement dinners or parties are particularly useful times to recognize the accomplishments of "old timers" and to reinforce the importance of the corporate values by telling stories, making speeches, and presenting appropriate gifts.

If a company does not ritualize these important events in a public ceremony, uncertainty and confusion will almost always result. This is especially true of firings or forced retirements, where unraveling can start if transition rituals are inappropriately staged or absent. If people tend to see the firing as arbitrary and unfair, they become confused and upset. In one fell swoop, the culture is called into question.

To bring these disturbing events under control, sophisticated companies provide elaborate rites. The rituals not only provide security during an unwanted transition but also put the culture on display and dramatize and reinforce its values and beliefs. Those managers who don't consider the dramatic aspects of a transition ritual will miss an opportunity to use it to extend the culture's influence.

One company we know has extremely demanding performance standards that, in effect, force significant turnover among employees at several critical stages in their career progression. Employees who fail to pass one of these "tests" are asked to leave. No one talks about the existence of these hurdles until this separation decision is made. Then, almost immediately, people are aware of the individual leaving. Lunches are arranged; virtually everyone who comes in contact with this "job divorce" offers suggestions and references; most go out of their way to begin conversations with words like "When I get around to leaving . . . "

The point of this ritualistic behavior among the remaining employees serves to remind the departee: "Don't feel bad. We set tough standards around here, and failing to meet them is not a bad mark at all." Indeed, a large and thriving alumni group of these former employees (who publish their own directory and arrange alumni dinners) gives eloquent testimony to the fact that the ritual gets its message across. Almost no one leaves harboring a grudge. In fact, some of its most loyal supporters are the former employees who exited gracefully and continue to value their experience with the company.

The Cultural Extravaganza

Some of the strongest corporate cultures elevate ceremonies to an extravagant level—grand festivals with no time or expense spared. Mary Kay Cosmetics stages "seminars" that are lavish multimillion dollar events at the Dallas Convention Center. The founder describes them as "a combination of the Academy Awards, the Miss America Pageant, and a Broadway opening! There are dazzling awards, competition, drama, and entertainment."

At these sales meetings, classes are conducted and the hundreds of Mary Kay salespeople learn something. But what they wait for are the different awards nights—more than thirteen hours of performances that educate, motivate, inspire, and entertain. One night the spotlight is on the team leaders and future directors who have been dubbed cultural heroes. They parade across the stage in bright red jackets, passing the microphone to tell stories about how they personally achieved success à la Mary Kay herself. To those in the audience the message comes through loud and clear: these people made it and so can I!

In another ceremony, awards for the best sales are given—pink Buicks and Cadillacs. One year the cars simply "floated" down onto the stage from a "cloud"—a weighty touch of hoopla that produced overwhelming response from the crowd. But the biggest night is a five-hour spectacular when the company crowns the Director and Consultant Queens (supersaleswomen) in each category. They're given diamonds and minks and surrounded by a court of women who have also achieved terrific sales. At the end of this extravaganza, everyone understands that the challenge of the company is in sales.

When Edwin Land still ran the company, Polaroid's annual meetings were extravaganzas just as lavish as the Mary Kay seminars, although very different in style and message. Polaroid was and is very much an R & D-driven company, and the meetings provided spectacular opportunities to inspire staffers and show the outside world what the company stood for. While most companies were content to hold their annual meetings in obscure places with a few hundred people—including most of their Wall Street analysts and stockholder gadflies—Polaroid staged its annual meetings in cavernous halls where more than 4,000 people crowded inside to see Chairman Land.

After a recitation of annual numbers, Dr. Land began to weave his spell. In 1977, for example, he introduced the new Polaroid movie camera as the "beginning of a new science, art, and industry . . . living images now at hand." A young girl appeared on stage and danced while he filmed. Ninety seconds later, the crowd viewed a full-color movie of the dance, exactly as it was seen on stage.

The shareholders not only shared in the profits, but also shared in the wonders of Land's technological innovation. After each was given an opportunity to shoot some film, Land reconvened the meeting by saying, "There's a rule they don't teach you at the Harvard Business School. It is, if anything is worth doing, it's worth doing to excess." Again and again Land stressed the symbolic importance of the technology, never mentioning marketing techniques or sales. He spoke generally and philosophically, all the while avoiding specifics. One shareholder interrupted and asked, "All of this is well and good. But what about the bottom line?"

"You think that the only thing that counts is the bottom line!" retorted Land. "What a presumptuous thing to say. The bottom line," he added, "is in heaven."

The annual meeting dramatizes the core values that have guided Polaroid since the beginning. Nothing can take away from the drama of that culture. In light of Polaroid's current problems with competition and bottom-line performance, the meeting also points to faults in the culture that appear to have come back to haunt it.

Managing Rituals

Savvy corporate leaders spend a lot of time on rituals, not just devising them but taking an active part in them. They participate in new employee indoctrinations, they orchestrate the celebration that takes place with a promotion, and they make sure that everyone knows why the person is being promoted. They take special advantage of retirements by anointing the retiree as a cultural hero—the embodiment of the company's core values and beliefs.

But there are more than the obvious unexpected opportunities for celebration. Good managers spend a lot of time instituting ritual under the guise of designing and fine-tuning the management process—such as an improved format for operating committee meetings, a revised membership for the executive committee, a new and improved strategic planning process. All of these are rituals through which management dictates what someone will be doing for some time. If we agree that management should have some idea of what it wants its employees to do (arguable, of course, in some quarters), then the attention to ritual is good.

Attention to ritual is also pragmatic. By dictating which individuals spend how much time on what process, senior management knows that it is continuing to control the company. It will influence what middle management talks about, what it thinks about, and the homework it will be doing. These rituals become powerful levers that top management can pull to maintain its control and exert its influence.

The real problem with managers today is that they are not aggressive enough in trying to influence the behavior around them. As a result, they aren't influencing their companies as much as they could. For example, in today's self-conscious world, where things are supposed to be "laid back" and "easy-going," few managers have the conviction to set any standard for behavior. As a result, the cultures of today's companies ebb and flow with the changing fads of society as a whole.

Setting Standards

We think that through culture managers can and should influence how employees act and how they spend their time. For instance, there are several social standards that managers can influence:

Language standards.   What is acceptable? Do people have to refer to their fellow workers using a formal prefix? Or can they call them anything? Is random swearing acceptable? Are exchanges between superiors and underlings easy or difficult? Much of what goes on in a company is simply people talking with one another. Setting standards for how they do this has a strong influence on the culture.

Public decorum. Can the company tolerate (or encourage) disruptive behavior? Can one group of workers interrupt another? Should an individual have the right to work quietly? Do people drink and party at work? Managers should decide what they want and then stick with it.

Interpersonal behavior. Does the company care who is sleeping with whom? Do romances intrude into the work place? Are there clear rules for people to follow? Are sexist jokes permitted or encouraged? Behavioral rituals determine who feels appreciated and who is downtrodden. A good manager will think them through and make the right kind of standard explicit.

Like the more social aspects of work, the management process can also be ritualized in ways that are more effective than is the norm today. Senior managers should recognize that the processes they institute occupy the time of employees and keep this clearly in mind as they review and revise their management processes. A simple example: everyone has a strategic plan but few companies are managed strategically. When they are, the managers first think strategically, and then eventually generate good strategic plans, not the other way around. A CEO designing a planning process should make sure that he or she will get managers to think strategically or it won't work well. The distinction seems miniscule, but it makes all the difference. Establishing these standards for strategic management shows employees very clearly what is expected of them. For instance:

Homework: Most managers will tell others *when* to join in a particular meeting, but they won't often tell them *how* to prepare for it. This can be accomplished simply with homework assignments.

Presentation and format. Companies with strong cultures set standards for presentations. At P&G, important things are stated on one-page memos. Because the format is well understood,

P&G explicitly manages the kind of preparatory work being done.

Explicit instructions.   Much management time is left to the whim of the manager. We see nothing wrong in a more heavy-handed approach. Middle managers should be told exactly what to do. After all, blue-collar workers are told what to do; why shouldn't managers?

We are not arguing for a return to authoritarianism. Rather, we believe that managers have a strong potential for positive influence if they will just exercise it. By paying attention to the rituals of the culture, they can make the values of the company coherent and accesible to every employee.

Rituals That Don't Work: The Assimilation of Women and Minorities

Day-to-day life in a company's culture revolves around countless repetitions of unwritten but well-understood rituals. Mostly social in context, one purpose they serve among others is to introduce newcomers to the culture. When the newcomer is different—a woman in a man's world, or a black in a white managerial eche-lon—no rituals exist to socialize this individual. In the place of comfortable rituals are taboos: "Don't hustle that woman"; or "Blacks are sensitive, so be careful not to hurt their feelings."

Entering the ritual life of a culture becomes a hurdle women and minorities have to overcome. The alien rituals of the main-stream culture make an outsider hypersensitive to things that hap-pen all around him or her: What did that gesture mean? Should I react to that innocent comment or not? How well am I really doing?

Membership in a subculture of outsiders affects women and minorities personally and professionally. But just as significantly, it affects overall corporate operations too. A company cannot get the best work from anyone who is an outsider looking in. The eco-nomic reasons should be quite apparent. Unless the barriers that keep women and minorities out of the cultural mainstream of cor-porate life can be overcome, there will be no way for the company or society at large to benefit from the huge reservoir of untapped human capital. The social reasons should be equally clear—we either believe in the individual rights and duties spelled out in the Constitution of the United States or not. If we believe in them, but recognize barriers that make people unequal, we need to work to remove these barriers. Finally, for political reasons, the needs of women and minorities must be met in due course, because these groups represent a huge constituency in society and a growing percentage of people in the corporate world.

But how do these doors that don't quite open work their damaging effects? The exclusion of women and minorities from the rich and supportive life of an organization's culture begins the day they walk in the door. Most don't even know it is happening to them at the time.

Consider the experience of a young and very talented black MBA in his first exposure to corporate life. "Throughout the recruitment process, I was much sought after. Maybe even more than the white MBAs around me. I had lots of offers and I got to pick from the choicest ones available. I was flying high at the time. Of course, not having worked before full time, I just didn't know what to expect. Neither did most of my classmates—several of whom joined the company I joined at right around the same time. I went to work day after day. Since I had no real expectations about work, whatever happened each day seemed normal to me. It was only a few months later that it dawned on me that what was normal for me wasn't what was happening to my white male classmates. I'd go to lunch with one of them. Or maybe we'd be off playing a little one-on-one to keep in shape. And they would tell me about having dinner with this VP or that. I hadn't met any VPs—except during the recruiting process—so I would ask them how they got to know the VP. Every time they would say something like—'Oh. I was doing some work with Charlie Smith and he just introduced me.'—sort of off-the-cuff, like it didn't amount to anything. In fact, it didn't amount to anything. It just wasn't happening for me. While it must have seemed normal to Charlie Smith to introduce his white buddy to the VP, the Charlie Smiths I worked with apparently didn't feel comfortable doing the same thing for me because I was different."

An isolated experience? Not in the least. Every black and woman we interviewed, and we interviewed several, described similar circumstances during their first days at work. For women, the primary initial exclusion was from after-work socializing. A common work-related social ritual—"let's go have a brew after work"—wasn't available to them. The men who worked around them all day were presumably concerned that an invitation for a drink would be a sign of a come-on. So they simply didn't make the request. If women wanted to drink after work, they did so with other women.

Exclusion from ordinary corporate life, was not just an entry-level experience of the women, however. Most complained this exclusion continued throughout their careers. And most—given the senior level of the women we talked to—were particularly concerned by exclusion from important, substantive events occurring around them. As one women said: "Most decisions are really not made on a golf course or in a locker room. So being cut off from social events is not really my concern. All decisions, however, tend to be made or influenced informally. And I do mind not being invited into or even accepted in informal hallway conversations about real business matters. But I am, because the males around me in the power structure just aren't comfortable behaving informally with a woman present. So if I join the hallway meeting, the subject switches off business and on to chit chat. Now I ask you, how am I supposed to do my job if I'm not made part of the informal sessions?"

One commented on the differing social perceptions of silence. If something sexually offensive occurred in the work environment, she said, her instinctive response was to ignore it, to be silent. As a young girl she had been taught to do so—it was not right to embarrass someone by commenting on their untoward behavior. Silence, with its implication of disapproval, was clearly much more appropriate behavior. But this was not so in business. Given male-inculcated standards of behavior as the norm, silence conveys a very different message: this woman is not assertive enough. Not aggressive like a man. Clearly, she will have trouble in the tough world of business.

Entries to Rituals

Ritualistic barriers to the assimilation of outsiders into corporate cultures—barriers that involve countless miniscule behavioral patterns—constitute one of the biggest problems women and minorities face in rising in the corporate world. What can be done to overcome these barriers and make traditional white, male-oriented cultures more open and accommodating to outsiders? Several tangible steps are possible.

Cultural Orientation. Much more care can be taken in the management of outsiders' career paths to ensure that people receive support from the culture when they need it. Some companies have instituted formal mentoring programs; whereby seasoned middle- to senior-level managers are made explicitly responsible for taking newcomers under their wings. When these turn into real and working personal relationships, they seem to be quite effective. Others try to manage job assignments to ensure a progression of sympathetic and supportive superiors. A third successful strategy is that of drawing up targeted (problem-solving or trouble-shooting) and short (usually six weeks long) task-force assignments. As a result of these assignments, new minority and female employees in particular form a series of relationships with their peers which sustains them in early years.

Explicit rules for treatment. Destructive ritualistic behavior can be neutralized by the development of explicit guidelines for behavior in situations involving women and minorities—and a procedure for making everyone aware of these guidelines. Above, we pointed out that in recent years managers have grown quite lax about conveying acceptable standards of behavior to govern life in the culture. Especially critical is the lack of attention to social rituals governing how various groups of people should behave toward one another. Nowhere is this gap more apparent than as it relates to social behavior vis-à-vis women and minorities. If women and minorities are to become comfortable, confident members in full standing of the company's culture, they will have to stop spending sizable portions of their time coping with the embarrassment foisted on them by others who do not know how to behave in a given situation. Managers who are serious about achieving real integration in the workplace will have to start by spelling out standards for social behavior in relationship to these new members of the culture.

Role modeling. The most obvious strategy is perhaps also the best—personal leadership and example-setting in appropriate treatment of minorities and women. Just as planning never seems to take hold until a chief executive provides leadership, so too behavior changes related to making women and minorities comfortable and welcome in a company's culture will not occur until chief executives and other senior managers lead by example.

Failure to accept women and minorities into the mainstream culture hurts not only those victimized but the long-term vitality of the business itself. The measures taken to date have been helpful but inadequate. Stronger action is needed—specifically action focused on the ritualistic cultural barriers to assimilation that are so hard to change.

The Legacy of Corporate Rituals

The rituals people learn in one culture mark them—in effect, train them—in a specific mode of behavior. This is especially true of managers. If they achieve success as managers in one environment using one set of management rituals, they are then more than likely going to carry these rituals to other environments or companies when they move on. Consider the case of Bob McNamara in his odyssey from Ford Motor Company to the Department of Defense and then to the World Bank.

McNamara, recently out of the Harvard Business School, started his climb to fame and fortune as one of the leading members of Tex Thornton's squad of statistical analysts who served the Air Force in World War II. Following the war, this group of talented analysts—soon to become the Whiz Kids—sold themselves, as a group, to the Ford Motor Company, then in the throes of a turnaround being engineered by Henry Ford II.

Given the nature of the automobile business—one in which good analysis can pay off, the penchant of McNamara and the other Whiz Kids for applying statistical-analysis techniques to management turned the Ford Motor Company around in the early 1950s. By 1954, Ford almost matched Chevrolet in the race for the most popular American car. This kind of high-quality staff work and financial control is one of the keys to good management in the automobile industry. It's an important value for the culture because it fits the demands of the marketplace.

Later in his career, McNamara moved on to the Department of Defense during the Vietnam War. He brought to the DOD many of the analytic approaches that served Ford so well.

McNamara soon became a symbol of national decision-making at a time when the war needed sound decisions. But then the statistics started to go awry. The numbers in the equation—the facts—were not always as solid or incontestable as one would like. There seemed to be unmeasured variables at work that produced gaps between the statistical bottom line and the actual progress of the war in the rice paddies of Vietnam. Our point is not that McNamara was wrong or even at fault vis-à-vis Vietnam; simply that his management rituals didn't work as well in Defense as they had at Ford. The conditions were not the same.

From the Department of Defense, McNamara moved on to the World Bank where his contributions were substantial. But, again, some critics challenged his techniques: "Somewhat like a go-go banker who pushes his subordinates to create impressive numbers rather than sound loans, McNamara sets high loan quotas and insists they be met," according to an article in *Forbes*. And *Barrons* reported that "The World Bank Staff Association denounces management for measuring effectiveness and productivity solely by the number of dollars loaned and projects processed . . . at the expense of both the quality and ultimate development impact of its work."

McNamara learned about business in Ford; indeed he assimilated a series of rituals built around complex financial systems and hard-nosed staff analysis. Using these rituals, he achieved great personal success and a measure of fame. We can hardly criticize him for equating the rituals of management he learned at Ford with management itself. McNamara himself is a brilliant man; he made a major impact on all the institutions he served in his illustrious career. Our point is simple: it was McNamara, not his management rituals, that did the job well.

The lesson? Rituals that work well in one culture may fail in another because of the differing business environments. But the ultimate lesson, of course, is that managers need to be fully aware of the ritualistic element of their own culture and not allow themselves to be captured by the magic of what they do day to day.

Strong cultures create meaning for people. Through their rituals they teach people how to behave, not just in their corridors of power but in the world at large. How do all of these elements of culture get transmitted, reinforced and blended into an overall corporate culture? Through the workings of the cultural network, to which we now turn.

5
Communications: Working the Cultural Network

Everyone in a strong culture has a job—but he also has another job. This "other job" won't get stamped on a business card, but that doesn't matter. In many ways this work is far more important than budgets, memos, policies, and five-year plans. Spies, story-tellers, priests, whisperers, cabals—these people form the *hidden hierarchy* which looks considerably different from the organization chart. In the hidden hierarchy, a lowly junior employee doubles as a highly influential spy. Or an "unproductive" senior manager gets the best office in the building, precisely because he does little but tell good stories—an ability that makes him tremendously valu-able to the corporation as an interpreter of events. As consultants, we've found that these "other jobs" are critical to the effective management of any successful organization. They make up what we call the cultural network.

This network is actually the primary means of communication within the organization; it ties together all parts of the company without respect to positions or titles. The network is important because it not only transmits information but also interprets the significance of the information for employees. The official announcement from the CEO may be that the vice-president resigned to pursue other interests. But half a day after the announcement goes out, the network has circulated the unofficial "truth": the vice-president missed his sales budget for the third year in a row—performance that is not tolerated in this company.

We have found that many "modern" managers only deal with the tip of the iceberg as far as communications are concerned. They send a flurry of memos, letters, reports, and policy statements, hold pre-meetings, meetings, and management sessions where they use flip charts, decision trees, and statistical analysis to accomplish . . . well, sometimes they don't accomplish much. We think that 90 percent of what goes on in an organization has nothing to do with formal events. The real business goes on in the cultural network. Even in the context of a highly controlled meeting, there is a lot of informal communication going on—bonding rituals, glances, innuendos, and so forth. The real process of making decisions, of gathering support, of developing opinions, happens before the meeting—or after.

In a strong culture, the network is powerful because it can reinforce the basic beliefs of the organization, enhance the symbolic value of heroes by passing on stories of their deeds and accomplishments, set a new climate for change, and provide a tight structure of influence for the CEO. Top managers need to recognize and tap into this cultural network to accomplish their goals. Especially in a large corporation, working the network can be the *only* way to get a job done.

As Franklin D. Roosevelt said: "The Treasury is so large and far flung and ingrained in its practices that I find it is almost impossible to get the action and results I want . . . there. But the Treasury is not to be compared with the State Department. You should go through the experience of trying to get any changes in the thinking, policy, and action of the career diplomats and then you'd know what a real problem was. But the Treasury and the State Department put together are nothing compared with the Na-a-vy. To change anything in the Na-a-vy is like punching a feather bed. You punch it with your right and you punch it with your left until you are finally exhausted, and then you find the damn bed just as it was before you started punching."

Roosevelt, one of the most powerful presidents ever, had the same problems every manager experiences in trying to move a bureaucratic organization. But, according to Arthur Schlesinger, FDR was a consummate networker. "The first task of an executive, as Roosevelt saw it, was to guarantee himself an effective flow of information and ideas . . . Roosevelt's persistent effort, therefore, was to check and balance information acquired through official channels by information acquired through a myriad of private, informal, and unorthodox channels and espionage networks. At times, he seemed almost to pit his personal sources against his public sources."

Characters in the Cultural Network

Like Roosevelt, top managers need to have a good sense of this informal system of checks and balances to gather and disseminate information. The whole process depends on people, not on paper. Let's take a look at some of the characters in the cultural network.

STORYTELLERS

People tell stories to gain power and influence—and because they enjoy doing it. Storytellers are in a powerful position because they can change reality. Storytellers simply interpret what goes on in the company—but to suit their own perceptions. And what is power anyway but the ability to influence people's perceptions—without their realizing it, of course. The image that comes to mind is that of the fable in which a fox tells long circuitous stories, lulling the raven off guard; thus the grapes were left up for grabs. The tales that storytellers tell, like myths in a tribal setting, explain and give meaning to the workaday world. For the corporation, storytellers maintain cohesion and provide guidelines for everyone to follow. It's the most powerful way to convey information and shape behavior. The beauty of a story is that just by remembering the punch line you can recreate the entire occasion.

Storytellers preserve institutions and their values by imparting legends of the company to new employees. They also carry stories about the visionary heroes or the latent outlaw over in the manufacturing plant. Storytellers will also reveal much about what it takes to get ahead in the organization. Thomas Watson, Jr., son of IBM's founder, often told a story about a nature lover who liked watching the wild ducks fly south in vast flocks each October. Out of charity, he took to putting feed for them in a nearby pond. After a while, some of the ducks no longer bothered to fly south; they wintered in the pond on what he fed them. In time they flew less and less. After three or four years, they grew so fat and lazy that they found it difficult to fly at all. Watson had discovered this story in the writings of Danish philosopher Sören Kierkegaard. And he always ended it with the point that you can make wild ducks tame, but you can never make tame ducks wild again. Watson would further add that "the duck who is tamed will never go anywhere anymore. We are convinced that business needs its wild ducks. And in IBM we try not to tame them."

Watson told this story again and again to impress upon people the value of deviance and the tolerance for outlaw heroes in a company well known for its conformity and standardized ways. Once, however, an employee reportedly told Watson that "even wild ducks fly in formation." This rejoinder quickly became part of the wild-ducks story precisely because it makes another important point about the culture: we're all going in the same direction.

The best storytellers are typically found in positions that give them access to a great deal of information. They are usually in the epicenter of activity and free to be as eccentric as they choose. A storyteller needs imagination, insight, and a sense of details—a story can't be abstract. While the position of storyteller is a powerful one, it's not a leadership role. Many people fear storytellers because everything—and everyone—is grist for their story mills. Yet colleagues revere them and often protect them.

A salesman who worked for a machine tool manufacturer "couldn't sell his way out of a paper bag," as his colleagues put it to us. Once, when a potentate flew in from Central America expressly to buy a new numerically controlled tool—a multimillion dollar transaction—this salesman somehow just didn't take the order. Why not? No reason, except that, as his colleagues put it, he couldn't ever seem to make a sale. On the other hand, this fellow knew so much about the company that the same colleagues told people, "Just go talk to X, he'll give you a lot of insight into the problem." This seemingly incompetent salesman was protected because he served a much more important function within the culture than just making sales.

PRIESTS

Like the church, companies also have priests. They are the designated worriers of the corporation and the guardians of the culture's values. They worry about the religion and keeping the flock together. This should be the job of the CEOs, but they're inaccessible; so the eminently accessible priests do the job. They always have time to listen to a confession, and they always have a solution to any dilemma, even a moral dilemma. This "other job" is one that requires the most responsiblity of any in the culture network.

To be a priest figure in a culture requires a maturity or seriousness beyond years. These people tend to be older than their colleagues, because people feel uncomfortable with priests who have not yet proven their worth by surviving in the company for some time. Priests are similar to storytellers, but priests seldom worry about details. Instead they deal in allegories about what once happened. If you ask about a current proposal, the response is to relate the issue back to another event.

Most priestly figures are human encyclopedias on matters of their company's history, just in the way that real priests have mastery of the Bible. The duty they are most often called on to perform is the provision of historical precedent for planned action. "Back in 1937 . . ." is how they invariably interpret the company's beliefs and values.

Priests also aid people in event of defeat, frustration, and disappointment. The person who handles worldwide assignments of managers is one company's favorite priest. A young manager will walk into his office and say, "My God, I've been assigned eighteen months with our South American division. I'll be away from the heart of the action, and I came here to get a lot of experience. What's the use?" By the time he leaves the priest's office, he will have been told indirectly about how the company's CEO spent ten years working in Brazil. The manager won't know what's happened to him because of the meandering, eccentric way storytellers work; yet he'll trudge off feeling, "Maybe I can spend ten years with this division and wind up as CEO." Stories are parables that motivate others and extend the power of the effective storyteller.

In the real hierarchy, you find priests tied into headquarters staff functions, three to five levels removed from the top, with a nonsense title like "Director of Economic Studies." In their formal job they usually have managerial responsibility but no staff and probably report to a vice-president. Yet good senior managers want them nearby so they can get the priests to bless a proposed venture, quickly. Such was the case for the head of the largest office of a multinational company. We asked him how he made personnel decisions to fill key slots in his organization. He told us, "The easy ones tend to fall right out. On the really close calls, however, I ask Harriet her opinion."

"Oh? Who's Harriet?" we asked.

"She's an administrative assistant here in personnel."

We were shocked. "You ask a low-level personnel person's opinion on close-call decisions? Isn't that an irresponsible way to make the decisions?"

"Harriet," he responded icily, "has been with this company longer than I have. She knows very well the kind of people who succeed around here. And she has extraordinarily good people judgment."

Harriet is a priestess in that culture, and, judging by the executive's tone, she was no one to belittle. Since then we have found a disproportionate number of priests in personnel departments. Roy Johnson, who was head of personnel at GE for years, was a priest of the GE culture. He was known to have enormous power, but he was invisible.

WHISPERERS

The whisperers are often powers behind the throne, people like Eisenhower's Sherman Adams, Carter's Bob Strauss, LBJ's Clark Clifford, or Nixon's John Ehrlichman. They are movers and shakers—but without formal portfolio. Sometimes they climb high in the organization, as these presidential aides did. But just as often, whisperers are buried in an obscure post, anonymous to all except the real cognoscente. The source of their power—the boss's ear. Anyone who wants something done will head to the whisperers.

Two critical skills are required of persons who play this whisper-in-the-ear role. First, they must be able to read the boss's mind quickly and accurately, with few clues. Their power is dependent on a symbiotic relationship with this key figure. Not surprisingly, intense loyalty is a strong part of their personal makeup.

Second, to get things done they must build a vast support system of contacts throughout the organization and work hard at staying current with all that transpires through this network.

Their knowledge is not as wide or developed as the priests'; but whisperers know where the bodies are buried.

Whisperers are frightening figures whom no one would want to cross. The classic example of a whisperer is Harry Bennett, the director of security for Ford in the latter years of Henry Ford, Sr.'s tenure. Over the years, Bennett ingratiated himself with the elder Ford and built a network of spies and enforcers throughout the company. As Ford reached his late seventies and suffered a considerable decline in health and acuity, Bennett conceived and executed shemes to remove from power all other senior managers not personally loyal to the security chief. Only the active intervention of Clara Ford—Henry's wife—and the wife of the then-deceased Edsel Ford, prevented Bennett from taking over the company completely. His bitter comment to Henry Ford II on the day Ford was installed as president was: "You're taking over a billion-dollar organization here that you haven't contributed a thing to!"

Not all whisperers play the Machiavellian role Bennett played at Ford. Those who do usually outrun the usefulness of their roles; they become prime candidates for "de-Stalinization" when new management comes in.

GOSSIPS

Gossips are the troubadors of the culture. While priests will only talk in analogues—that is, tell you the scripture—gossips will know the names, dates, salaries, and events that are taking place in the organization, *now*. The trivial day-to-day happenings are carried by gossips whom most people appreciate, even if they are wary of gossips' tongues. After all, without a steady diet of news about people one knows, life in most companies would be grim— and pretty dull.

Gossips are not expected to be serious people; and they are not always expected to get the news right. They are expected simply to entertain. For this entertainment value alone they are tolerated, even liked.

Their role in reinforcing a culture is vital. Storytellers create the legends of the company and its heroes, but the gossips help the hero-making process flourish by embellishing the heroes' past feats and spiffing up the news of their latest accomplishments.

While storytellers and priests deal one-on-one with individuals, gossips can spread their news more quickly because they talk to groups at the lunch table or during coffee break. They also have the unique ability to penetrate all levels of the organization.

Unlike whisperers, gossips have no proximity to power. But their usefulness in helping one raise one's status can be invaluable. A senior executive at the Foxboro Company, a leader in the field of industrial-process control instrumentation, was transformed by company gossips into a legendary figure. The stories they told, which we heard, certified him as one of the nicest people in the world but also one of the most frugal.

Ben, the executive, had been sitting in his office when Foxboro's chief technical officer ran in, exuberant. "I did it!" He showed Ben the small sensing device that represented the successful end of months of intensive work. "Wonderful, absolutely wonderful!" Ben said. "That deserves special recognition," but as he began searching feverishly in his desk for a reward, he realized it held nothing on a par with the engineer's discovery. Finally in desperation he stuttered, "Here, have a banana," retrieving it from the bottom drawer. "Why, thank you," said the startled engineer and turned back to his lab, technical device in one hand, banana in the other. "Where did you get the banana?" people asked him in passing. "Ben gave it to me when I showed him the new device," he told them with a confused look still on his face.

The gossips got hold of the story and repeated it throughout the company. For years they didn't let go of it, and the storytellers picked it up. A decade later, when the engineer retired, he was presented not with a gold watch but with a gold banana.

At the same time, gossips can become the leaders of the pack when it comes to de-Stalinizing a hero. They are the ones to provide the "real" story behind the official announcements and memos.

SECRETARIAL SOURCES

Clerical workers penetrate a different level of the company than managers do, and they're often more observant. You may value the high-ranking bureaucrat in your social order, but in your cultural network, a clerk or secretary can be much more useful.

When we as individuals want to tap into the network, the people we go to first are the key clerical people. They tell us more about what the organization is *really* like, what is *really* going on, who's angry with whom, and so on, than anyone else, including the CEO. They can do this because secretarial sources form a stable network of relatively noninvolved and therefore unbiased players.

This is particularly true of the army of professional secretaries who move up the corporate ladder concurrently with the managers for whom they work. By the time they become secretaries to senior executives, they are tremendously savvy about all the serious affairs of business and all the hijinks as well. This is precisely why managers on the rise pay such attention to moving their secretaries with them as their own careers progress: the secretaries keep them tuned in to what's really happening. They'll tell the boss about the argument around the water cooler, a memo another boss's secretary is about to send, who pulled an embarrassing prank on whom. As noninvolved players, they invariably have excellent judgment, and for this reason they sometimes play the priestess role.

Also, as managers move up the ladder, they invariably lose touch with the rumor mill. Their secretaries are invaluable in keeping them tuned into the latest interpretations of official events. The secretaries also can help their bosses by passing stories of their deeds on through the gossip network.

SPIES

Almost every good senior manager has spies. Typically a spy is a well-oiled buddy in the woodwork—someone loyal enough to keep you informed of what is going on. The best spies are people who are liked and have access to many different people; they hear all the stories, and they know who's behind them. Often the best spies come from the ranks of the company storytellers. Most tend to be unthreatening people because they are not likely to get ahead. Yet spies know that while they're not going to progress any higher in the organization, they'll always be taken care of as long as they keep the channels of information open.

These are not spies in the cloak-and-dagger sense of infiltrating the boardroom or snooping in the files. Truly effective spies never say a bad word about anybody and thus are much loved as well as much needed. They are so careful that they won't attempt to color the organizational climate in any way that might impinge on the careers of others. They do this carefully and precisely to keep those valuable channels open.

Instead, sharp spies keep their fingers on the pulse of the organization. Smart managers on the way up latch onto spies and develop special friendships with them. They lunch with them once a month and find out from them what is transpiring in their little corner of the cultural network. They use spies to verify the rumor mill or to balance the information they get from their secretary.

Recent arrivals to the company are very effective, if unwitting, spies. A newcomer has the freshness of perspective to judge events more clearly than a habitual player. And the newcomers don't know enough to filter out information that someone more savvy thinks the senior manager shouldn't hear.

Senior managers often cultivate these new workers as spies. They might ask. "How have you found your first six months here?" Or, "What's going on out there?" Or, "What do you feel about these changes?" The junior employee, flattered by this unexpected favoritism, will say: "Well, we've got to change something about such and such." And the senior manager will ask, "Oh, why's that? Tell me about it." The junior person will tell the senior manager everything he or she wants to know about what's going on; after this initial, rather intimate conversation, the newcomer is very likely to come back to the senior manager again and again with more insight and information.

CABALS

A cabal is a group of two or more people who secretly join together to plot a common purpose—usually to advance themselves in the organization.

Why this should work is due to a little-known trick of behavioral logic. It's become known as the Dummy Theorem, invented and told to us by software developer John Munzer some twenty years ago. The Dummy Theorem states that in any group of 'n' people, 'k' of them are dummies, and the ratio of 'k' over 'n' is a constant greater than or equal to 2/3. That is, in any group of people, 2/3 of them will be dummies.

Why are there so many dummies in the world? The Dummy Theorem explains that within a peer group, people self-select themselves into dummy or nondummy status based on their perception of themselves, vis-à-vis their peers. This is the only possible way to explain the large number of dummies who earn large salaries in the corporate world. Here is how smart managers put the Dummy Theorem to work:

The chairman of Mitsubishi was once interviewed on the subject of lifetime employment in Japanese industries. "What do you do if a middle manager starts misperforming? What do you do with him, given that you're committed to employ him for a lifetime?"

The chairman responded immediately, "Oh, that's a problem we've studied a great deal. First, we check out the situation to find if there's something we could change to improve his performance. But if we really don't understand why he's performing badly, we promote him. Because in 72.4 percent (or thereabouts) of the times we promote someone, their performance immediately improves."

By promoting him, you improve his perception of himself in relation to his peers. And so, obviously, he stops behaving like a dummy; he behaves like a nondummy.

But in some businesses there are even more clever uses of this theorem. The Dutch Admiral's Paradigm, for instance, told to us by Peter Kraljic, is a corollary to the Dummy Theorem. As Kraljic reported to us, it postulates that within a peer group a cabal can influence the perception of people as to who in the group is a dummy or a nondummy. It's simplicity itself.

Not long ago, there were two junior officers in the Dutch Navy who made a pact. They decided that when they were at the various navy social functions, they would go out of their way to tell people what a great guy the other guy was. They'd appear at cocktail parties or dances and say, "What an unbelievable person Charlie is. He's the best man in the Navy." Or, "Did you hear about the brilliant idea Dave had?"

They revealed this pact to the public the day they were both made admirals—the two youngest admirals ever appointed in the Dutch Navy. Their cabal had influenced the perceptions of the peer group in the organization. In addition, it aided the process of hero-making. The point here is: BELIEVING IS SEEING. It's much more effective than the old notion that seeing is believing.

The Dummy Theorem is a vast improvement over the Peter Principle, which states that people are promoted until they reach their level of incompetence, where their careers stop. The Dummy Theorem says just the opposite: *As long as you can advance your perception of yourself* in comparison to others, *you'll continue to advance* and you'll always rise to the higher occasion. But crucial to advancing your estimation in others' eyes is the role of the cabal and the peer group.

Cabals are everywhere in organizations. Cabals can be large—for example, the membership of the Republican Party. Or a cabal can be as cozy as two people who always second one another's ideas in meetings. We two authors are a cabal in the world of organizational effectiveness. When Terry attends a conference where he is surrounded by alien figures, he might say, "My friend Kennedy, the consultant in McKinsey, agrees with my argument." And when Allan goes to a workshop and wants to give credibility to what he says, he begins with: "Dr. Deal of Harvard said . . ." and then finishes the sentence himself. We know each other well enough to do that, and neither would abuse the trust.

The cabal is a useful lever for elevating your status, but it's also important as a protection mechanism; it offers you strength and backing. In fact, in strong cultures people unconsciously create and nurture cabals that reinforce their ideas and positions in the company. That is, some people are semiconscious of the Dummy Theorem and how it works; and they manage by those principles rather than by more formal principles.

Trust and loyalty to the group is crucial, whatever the cabal's size. A cabal can be infinite in size, but it must have clear identification of interests within it. A cabal is by definition focused on something. The members of the cabal can borrow the reputations or ideas of the other members to further their own purposes. Within the cabal, this is acceptable. It's a fair trade. Shared values and experiences nurture a cabal.

A strong culture company will deliberately develop cabals, because when its interests match the cabal's interests, the result is a strong management lever. IBM uses the cabal very adroitly, by setting its quotas so that roughly 80 percent of its sales force wins its way into the Hundred Percent Club. In reality there is no real distinction to becoming a club member. IBM simply wants to weed out the 20 percent worst salespeople. But the club is a cabal that IBM manages by defining a good salesperson as someone who is admitted as a Hundred Percenter. These people feel as though they have special status and often will note the Hundred Percent Club on their resumes.

GE invites a select cabal to its Bel Air Conference, which former GEer Kurt Vonnegut referred to as "the company picnic" in *Slaughterhouse-Five*. The conference takes place in January of each year, and everyone from general manager on up is privileged to attend. It's now so large that some people only get to go every second year. But the real point of the conference is not to accomplish work or promulgate ideas or even to play golf—it's to celebrate being a general manager in GE, which is a promotion all the ambitious up-and-comers want. If you're going anywhere in GE, you've made general manager by the time you're thirty-five. The conference is therefore a cabal with which everyone up for promotion wants to be identified. They'll ask one another, "Are you going to Bel Air this year?" And those who go to Bel Air return home deliberately mysterious about what transpires there.

In creating a huge cabal, GE speaks to these managers as insiders. It's more effective than addressing each manager separately with a suggestion or request. "We" is a clever ploy for communicating company principles. To stir the emotions of a cabal by saying "Here's what *we* are all about" is to make people identify themselves as a group, not as individuals. Strengthen the cabal and you strengthen the culture. Smart managers use cabals for their motivating effect.

A manager's real interest in cabals has to do with the fact that a cabal is a strong subculture within an organization; because it's very hard to deal with 100 or 100,000 people all at once, managers actively foster cabals and then weld them together so all will move in one common direction.

Yet this attempt can backfire. Harold Geneen created a cabal of managers at ITT who hated him, who commiserated among themselves, and felt closer to each other than to anything associated with the company. Geneen found this useful, because he believed in a very competitive model of management. Yet had he wanted to use the cabal in his favor, he would have relaxed the tightness of his control and allowed the cabal to win on a major proposal, thereby encouraging it to fight him. This would have made for better management at ITT. There would have been a sense of shared purpose, and as a result, the organization would have been more cohesive and would not have struggled once Geneen left.

In certain industries—high-tech companies in particular—cabals are disruptive because they cut across company lines. Computer programmers, for instance, tend to have much greater loyalty to their profession than to any individual organization. So they change jobs without a thought, always focusing on the next challenge. The result is very high turnover in fast-growth companies and often a major loss of initiative.

Managing the Cultural Network

It's clear by now that the cultural network is a powerful means of communication within the organization. Every company, no matter how small, will have its share of storytellers, priests, gossips, spies, whisperers, and cabals to broadcast, embellish, and reinforce values. Within large corporations, each subsidiary or division will have its own cast of characters. Yet they will still be linked to the wider organization. In weak cultures, networks are served exclusively by spies and pretenders, vying with each other to do someone in and take over. But in strong cultures, networks carry the beliefs and values that keep the culture alive and shared across levels, divisions, and among people.

The cultural network is informal, yet its rules are nonetheless rigid—they're just not written down. You've got to learn them all or you can't survive in a culture. If you forget even one, you stand out as someone who doesn't know her or his way around the company. A new employee isn't handed a booklet called: "The 50,000 Informal Rules You Need to Survive Here." Nor do managers explicitly try to manage by these rules; yet they dictate the bulk of the activity that goes on in an organization. Our point is that there is no avoiding your involvement with the cultural network. It's simply a matter of using its activities in your favor.

Consider how the cultural network operates at one company. The aggressive new CEO of this large company was concerned about lagging productivity. The company's markets had suddenly become very competitive and the company was losing share. No shrinking violet, the CEO launches a process that soon leads to a set of recommendations to reorganize the sales force and institute a new set of sales incentives. These recommendations are written up and announced to the organization at large. Effective communication? Definitely not. The reason? Any such announcement and its distribution are only the beginning of the communication process. Here's what happens when the word arrives in a field office:

The first people to see it are the secretaries. They receive their own copies and note with interest that their boss is getting a copy too. Each dutifully takes ten minutes to read the memo through. After all, they don't receive all that many memos directly from the CEO. So far so good.

The first secretary finishes reading and waits for the others to finish as well.

"What's this about?" they all want to know.

"I have no idea," responds one. "Maybe the company is in trouble. Hmmm. I hope I'm not going to have to start looking for a job." For the next forty-five minutes not much work gets done as the pool of secretaries, working their end of the cultural network, debate whether or not the company is going under. The debate comes to a close when the priest—a woman who has been with the company for seventeen years and has seen it all before—says "It doesn't mean anything. Al sent out the same memo back in 1976 and nothing happened. Nothing."

So ends round one. Score:

> Communication: 10 minutes reading time
> Cultural network: 45 minutes discussion time

Round two begins when the boss arrives and picks up his mail. The secretaries are alert to see how he responds to the memo. He goes into his office, spends five minutes scanning the memo, and then reaches for the phone. The secretaries seem visibly relieved.

"Hello, Charlie. This is Bill. Did you see Henry's announcement? Old Fred really lost out in that shuffle. I knew he had blown it when they left him off the speaker's list for the annual sales meeting." For the next half hour, the two friends talk about the politics of the reorganization, as well as how they will personally fare. They conclude that nothing will really change in the sales force as a result of these moves since the salespeople in the field will still face the same conditions day-to-day in the marketplace.

End of round two. Running score:

> Communication: 15 minutes total
> Cultural network: 75 minutes total

The incident is not over, however. The CEO of this company understood how the cultural network worked and was suitably cynical about the direct effects of reorganization on the field sales-force's performance. He also thought he knew what the problem was: his salesforce had grown accustomed to taking orders without facing head-to-head competition. That's where his incentive plan came into play and the third round of communication began. This third round was designed to feed tangible examples directly to the salesforce through the cultural network.

To start this third round, the CEO first asked the field to send him weekly lists of competitive sales situations they were facing. Then each week he would allocate a day for work in the field on one of these accounts. A strange allocation of time for the CEO of a multi-billion dollar company? Not really.

The CEO had started his career with another very competitive sales-oriented company. And, he was a first-class salesman. So soon, the cultural network was abuzz with stories like "Did you hear how Charlie (not his name) knocked over that oil distributor's account in Omaha last Friday? We were almost out on our ears when he shows up and lands a ten-unit order. The account sales-man even got a $500 bonus payment out of the deal. They actually convinced the customer that our machine was twice as reliable as those Japanese models they were about to buy."

Score: The cultural network wins again—but this time because a manager knew how to use it. The stories about the CEO's exploits in the field were told over and over again in the company. They are still told today, years after the fact.

Tapping the Network

Our own message is that managers who want, *first*, to know what people in their organization are *really* thinking and, *second*, to influence their behavior day to day must be deft at working the cultural network.

How does a manager tap into this network? You could make the rounds of people in the company. Consultants do this all the time. Ask twenty people, "How do you feel about your work load?" Just listen to what they say, and infer from it their true sentiments. Or ask a neutral party to question them: "What do you think so-and-so's real priorities are? How well do you think Dave is spending his time on these priorities?" See what the answers are.

But in the real world, people don't in fact ask their subordinates or even their peers "What do you think?" because they get stilted, artificial answers. Instead, a smart networker will cut across these hierarchical lines into the hidden hierarchy.

Working the cultural network is a simple and straightforward procedure. Effective managers who use it to their best advantage follow a pattern:

They recognize the network's existence and importance instead of feeling above it.

They make sure they are part of it by cultivating a network of appropriate contacts themselves—especially among key storytellers and priests. There are four major points to keep in mind in cultivating such a network.

- Treat each person with whom you come in contact with deference you would reserve for the CEO of the company. A person's formal, hierarchical title may suggest that he or she is a person of no particular import. However, each person in an organization has other hidden but culturally important roles which no outsider can know. So treat each person you come in contact with as though that person were the high priest(ess) of the culture. He or she may be.

- Ask people you meet to explain the meaning of what you have seen. Ask them about history. The storytellers and priests of the cultural network do not wear badges announcing their cultural roles. You have to judge from their response to questions who they are. Thus, if you ask what something means and your contact responds with a few anecdotes, you probably have found a storyteller. If you ask for history—and almost everyone appreciates such questions—the person who can best recount it and interpret it is likely in the ranks of the clergy. You won't find out unless you ask.

- Ask each contact for the names of others to talk to. A good practice is to ask every contact who else you ought to approach to learn more information. The odds are high that if you ask five people "Who else?", some of the names they mention will be similar. The odds are even higher that some of these names will be those of the storytellers in the cultural network.

- When you find the storytellers, cultivate a special relationship with them. If you are alert as you work your way through your initial round of contacts, it is only a question of time before you find the storytellers and priests. Once you find them, be nice to them because they are important to you and let them do their job. Their job is to carry news and interpret events. If anything happens that you can't explain, ask them for an explanation. They would think it strange if you didn't.

Culture networkers cultivate a lot of exposure to people at all levels in the organization. You can't influence the network without frequently touching the lives of its people. This is particularly true of old-hand secretaries. Always take the time to pass the time of day. Knowing personal details—family, hobbies— will almost always encourage reciprocity. If you keep at it and are sincere about the respect you pay this key subculture, over time it will do wonders for you in helping you get your work done well.

Culture networkers make extensive use of anecdotes and stories to reinforce values they themselves care about. Or they put themselves into situations where, with any luck, a story will emerge (such as going drinking with the troops).

They seek out friendships. Organizations are collections of people. Particularly in the business world, people are not necessarily together because they want to be. Despite this, humans as social animals make friends with others around them. And these friendships—small cabals, in effect—become an important part of each individual's support within the culture.

Friends keep you tuned in to what is going on that may be relevant to your own situation. Good friends represent you in a favorable light to others in the culture. Friends buck you up when you are down. They laugh with you when the barriers seem unsurmountable. They run interference for you when they can, and when you need it. Almost everyone needs the support of friends in a culture.

Culture networkers rely on the network to work for the bulk of their communications with the people in the organization. More important, they believe in the cultural network and they trust it to do their bidding in the most effective way.

Part II

PUTTING CULTURES INTO PRACTICE

6

Corporate Tribes: Identifying the Cultures

In the last several chapters, we looked at the components of corporate culture. Now it is time to put all of these factors together—values, heroes, rites and rituals—and see how they actually work within the corporation. The focus in this section of the book is on managing cultures—that is, on understanding them, analyzing them, shaping them, and retooling them when change is necessary. Most of the information here is suggestive, not prescriptive. We intend it as a different way of looking at management within an organization and we hope that it will offer a new perspective for both managers and employees.

As we've said before, the biggest single influence on a company's culture is the broader social and business environment in which the company operates. A corporate culture embodies what it takes to succeed in this environment. If hard selling is required for success, the culture will be one that encourages people to sell and sell hard; if thoughtful technical decision-making is required, the culture will make sure that that happens too.

After examining hundreds of corporations and their business environments, we have come to see that many companies fall into four general categories or types of cultures. These categories are determined by two factors in the marketplace: the degree of risk associated with the company's activities, and the speed at which companies—and their employees—get feedback on whether decisions or strategies are successful. From these market realities, we have distilled the four generic cultures:

The tough-guy, macho culture. A world of individualists who regularly take high risks and get quick feedback on whether their actions were right or wrong.

The work hard/play hard culture. Fun and action are the rule here, and employees take few risks, all with quick feedback; to succeed, the culture encourages them to maintain a high level of relatively low-risk activity.

The bet-your-company culture. Cultures with big-stakes decisions, where years pass before employees know whether decisions have paid off. A high-risk, slow-feedback environment.

The process culture. A world of little or no feedback where employees find it hard to measure what they do; instead they concentrate on how it's done. We have another name for this culture when the processes get out of control—bureaucracy!

This division of the world of business into four categories is, of course, simplistic. No company we know today precisely fits into any one of these categories. In fact, within any single real-world company, a mix of all four types of cultures will be found. Marketing departments are tough-guy cultures. Sales and manufacturing departments work hard and play hard. Research and development is a world of high risk and slow feedback. And accounting sits squarely in the upper reaches of bureaucratic life.

Moreover, companies with very strong cultures—the companies that most intrigue us—fit this simple mold hardly at all. These companies have cultures that artfully blend the best elements of all four types—and blend them in ways that allow these companies to perform well when the environment around them changes, as it inevitably does. However, we do think that this framework can be useful in helping managers begin to identify more specifically the culture of their own companies. Let's take a look at each type of culture and how it works within an organization.

The Tough-Guy, Macho Culture

Fortunes and flops are made overnight in this world of high-risk stakes and quick feedback, the most grueling of all business cultures. Police departments are the essence of this type of culture since the stakes there are often life and death. The same is true for surgeons. But the marketplace also provides a variety of other organizations that fall in this category: construction, cosmetics, management consulting, venture capital, advertising, television, movies, publishing, sports—in fact, the entire entertainment industry.

The financial stakes are high—big advertising campaigns, expensive construction projects, the fall television season, a $32 million movie, the World Series. And the feedback is quick. A year is probably the longest it takes to get feedback; more likely, companies will know whether their products will make it or not in a single season. In extreme cases—like a Broadway show or a movie opening—feedback comes right away.

In construction, for instance, a team digging a tunnel described for us the process of exploding the last stretch, called the "plug." They have only one shot to "blow the plug." If their sense of thoroughness or anxiety leads them to be overly generous in their use of explosives, they could destroy the surrounding terrain. If, on the other hand, their sense of caution prevails, they could damage the tunnel by flooding it, making all their previous work—the engineering, the hardships, the time—disappear on one throw of the plunger. High risk, very fast feedback.

Tough-guy, macho cultures tend to be young ones with a focus on speed, not endurance. Not taking an action is as important as taking one. If the automobile executive puts off the decision on design changes and the old model doesn't sell, chances are the executive will get fired. If changes are made and the car is a hit, the executive will become a star. The financial rewards also come early; all of those twenty-eight-year-old millionaires walking around probably come from tough-guy cultures. But the intense pressure and frenetic pace of the culture often burns people out before they reach middle age.

The all or nothing nature of this environment encourages values of risk-taking and the belief that "we can pull off the big deal, the best campaign" . . . whatever. Slogans of these companies reflect the value of best, biggest, and greatest. "Make great ads," (Leo Burnett Advertising); "The Last Smart Move," (an inventive technology company).

THE SURVIVORS/THE HEROES

Tough is the by-word in this culture. The need to make a quick decision and to accept the risk that very soon it may be proven wrong requires a tough attitude. So does the internal competition.

Every meeting can become a war game where the most junior person in the room has to best the most senior person in order to win respect. If the junior person doesn't fight, he or she will be dismissed out of hand as a lightweight. A comer is the one who's aggressive whether right, wrong, or indifferent.

Survivors also must maintain a tough attitude in this culture because anyone will go after you given the right opportunity. A newcomer in one macho business asked what sorts of things needed to be learned in order to succeed. The senior staffer replied, "Learn that you never cry in public. No matter how bad it hurts, go back to your office and cry in private."

The junior staffer seemed mystified by this: "But why do you have to cry?"

"Ah, because the bastards will get you when you're down."

"Who are the bastards?"

"They're all over the place," said the senior staffer. "They're your colleagues, your customers. They'll get you down, especially when you're depressed. But don't cry. Cry and they'll just tear you apart."

"Well, what else is there?" the junior staffer felt brave enough—or perhaps just scared enough—to ask.

"It's o.k. to shout, scream, and curse. It gets frustrating, and while you're not allowed to cry in public, it's all right to express emotion—particularly emotion that can forcefully affect the situation. So, if you really get upset, say some outrageous curse word and storm out of the person's office, rush back to your own office, and then cry. Just remember, don't do the crying first."

Persons who survive this culture best are the ones who need to gamble, who can tolerate all-or-nothing risks because they *need* instant feedback. This is a world of individualists. For these people there is no reward in being part of a team; their goal is to become a star. In this culture it is very possible to become a star overnight—the genius who finances the last big deal in venture capital, the player who scores the winning point in the hockey game, the management consultant who totally reorganizes the Fortune 500 company, the book editor who plucks a first novel out of the slush pile and makes it a bestseller. Of course fame can fly just as quickly as it comes. When a deal sours and the star is to blame, he can be out on his ear. As the old saying goes, "You're only as good as your last movie."

Stars are temperamental. But the tough-guy culture tolerates them because it would be nothing without them. In fact, outlaw heroes are the norm for this culture. They may behave outrageously, but as long as they hit the success button every time they go out, they'll be heroes. Although this is called a tough-guy, macho culture, it probably discriminates the least against women of any of the four types. After all, a star is a star.

THE IMPORTANCE OF RITUALS

Chance plays a major part in tough-guy cultures. What worked once may not work again, so employees devise rituals that tend to "protect" them from the vagaries of the environment. As an example, people in tough-guy cultures will wax poetic about the importance of "problem-solving" or "strategizing" in their work. Don't believe them. These are only security blankets used to slow the work routine down and give employees a sense of safety. Any procedure becomes a temporary haven from the fear of taking risks and making the BIG mistake. That's how surgeons work on a difficult case. When they operate, they follow a procedure, even if it's experimental. If the patient dies, surgeons say "I've done everything I can." To further protect themselves, doctors display degrees on their walls and bound editions of medical journals on their shelves. What they communicate is "I'm reading all the time. I keep up with what's new. I did all the procedures right." You will recognize that if you are dead as a result, you will not be too convinced by these arguments. But the surgeon will be.

Such rituals become superstititions in a tough-guy culture. They help individuals believe that they can, in fact, do the things they are supposed to do. In the winter of 1982, the ratings for CBS Evening News were sagging. Walter Cronkite was gone, and he was obviously a difficult act for anchorman Dan Rather to follow. ABC and NBC moved in quickly and started taking viewers away from the formerly preeminent CBS. News executives were becoming alarmed. In the dead cold of the winter, Rather started wearing a sweater under his jacket on the air because the studio was chilly. Soon after he donned the sweater, ratings began to climb. Rather quickly developed a superstition about the connection between the sweaters and success, even hinting that he might continue wearing them during the summer.

Steve Carlton, the Phillies' Cy Young award-winning pitcher, clung superstitiously to the belief that he could only pitch to catcher Tim McCarver. He kept McCarver in the major leagues for five years after the catcher was over the hill. What did McCarver have to do with throwing baseballs? Nothing. There was simply a fast bond between the two that was exactly like the magnetic pull between partners in a police force. The partner is the one person you'd trust to cover you in a dangerous situation.

Bonding is often exclusive and exclusionary. Stars in some cultures band together so that the "magic" won't be diluted. A group of venture capitalists who have financed a string of successful projects form a tight little cabal. They claim that it is their magic that makes their work so successful. No one else can join the group because the luck might go sour—they call it "being in the deal stream." It's a ploy as old as Napoleon, who insisted on taking only "lucky men" with him to the front lines—just in case.

STRENGTHS AND WEAKNESSES

Tough-guy cultures enable companies to do what needs to be done in high-risk, quick-return environments. Successful companies in such industries try to buffer individual stars from the agony and uncertainty of high-stakes ventures, then reward them handsomely when heart-stopping gambles pay off.

Through rituals of bonding and problem-solving, and with values that make taking sensible risks a virtue and relying on the safe and sure an unpardonable sin, star cultures move industries ahead. They promote employment for the risk-takers we need, whether it's Reggie Jackson, Henry Ford, or Helena Rubenstein.

But their very strength is the source of real weakness. The tough-guy emphasis on quick feedback diverts resources from long-term investments, thus there is no value placed on long-term persistence. This short-term orientation has several consequences. First of all, the competition to become a star is so keen that the virtues of cooperation are forgotten. Also, because the culture is superstitious, it breeds out the ability to learn from mistakes. Tough cultures foster immaturity by tolerating tantrums; often top management encourages this attitude and delights in watching everyone trying to score points off the other guy. The result of all this is a culture that rewards individuals who are temperamental, short-sighted, and superstitious; and that devastates people whose careers might blossom over time. Because of the high turnover created by people who fail in the short-term, building a strong, cohesive culture can become quite difficult in the tough-guy climate.

Work Hard/Play Hard Culture

This business kingdom is the benign and hyperactive world of sales organizations: real estate, computer companies, automotive distributors, any door-to-door sales operation—such as Avon, Mary Kay Cosmetics, and encyclopedia companies—mass-consumer-sales companies like McDonald's or Frito-Lay, office-equipment manufacturers such as Xerox or Pitney Bowes, and all retail stores (except Bloomingdale's, which has placed itself squarely in the tough-guy culture).

The employees of these companies live in a world of small risks—no one sale will make or break a sales rep—and quick, often intensive feedback—a rep either gets the order or doesn't. Activity in this world is everything. As long as employees can keep up, the work will get done. Success comes with persistence. Go back to the customer one more time. Make one more telephone call.

Of course, within any single corporate culture, the sales division fits this mold. But manufacturing also falls within the culture. Most factory workers have to keep at the job, day after day. The feedback is quick—everyone knows when something isn't working right away. But the real risks are comparatively few; the system is full of checks and balances to keep the job from becoming a big risk.

The primary values of this culture center on customers and their needs. If the tough-guy culture is built on "find a mountain and climb it," then work hard/play hard rests on "find a need and fill it." The idea of good customer service is one that permeates most of these organizations; "IBM means service" is probably the hallmark slogan. Digital Equipment has taken the IBM idea one step further by developing "warm armpit marketing"—a concept where the sales representative stays in the field and gets closely involved with the customer's problems.

But also consider McDonald's—experts say the company's success does not come from better burgers, but rather a faster turnaround at the counter. The secret: volume against fixed cost.

But that isn't the whole story. McDonald's creates a mystique of quality, service, cleanliness, and value—QSCV—among its employees and franchisees. This theme is repeated and repeated from the day a new franchisee first goes to Hamburger University. Employees become true believers and the culture's intensity is McDonald's secret. While all companies aren't sales driven, some of the best companies in America have gravitated some or part of the way towards an action culture. The rationale for this is simple. In a dynamic environment, the worst thing that can often happen from a performance point of view is to stand still. To protect against this natural human tendency, good managers work hard to instill an action orientation. "Try it; fix it; do it" becomes the operative ethic of companies like Hewlett-Packard (H-P), Intel, DEC, and others. The managers of these companies are saying to their employees that the race is to the quick; and they demand a high level of activity and initiative to make sure they stay in the race.

THE SURVIVORS/THE HEROES

The heroes of this culture are the super salespeople, the silver-tongued charmers who could sell an igloo to an Eskimo *or* a sun worshipper with equal ease. Unlike the tough-guy heroes, the work-hard heroes measure the worth of their activity in volume, not high stakes.

The best of the workers/players are friendly, carousing, hail-fellow-well-met kinds of people. They aren't worried or superstitious. While anyone who succeeds in a tough-guy culture becomes a star; here the team beats the world because no *individual* really makes a difference. The team produces the *volume*. That's why salesmen's clubs and contests are so important—everyone wants to be part of the group that goes to Hawaii.

RITES AND RITUALS

This is the play-hard aspect of the culture; fun becomes the flip side of an intense day of selling. More than any other culture, this one revels in energetic games. Contests, meetings, promotions, conventions. Anything that will work to keep motivation up. Tandem's weekly beer busts, Tupperware's rallies, and Mary Kay's conventions are good examples. IBM's yearly gatherings find salesmen joining forces to reaffirm spirit, growth, and conquest, the core values of this culture by singing the IBM song:

EVER ONWARD-EVER ONWARD

That's the spirit that brought us fame!
We're big, but bigger we will be
We can't fail for all can see
That to serve humanity has been our aim
Our products are now known in every zone
Our reputation sparkles like a gem
We've fought our way through and new
Fields we're sure to conquer too
Forever onward IBM.

Language plays a big part in the business rituals of the work-hard culture. The perfect sales pitch enjoys a special position in the folklore. But so do salesmen's jokes, sports metaphors, and, of course, exaggeration, as when salesmen tell how much damage they did to the hotel room last night. Boasting, by contrast, is a tough-guy game because it's a form of self-aggrandizement. A star will say "That's the best goddamn project I've ever done," while the super salesperson will say, "That customer was the worst creep in the world, but we made the sale!" They'll both be talking about the same thing.

STRENGTHS AND WEAKNESSES

Work/play cultures get a lot done. If the objective is to make or move some quality item fast, a work/play culture can do it. The environment is ideal for active people who thrive on quick, tangible feedback. The action culture makes available the mass-produced goods the American market wants—better than anyone else can.

But action also carries great disadvantages. Volume can displace quality in the culture's pell-mell rush to produce and sell more. The worst of the culture comes out in lack of thoughtfulness or attention; the tendency is toward the kind of back-of-the envelope calculations that can backfire. Also, work/play-hard cultures often get fooled by success, forgetting that today's successes may become tomorrow's failures. High-tech companies, especially, grow enormously overnight but often face the prospect that the growth was just a one-time spurt.

When they get in trouble, these cultures often go for quick-fix solutions. Like tough-guy cultures, they tend to have a short-term perspective. Companies with this culture can suffer dramatic turnover when their sales forces become disillusioned and easily cynical. When their activity doesn't produce, they go somewhere else rather than search out the root of the problem. The troops don't stick to the company long enough to weather the tough times because they are often more committed to the action than to the company.

Also, high-energy enthusiasts can drift into cynicism when their quick-fix existence has lost its meaning. The work hard/play hard culture requires stamina that ebbs as we age. These cultures are often cultures of young people who are looking for places to prove their worth. The action's attractive. These people are young chronologically; by contrast, tough guys are young emotionally. And unless a company can retain older people, the culture loses some of its most important lessons.

Savvy companies spend a lot of time trying to counteract all of these tendencies. First of all, they aim to keep product quality on par with customer wants and encourage the worker/players to slow down and make more considered decisions. IBM counteracted the high-energy sales attitude by placing "Think" signs all over the company. They were trying to find a good balance between quality and activity, identity and growth, a difficult trick.

Bet-Your-Company Culture

Life in this culture means a diet of high risk, but slow feedback. Slow here doesn't mean less pressure; instead it means pressure that is as persistent as slow-drip water torture. It means investing millions—sometimes billions—in a project that takes years to develop, refine, and test, before you find out whether it will go or not. Mobil or Exxon considers sending a $500 million drilling rig to explore for oil off Georges Banks; Boeing Aircraft spends several billion to build the 757 and 767; NASA commits billions to the Space Shuttle Program. All very high stakes. And all with feedback years down the line.

Industries in this culture include capital-goods companies such as Cincinnati Milacron or Caterpillar Tractor, mining and smelting companies like Alcoa and Kennecott, large-systems businesses, oil companies, investment banks like Morgan Stanley and First Boston, architectural firms, computer-design companies, and the actuarial end of insurance companies. We also include the Army and the Navy because they spend billions of dollars preparing for the war they might never have to fight.

Instead of putting their careers on the line—as tough guys would—corporate bettors often risk the future of the entire company. These corporate giants may not flounder on one bad investment decision; but it's possible for two bad decisions to sink a company.

The importance of making the right decisions fosters a sense of deliberateness throughout the companies. The world of bet-your-company cultures moves in months and years, not days and weeks. Once, at a meeting in a capital-goods company, someone raised a question that couldn't be answered then and there. No one batted an eyelash. The meeting was stopped while the participants went off for two weeks to find an answer, and then resumed later, answer in hand. Other cultures would have "put that one aside for now" and moved quickly on to finish the meeting. In faster feedback environments, managers typically have one hundred pages to review in a two-hour meeting. In the bet-your-company culture, the agenda will include ten pages for review, but the meeting will spend two hours on each page.

The primary ritual of this culture *is* the business meeting. Although people from all levels of the organization might attend, seating will be strictly prescribed by rank, and only the senior members will talk. Decision-making comes from the top down—once all the inputs are in. In a shorter-cycle business, by contrast, decisions are made more quickly because the organization is flat and less formal, and it doesn't really matter if the decision is wrong; it can always be corrected.

The values of this culture focus on the future and the importance of investing in it. "Progress is our most important product" (GE), "Better living through chemistry" (DuPont), "Alcoa can't wait . . . for tomorrow." The beliefs center on the attitude that good ideas should be given the proper chance for success. A saying at 3M goes, "Never kill an idea, just deflect it." People at 3M say a coherent sentence is an acceptable draft of a new product proposal.

THE SURVIVORS/THE HEROES

People don't make it as bettors unless they have a great deal of character and confidence that can carry them through the waiting period. They are just as self-directed and tough as people in the macho culture, but they have the stamina to endure long-term ambiguity with little or no feedback.

Bettors' moves are measured and deliberate because they need the assurance that they're right. They take time to make a decision, then double check every component of it. And once they have made up their minds, bettors don't change their convictions easily.

Survivors all respect authority and technical competence. When the organization can't afford mistakes, those who have proven themselves gain great respect. The heroic figures tend to be hunker-down heroes, the people who were fired or shuffled off to the corner but who kept working on the big project until it became a reality. Heroes take on great importance because they provide psychological support during all the rough times.

Immaturity is not tolerated in this culture. Young bettors will do trivial jobs for years and still take them seriously. Evaluations of employees are made over decades. Top management says: "He's just a young fellow, give him a chance." Or, "He's only been here five years; it's too early to tell." In the work/play culture, if someone says, "He's been here a month already and nothing's happened," they mean, "He's on the way out."

Sharing hard-won knowledge is another component for success, so bettors become highly dependent on one another and treat one another with infinite politeness. It's like getting married—they have to preserve links in the bettor culture. There is none of the denigration that runs rampant in the macho world but instead a reliance on respect for authority. Younger employees look to mentors, who become the backbone of the system. For example, people happily defer to their boss because they know he has likely been through the waiting period on more than one important project—and made the right decision. That experience is something they can look up to.

STRENGTHS AND WEAKNESSES

Bet-your-company cultures are ideally suited to the environment in which they operate. After all, the quick fix/immediate gratification needed by the first two cultures could spell disaster in the nuclear arms division of the U.S. Army. Many nuclear engineers never know whether they are right or wrong; nor do we want them to know since our lives and property would be part of the feedback.

Bet-your-company cultures lead to high-quality inventions and major scientific breakthroughs—they help move the country's economy ahead. But they also move with awesome slowness. They do not produce on a mass scale, nor perform with the speed and decisiveness of a quick-feedback environment. In addition, because of their long-term perspective, these companies are vulnerable to short-term fluctuations in the economy and cash-flow problems while they wait for major ventures to pay off.

In the end, however, these companies may be the ones our economy needs most desperately. Careers, products, and profits don't develop quickly. But when they do, they last a long time.

The Process Culture

This low-risk, slow-feedback corner of the world is populated by banks, insurance companies, financial-service organizations, large chunks of the government, utilities, and heavily regulated industries like pharmaceutical companies. As in the work/play culture, the financial stakes here are low: no one transaction will make or break the company—or anyone in it. But unlike worker/players, the employees here get virtually no feedback. The memos and reports that they write seem to disappear into a void. As a result, they have no idea how effective they are until someone blames them for something. In a government agency, for instance, employees may work like crazy, but the only time they get any recognition is when a legislator decides to kill their agency or indicts it for violating the public trust or for promoting inefficiency and corruption.

This lack of feedback forces employees to focus on *how* they do something, not what they do. They start developing artificial ties to elements of the world in the organization; small events take on major importance—a certain telephone call, that snippet of paper, or the section head's latest memo. People in these cultures tend to develop a "cover your ass" mentality. The most trivial event becomes the subject for a memo. They describe the incident in minute detail, giving the best explanation for their actions. Then they copy the world with it. Those fellow sufferers who receive the memo don't want to acknowledge that they've missed anything. So they send an answer, often as detailed as the original. Everything goes into a file so that they can prove that they didn't make the mistake, should someone mention it five years from now.

The values in this culture center on technical perfection—figuring out the risks and pinning the solutions down to a science. In other words, getting the process and the details right. "Underwriting Excellence," the Chubb Insurance slogan, is a good example. So is "Strive for Technical Perfection" (Price Waterhouse & Co.). Again, these values are particularly well suited to the business environment of the culture. What we describe may just sound like so much red-tape. But if banks, insurance companies, or governmental agencies responded to every fad or fashion, we would all suffer. Imagine a major change each year in the driver's test. Or a new procedure for income taxes. And would anyone really want a work hard/play hard type keeping track of his or her checking account?

THE SURVIVORS/THE HEROES

Protectiveness and caution are natural responses to the absence of feedback. If process people don't know where or when they will be attacked, they try to have all of their flanks covered. But caution in this culture isn't personal, rather it becomes related to the end product. So, how neatly and completely workers do something is often more important than what they do. If the pink slip isn't filled in correctly, the world comes to a standstill. If the job application has a typographical error in it, then the job seeker is shown the door. People who are valued in this culture are those who are trying to protect the system's integrity more than their own.

The real survivors learn to live within this artificial world. They are orderly, punctual, attend to detail, and survive on their memories. They carry out the procedures as they are written down without asking whether they make sense in the real world. In fact, the real world ceases to exist, and most successful bureaucrats have trouble dealing with it when it infringes on their turf.

Since these organizations are often vulnerable to political whim, the ability to survive one or two storms becomes a heroic trait. Stories center on hunker-down heroes. Such as the G-12 in GAO who lost her secretary, her telephone, and her furniture and still reported for work promptly at 9:00 A.M. staying until 5:00 P.M. (except for the hour lunch break, of course). Or the one about the G-13 assistant to the section head, who has been promised that promotion to G-15 for years, but simply watches as the boss above her keeps getting transferred—only to be replaced by someone equally obnoxious and incompetent. The assistant does most of the work and is loved by all. Process cultures thrive on stories like this.

These hunker-down types often win out when the political winds shift for the better. But the lack of *identifiable success* for these figures means that heroes for some employees are often functions—not people. In other words, the post may make the hero.

RITES AND RITUALS

Rituals center on work patterns and procedures, and there is a great deal of discussion about these matters. Long, rambling meetings focus on the way in which a decision should be made: Who is best at keeping track of milestones in resource allocation and management plans? Or which way is that reorganization going to go? Is one department going to be collapsed into another? Whose job may be threatened? Reorganization becomes a strong candidate for the most important ritual in a process culture. But there are others, like retirement ceremonies honoring those who have stuck it out the longest.

Like corporate bettors, process people also pay inordinate attention to titles and formalities. Their tightly structured hierarchies come very close to a class system. At a major insurance company, for instance, the hierarchy runs from "Class 19" for those with a high-school diploma, all the way up to "Class 49" for the highest vice-presidential level.

One of the company's managers described the system this way:

Classes 17–27: "In tray/Out tray people." The work is a never-ending process and there is a lot of job burnout.

Classes 27–33: "The professional/technical grunt group. They have college degrees and do the brunt of the paper work."

Classes 34–39: "The 'men in the middle,' the department heads. They are a highly stressed group."

Classes 40–49: "The group that's made it. They identify with top management. I'd say these guys work sixty-hour weeks."

This system is so strong, he said, that "People want a class change over a salary increase any time. They feel movement up through the class system is a better indicator of success. I've literally had people refuse a raise if it meant staying at the same class rank."

The system is also highly visible; at this company your office furniture shows exactly where you are in the pecking order. Classes 17–25 have small steel desks and one chair with no arms. Classes 26–29 have the same chairs behind their desks but have an additional typewriter wing and one chair with arms. By contrast, classes 30–34's desks are known as "aircraft carriers" or "flat-tops," so much larger are they; and—hallelujah—they come complete with armchairs (two). Managerial classes 34–39 are offered wooden desks, three-quarter-length walls, a conference table, and a bookshelf. Classes 40–42, assistant vice presidents, get that same bonanza plus a choice of a sofa and chairs, or a round table and a credenza. Classes 43–49, vice presidents, have floor-to-ceiling offices. They also have a choice of upholstery from a fabric book updated and controlled by the company, so that their couches and chairs are sure to look distinct from those belonging in the offices of assistant vice presidents.

These distinctions are no small part of the company. The very day a person's promotion is placed before the board of directors for ceremonial final approval is the day the furniture men move in with the right trappings to match the new rank. As one vice president commented, "The furniture is never a day earlier or a day later."

STRENGTHS AND WEAKNESSES

The process culture has become a scapegoat for much that is wrong with the modern world. President Ronald Reagan is trying to make his mark by "getting government off our backs." No one can say they really *like* an efficient administrator. And we all complain about how hard it is to get anything done in a world of red-tape.

Yet, these cultures did not simply spring forth full-blown. Special creations designed to fit special circumstances, they offer a perfect counterpoint to the high-risk world of the star culture or the quick, sometimes thoughtless energy of work/play. Process cultures put order into work that needs to be predictable. In many ways, good process cultures make sure the world works for the stars, worker/players, and bettors.

Tribal Habits

Although this is admittedly a very general, very brief look at the four types of cultures, we think it should give you a good start in identifying your own, or at least parts of it.

The type of culture you work in is important for many reasons. It even influences people's preferences, styles, and habits—how they dress, where they live, and what they do outside the corporation. Let's make a few distinctions in tribal habits among the four cultures, however fanciful:

Dress.   Tough-guy cultures are studiously "in fashion" all the time; the stars of the culture often make a real effort to look different from their peers—but not too different. If everyone else has a Gucci briefcase, the star will come in with a Mark Cross briefcase. Pretty soon everyone else will have one too, then the game begins again. Worker/players on the other hand, avoid extremes in dress, choosing instead to stay with the norms of middle America—

sports jackets, plaids, shirt sleeves, and in the computer companies, jeans. Bettors and process-people are conservative dressers, and what they wear tends to coincide with their rank. Junior people *look* like junior people. The higher ranks often appear in dark, three-piece suits.

Housing. Tough guys live wherever the "in" place is; they're the ones who have revitalized the cities because they decided that was the newest place to live. They also spend a good deal of time finding a "different" (but not too different) spot for their vacation house. Workers/players live in tract houses and they're proud of them. They'll stay in the same house for twenty years, but upgrade the playroom into a den. One employee of a high-tech company moved from his tract house into a much fancier one across town. His fellow employees just shook their heads, "He's getting awfully uppity lately." In the bet-your-company culture, housing matches the hierarchy. This is especially true in company towns like GE's Schenectady or DuPont's Wilmington, where the top managers literally live at the top of the hill. Bettors go for suburbs that are relatively far out of town and they like the Old World charm of Tudor design. Process people live in apartments or in simple, no frills homes. They tend to cluster in the same suburbs close to town because they usually either car pool or take public transportation to get to work.

Sports. The individuals of the tough-guy culture like one-on-one sports such as tennis. They especially like squash because it's "in" and because it relies heavily on the killer instinct. Worker/players like all team sports, plus they like any sport that requires a lot of action or movement, such as basketball or touch football. Bettors play a great deal of golf, because in a good game you don't know if you've won or not until the eighteenth hole. And process people like jogging and swimming, which are, after all, process sports.

Language. People in macho cultures like to use words that no one has ever heard of. They also take common words and make them uncommon. A speech by Alexander Haig will give you a good idea of what we mean by this. Worker/players use acronyms all the time; they also rely heavily on sports metaphors. Bettors are constantly referring to history, "Back in 1937 . . . ," and they call everyone Mr. or Mrs. Process people answer any question with a detailed explanation, and delight in asking the specific question that no one can answer.

Greeting Rituals.   You'll know you're in a tough-guy company when the receptionist hardly pays any attention to you and you have to wait a minimum of twenty minutes to see your appointment. In a worker/player company, your appointment will meet you at the door, slap you on the back, take your coat, and have a cup of coffee waiting. At both the bettor and process companies, you'll go through an elaborate sign-in procedure and you'll probably have to wear a visitor's tag. At the bettor company you may think you'll meet with one person, but you'll actually meet with at least five. In the process culture, both you and your appointment will relate to each other through paper.

Co-worker Rituals.   Tough guys score points off one another; worker/players drink together; bettors mentor each other; process people discuss memos.

No one company fits perfectly into any one of these molds, and different parts of the same organization will exhibit each of the four types of cultures. Still, most companies will have overall tendencies toward one of the cultures because they are responding to the needs of their marketplace.

Some companies, however, have two very strong—and competing—cultures. The automotive industry is a good example where a bet-your-company culture runs smack into a process culture. The new-car-design side of the industry is a classic bettor culture; decisions on what kinds of cars to make must be made years in advance to allow for retooling the manufacturing plants. Feedback doesn't come until considerably later—when the cars hit the marketplace. And the consequences—as we all know by now—can be disastrous.

The competing culture is the one of statistical technicians, the number crunchers left over from the days of Ford's whiz kids, who believed that *anything* could be quantified. These people swarm all over the company trying to knock off 50 cents from the manufacturing price of the bumper and another 75 cents off the price of the fender—cost savings that can save the company millions of dollars. But this very process collides with the bettors who are trying to get out the best car with the most new features.

Unless the company has a very strong system of overall values that encourage everyone to work for the same, identifiable goals, these competing tendencies can easily turn into internecine wars. Where key people focus more on internal wars and less on keeping their organization in tune with the business environment, then it's very possible for the marketplace to pass them by.

While some companies have competing cultures, others deliberately shift their focus to a different kind of culture to give themselves a leg up on the marketplace. For instance, Procter & Gamble, Pepsi Cola, and Bloomingdale's department stores should—by all accounts—fit nicely into the work hard/play hard culture. For the most part, they produce or sell low-cost consumer products and depend on volume sales for their income. However, each company has deliberately cultivated elements of a tough-guy, macho culture to increase internal competition. Employees in these particular cultures feel as though they're making high-risk decisions all the time.

Why the emphasis on competition? For these companies, that's all there is. They have turned simple products like soap or soft drinks or clothes into gold mines through aggressive marketing. It's not all that difficult to manufacture a new soap bar or a new suit. So these companies choose to differentiate themselves in a dramatic way from similar companies. To them, success is based on beating out your competitor. So fighting outside the company is nurtured by fighting inside.

Although most companies switch to tough-guy cultures to become more aggressive in the marketplace, some choose to switch to a work hard/play hard culture. Citibank is a good example. Most financial institutions are passive, like utilities with money in them. But Walter Wriston wanted his bank to become the world's largest (it was then third or fourth). To grow, Citibank had to take market share away from other banks. So, Wriston created an action-oriented environment where active sales and service became the standard. Soon financial officers were ringing figurative doorbells saying, "Leave your money with me" or "I could make you the greatest loan." Citibank thus forged new values for the industry.

As we will see later on, switching cultures within a company is a very difficult and tricky business. But if it is done correctly, it can make a big difference in the fortunes of the corporation.

So, as we have said, it is important for all managers—or employees for that matter—to have a good and precise sense of the culture of their companies. Once you know more exactly the type of culture that you're dealing with, you will have a better idea of how to get things done in an effective way. Let us turn therefore to the techniques for diagnosing culture.

7

Diagnosis: Learning to Read Cultures

A culture is its heroes, values, networks. It is all these things, but something else besides. Culture is a money-in-the-pocket investment—for CEOs, financial analysts, even job seekers. Experience tells you only so much about a company; its culture tells more. One can, in fact, predict a company's performance by diagnosing the character of its heroes, values, and so on.

Culture, even roughly defined, has a very strong influence on a company's behavior over time. And that influence is predictable. CEOs and senior managers can read a culture for early warning signals of people out of synch with the aims of their business. Investment analysts can turn to culture for greater accuracy in forecasting. Even executives in search of new opportunities would do well to match-make their personality to that of a company. Yet where should the neophyte cultural observer begin?

Although any superficial analysis runs the risk of being incomplete or even wrong, surprisingly much can be learned in a limited amount of time about a company's culture. How? By using the techniques consultants rely on. The process begins at the surface and proceeds inward, toward the company's unconscious. Almost like a psychoanalyst, the culture analyst places a company on the couch. Here are the most basic routes we follow:

Study the physical setting.   However irrelevant to the conduct of business, a company's investment in bricks and mortar—its building—inevitably says something about its culture. After all, building investments are made or at least overseen by senior management. As much as they'd like to avoid the thought, most senior managers recognize that the buildings will likely outlive them;

129

thus they try to create a setting that makes a statement to the world about their company, both deliberate and otherwise.

A company that is proud of itself and its culture will reflect this pride through its environment. Around the world, city after city proudly displays its IBM building—a bright, clean, modern statement about a proud company. General Electric's fortress-like headquarters in Fairfield, Connecticut, is a monument to corporate stability and importance. Citibank's gleaming Citicorp Center expresses the company's sense that, "we're important and we're different." (Citicorp is located in a section of Manhattan not frequented by banks). Digital Equipment's refurbished mill site conveys that they're a modern company, but their roots are in New England—thus they respect tradition. Contrast these bold statements of strong culture companies with the nondescript locations of many other companies.

Consistency among sites is also important. A slightly more subtle look at a company's culture can be gleaned by contrasting sites. Today it is not uncommon for corporate headquarters to look spiffy—senior executives do know how to look after themselves, after all. But are division sites consistent with the standards of headquarters? Are sales offices in say, Toledo, tucked into the upstairs level of a warehouse? Is the factory in upstate New York in danger of collapsing? The careful observer must factor in elements of age or use of environs, but usually the signs are unmistakeable.

One should also look for consistency across classes of employees. Department by department, physical settings indicate a company's attitude toward different classes of employees. When NCR's John Patterson discovered the terrible working conditions in his plants, he immediately refurbished them and planted grass and trees in an attempt to make people proud they worked for NCR. Similarly, the Ivorydale complex of P&G was a model of its kind when it was built before the turn of the century. Contrast this with Ford's River Rouge complex in Dearborn, Michigan: This massive industrial complex stood for decades, to some a stark reminder that workers were tools of industrial progress to be used, coerced, and discarded when no longer needed.

Culture is a human phenomenon. Strong culture companies care about all of their people and take pains to see they are all treated appropriately. Discrepancies in the way physical sites are arranged for different classes of employees is one sure sign of a weak or fragmented culture.

Read what the company says about its culture. The company's own statements about itself—annual reports, quarterly statements, press releases, comments to financial analysts—reveal more than one would expect. The rule seems to be: if you've got it, flaunt it. Companies with strong cultures recognize the importance of their values and their people and they continually report this to the world. When Wheelabrator-Frye goes to the trouble of producing a child's version of its annual report, people recognize that the company is a bastion of conservative free enterprise thought and has a culture that strongly reflects this religion. By contrast, companies with weak or fragmented cultures make much ado about the business and its performance—almost as though it operated without the help of human hands. What the company says about itself should be carefully checked for consistency. It is often possible to track company statements over time and watch how its culture evolves, a procedure called content analysis. It can be done by simply tabulating the number of times a particular phrase or belief is articulated in the annual report. The surprise is that even such a simplistic analysis will show a clear trend in the evolution of a company's beliefs about itself.

Yet published statements are only a clue to the culture, and not a very definitive one. All too often management says it believes in certain things, but a careful review of other clues suggests the belief is little more than lip service.

Test how the company greets strangers. Your first exposure to the company will be its reception area. Is it formal or informal? Relaxed or busy? Elegant or nondescript? Whatever the case, you must assume it reflects the values of the culture.

For example, around New England and the Midwest, the receptionist will, almost invariably, have other duties (such as casual typing) than simply greeting visitors. This reflects the ethic that at work you must be busy. By contrast, in New York City the emphasis is often more on the receptionist's style; appearance is all important. The receptionist's attitude tells you still more about how work gets done. In a very service-conscious company, you might have your coat taken and be offered coffee. In a more bureaucratic environment, you probably will have to endure an elaborate sign-up procedure. In a tough-guy company, you may be ignored while you cool your heels waiting. The message is, "You don't look like a star, so why should I pay attention to you."

While you wait, observe what is happening around you. Are procedures rigorously followed for everyone who passes through the lobby—employee or visitor? Tom Watson at IBM and Ed Land at Polaroid were occasionally stopped from entering company buildings because they did not have the right badge with them— though the receptionist knew perfectly well who they were. Companies with strong cultures take their rituals *very* seriously.

In testing the culture, we usually strike up a conversation with the receptionist. We ask what the company is like and whether it's a good place to work. True, no one tells us they hate the people around them. But the way these questions are answered are important, because they are *rehearsed answers.* If the receptionist dwells on the wonderful opportunities available in the company and explains that three relatives work there, you will get a vastly different impression than if you're told it's steady work and only five minutes from home.

Interview company people. In almost any company, an employee with even a few months tenure can respond adequately. We look for both consensual and conflicting perceptions. In taking our own diagnostic profile of a culture, here's what we ask:

- Tell me about the history of the company. What were its beginnings? People are generally eager to recount the past. Often their facts—if you bother to check—will be wrong. Instead they communicate the mythology of the company as they understand it (and as it was passed to them).

- Why is the company a success? What explains its growth? People tell us what they think is important in the company. They may not be substantively correct, but they are reflecting their impressions of what the culture values.

- What kind of people work here? Who really gets ahead in the long term? Since culture is fundamentally a human phenomenon, people are most eloquent in characterizing their fellow workers. What they invariably describe is their picture of a hero in the culture.

- What kind of a place is this to work in? What is an average day like? How do things get done? The answers will typically characterize the important rituals, meetings, or bureaucratic procedures. You can be sure these elements are taken seriously. If the response is hierarchical—"the boss is a good person to work for"—assume that this bet-your-company aspect of cultural life is important.

Observe how people spend their time. What people do is determined by what they value. Comparisons between what people say and do is a good measure of cultural cohesion.

Having gathered such clues, use them to determine the direction of the company. If, for example, a culture is focused inward—in other words, all the beliefs, heroes, and rituals relate to internal matters and political debates—then it is predictable that it will be slow to respond to events that occur outside it in the marketplace. This in turn will warrant a closer look at whether the company's growth is real or merely an appearance. It will help an observer distinguish which manufacturers within related industries will survive, and which won't. Knowing corporate culture, an investment analyst could gain important insight into a company's aims. Assume, for example, such an analyst is debating the strengths of a recently opened GE division. The analyst knows orders are being cancelled, that the business is foundering. Experience would tell the analyst to pass on this company. But knowledge of GE's culture would create an expectation that GE would carry out its commitment and work toward making the division strong. GE's culture is built upon sticking with a business and making it work—just as it almost never walks away from a customer.

DIAGNOSING CULTURE FROM THE INSIDE

A company insider can go much deeper in diagnosing culture, and with much greater precision. But there are a few pitfalls to achieving an accurate reading of one's own company's culture.

Objectivity is of the first importance. It is easy to analyze the shortcomings and strengths of a competitor company. But to understand your own company's culture you have to make one important distinction: Forget whether you believe that "X" is the right way to make business decisions. Concentrate on how you and your colleagues typically make the decision. To be an effective observer of your own culture you must avoid making value judgements about what is important and what is not. Just observe what is—not what you think should be—and remember that the patterns are subtle.

On the job, this distinction tends to get muddied. When we consider what is important, we point to the product, the budget, what we got done yesterday. But how did we deal with the last issue concerning the product, or the budget, or yesterday's chores?

Culture deals with people—what they think, what they feel, what they do with their time. Five minutes spent gossiping with a friend in accounting may have had a greater influence on a product decision than did fifteen minutes in a meeting on the subject.

With these admonitions in mind, what are some of the tools an insider might use to sharpen perspective on a company's culture?

Understand career path progression of employees. Who gets ahead? If all important positions are filled by ex-salespersons, then it is pretty clear what the culture believes in and values.

What does an employee have to do to get promoted? Does the culture reward competence in key skills, performance against objective criteria, tenure, and loyalty? The beliefs of the culture are primarily shaped by people's perceptions of what it takes to get ahead. If you've already made it and you know the reason was that you were a good team player, not a superstar performer, that is what you will look for in others and what others will emulate. John DeLorean was most critical of a GM practice he characterized as "promotion of the unobvious candidate" as a symbol of the deterioration in GM's culture through the 1960s and 1970s.

How long do people stay in jobs—particularly middle-management jobs? Tenure is critical in assessing culture. Short tenures mean people are motivated to make their mark quickly (and hence get promoted again) and will steer clear of longer-term, slower-payback activities. In such a culture a short-term focus will likely dominate.

Look at the content of what is being discussed or written about. People in management spend an enormous amount of time reading and writing memos, but what are the memos about? Take your in-box some week and simply tabulate what's in it by subject matter. You may surprise yourself.

Similarly everyone spends a lot of time in meetings. Forget the stated purpose of the meeting. Instead, keep track of what is actually discussed—and who talks, and to whom. Track how much time is spent on each subject. However surprising the result—and we guarantee you will be surprised—you'll discover that the culture spends its time on what it values most.

Pay particular attention to the anecdotes and stories that pass through the cultural network. When people want to share their experience, they relate it through anecdotes and stories. The same stories told by many different people are especially significant.

Ask yourself what was the point of any given story. Inventory the anecdotes to determine how many relate to customers, to political infighting in the company, to individual initiative taken and rewarded (or punished). You will then have indisputable evidence of what this culture thinks is important. Its accuracy outdoes almost any other barometer.

How do you interpret these findings? When do the signs, stories, meetings, settings, and so much more signal a weak culture? To find out, the diagnostic profile must be taken one step further.

Signs of a Culture in Trouble

Throughout this book we have written extensively about the characteristics of companies with strong cultures. We have not elaborated on the opposite—companies with weak cultures. Nor can we, because the truth of the matter is that companies with weak cultures simply lack some or all of the characteristics of their stronger counterparts, specifically:

- Weak cultures have no clear values or beliefs about how to succeed in their business; *or*

- They have many such beliefs but cannot agree among themselves on which are most important; *or*

■ Different parts of the company have fundamentally different beliefs.

■ The heroes of the culture are destructive or disruptive and don't build upon any common understanding about what is important.

■ The rituals of day-to-day life are either disorganized—with everybody doing their own thing—or downright contradictory—with the left hand and the right hand working at cross purposes.

What are the symptoms of cultural malaise we worry about most?

Inward focus. Companies invariably get in trouble when they stop paying attention to what is going on in the real world, particularly when they start doing things to placate the boss or to look good or to score points off others around them. Such short-sighted actions can take the form of overemphasis on internal budgets, financial analysis, or sales quotas and no talk about customers, competitors, trends, or other real-world matters. If you find that a large portion of people's time is spent serving internal masters—politics, apple-polishing, etc.—beware. When a culture focuses inward, the company is in great danger in the marketplace. It is usually only a question of time before the company's economic performance suffers.

Short-term focus. The great American businesses are great because they have survived and prospered for decades, through good economic times and bad. Setting high performance standards is important for success in any business. But if all the time and attention in a company is devoted to meeting short-term targets, then sustainable business receives no support. Again, the cultural clue is what people spend their time on. How much time spent on short-term results is too much? You be the judge.

Morale problems. A culture gets in trouble when its people are chronically unhappy. Before long, unhappy people leave. Therefore one of the indicators to watch closely in companies is turnover. Some turnover is inevitable. But if turnover is high or trending upward, something is wrong in the culture. This can happen in a division or across a whole company. It can happen in a function or a location. When we recently spoke to someone in a seemingly successful company, we asked, "How's the job?" He replied, "Ah, it's a job." Morale problems stemming from cultural malaise are often first expressed as just such subtle signals. In later stages, weak culture employees become readily and loudly critical of the organization.

Often a useful technique for recognizing this problem is a confidential survey of employees. People can be very eloquent in characterizing the problem in the culture around them if you just take the time to ask.

Fragmentation/Inconsistency. Often these differences within a culture are visible: different standards of dress and speech, different physical settings, different work habits and rituals. The problem with fragmented cultures is that they do not mesh well when they need to. When people from the different cultures come together, each listens to different drummers, and confusion and frustration results from their inability to see eye to eye on matters that need to be discussed and resolved. The frustration in turn deadens motivation and affects performance. When a division expresses discontent about how "headquarters" works and/or tells jokes about what goes on there, it may be a strong sign that the cultures of the parts are not integrated into a coherent whole. It is not surprising to us, for example, that conglomerate performance has been spotty at best. There must be so much energy lost to misunderstanding and frustration in these diverse organizations that it is a wonder any work ever gets done.

Emotional outbursts. The final and most serious symptom of a culture in trouble is rampant emotionalism, to a degree outside the norm for the company. A company's culture is like a security blanket for its people. It tells them what to do and reassures them that if they do it they will be not just accepted by the people around them, but also rewarded. When the culture is weak or in trouble, people get frightened. And this fright shows up in emotional outbursts in the workplace, such as denouncement of a company policy at a meeting or visible displays of anger, and through evidence of dissolution in personal affairs—such as a wave of divorces or drinking problems. When these become apparent in a company, usually there is something seriously and urgently wrong with the culture.

To be watched even more carefully is the evolution of strong and sometimes destructive subcultures. A CEO's tools for understanding subcultures are, of course, the same as those all of us should use to look at the culture itself; the trick is in deciding when differences among parts of the company are healthy and not divisive.

In any company, there will be strong variations in the behavior of different parts of the company. For example, different divisions will have different cultures to some extent, depending on the different requirements for success in their basic businesses. In addition, different functions will have different subcultures: you don't pay finance people to be the risk-taking macho-types you may want in marketing. Then too, different age cohorts in the company will vary because of differing social and other influences on them in their formative years. Older employees will see the world differently than youngsters; similarly, older businesses probably set different standards that the newest divisions.

When do these natural cultural differences become problems for the larger company culture? There are several trouble signs to watch for:

When subcultures become ingrown. If there is no regular formal or informal commerce among subcultures, they can become ingrown and begin to work to the detriment of the company as a whole. Watch out for transfer programs and regular signs of open access to different subcultures.

When subculture clashes surface. A clear sign of subcultures becoming too strong is when they publicly try to undermine each other—meetings where finance tries to "show up" marketing; campaigns by a group of young turk engineers to overstep the authority of their older bosses. A healthy tension among subcultures is desirable, but when the tension becomes pronounced and destructive it can signal a problem.

When subcultures become exclusive. A sure sign of problems arising is when subcultures take on the perquisite of exclu-

exclusive clubs—restrictions on membership, arbitrary exclusion of individuals, rituals for members only. Companies work best when all employees pull together, not when some place their own collective interests over others.

When subculture values preempt shared company values. In any company with a strong culture, any employee at any time can tell you what the company stands for or believes in. When subcultures start touting their beliefs as superior to overall corporate beliefs it is all too easy for the tail to wag the cultural dog.

Balancing the legitimate differences of subcultures with the legitimate and desirable elements of a company's culture as a whole is one of the trickiest parts of diagnosing and managing culture. At a minimum, managers must know what is happening in existing subcultures and be alert to new ones that may emerge.

Cultural diagnosis will give managers a fix on the state of the culture, particularly whether it is weak or strong, focused or fragmented. Given this fix, a manager can then sharpen the focus of his or her managerial efforts. Managing culture differs from managing other aspects of business such as presiding over strategy, pricing issues, and so on. To see where these differences lie, let's now turn to the role of the symbolic manager.

Symbolic Managers: Managing the Culture

In strong culture companies, managers take the lead in supporting and shaping the culture. We have dubbed these people "symbolic managers," because they spend a lot of time thinking about the values, heroes, and rituals of the culture, and because they see their primary job as managing value conflicts that arise in the ebb and flow of daily events.

What distinguishes these symbolic managers from others less attuned to the importance of culture is a number of factors:

Symbolic managers are sensitive to culture and its importance for long-term success. Symbolic managers are always speaking about their company's culture, writing about it in their annual reports, and crediting the strength of the culture for their marketplace success. They do this without hesitation or embarrassment; more conventional managers shy away from this "soft side" of organizational life.

Symbolic managers place a much higher level of trust in their fellow employees and rely on these cultural fellow travelers to ensure success. The ethic in companies with strong cultures is "we'll succeed because we're special." Symbolic managers recognize the power of this "us against the world" mentality and conduct themselves in such a way as to nurture extra effort and initiative from those around them. Thus they take on a high degree of personal initiative and responsibility for guarding the culture—reinforcing its beliefs, deciding who belongs and who doesn't—and they tend to delegate other matters some might consider more important—even a major strategic decision—to

141

employees around them. Given the high level of trust involved in this readiness to delegate, the employees respond accordingly, accept responsibilities willingly, and get on with it. By contrast, the mythology of modern rational management suggests a macho view of the manager sitting at the strategic apex of the company, making the major decisions as they come along. For a symbolic manager the reality could not be more different.

Symbolic managers see themselves as players—script-writers, directors, actors—in the daily drama of company affairs. Indeed, we call them symbolic managers because of their recognition of the importance of the symbolic influence they have on cultural events around them. Each day is a new scenario; each meeting a new setting for dramatic action. No events are too trivial for the great actor as he strides across the stage of the corporate set; no bit player is too trivial to ignore in this great symbolic drama. Henry Mintzberg, in his landmark study *The Nature of Managerial Work,* pointed out that typical senior managers spend a median of nine minutes on each event that occurs during a typical workday. Think of it: nine minutes. What could anyone get done in nine minutes? To the symbolic manager this fragmentation of a typical workday is a goldmine—the manager gets literally hundreds of different events to use in influencing the culture around him or her.

Symbolic vs. "Rational" Managers

A day in the life of any modern manager is chock-full of little things that don't matter, little things that matter some, and big things that matter a lot. We call the first trivia, the second events, the third dramas. One of the chief skills of a symbolic manager is to distinguish among the three. The culture helps because it defines in large part what is important and what is not. But it is the symbolic manager's native intuition and judgment that help to pick the right moment to make a big deal out of something. To dramatize trivia is to look like a fool. To overlook drama is to become a victim or villain. To miss an event or miss one's cues when something is fairly important is to look insensitive or, worse yet, stupid. Symbolic managers become adept at separating the rush of corporate life into these different categories. And for events and dramas, they become dramaturgical experts—actors and directors of recognized repute. They never miss an opportunity to reinforce, dramatize, or involve the central values and beliefs of the culture.

In short, their approach to management is different—sometimes dramatically so—from the smart, rational managers who fill many companies today. Let's look at some examples:

Managing people. Modern management practice would have us believe that the key to effective management of people is the development and use of human-resource systems. In other words the scientific management of people. Formal career planning. Thoughtful performance-appraisal systems that are really used. Specific plans for management succession in key jobs. And so forth. No manager—"modern" or symbolic—would run a company today without such systems and procedures. However, symbolic managers go a step further. More often than not they ignore the formal systems for human-resource management and do what seems right culturally, regardless of what the system says, and they spend much more time than their more rational peers on people-management issues.

Some examples: Fletcher Byrom, the CEO of Koppers Corporation, reorganized that company into twelve profit centers to create twelve jobs for twelve up-and-coming managers of the company, although the nature of the businesses did not really warrant the reorganization. General Electric has long had a program in which senior managers mentor junior managers about their careers—including specific advice on how to beat the formal systems. The 3M company has a formal program whereby junior employees with an idea can go sell it and themselves to other divisions if they feel they are being overlooked in their own operation. All of these are examples of obsessive attention to people and established procedures for breaking the personnel rules when appropriate to the culture.

Hiring/firing people. Conventional wisdom about the hiring of new recruits, particularly at junior levels, is that the personnel department is supposed to do it. But that's not how Jack Welch of GE sees it. He personally went to the Harvard Business

School to talk with the students there about GE's values and his own management philosophy. Other symbolic managers we know make sure they participate in the interviewing and selection of new employees. Similarly, symbolic managers are equally involved in firings. Conventional wisdom says to establish objective and tangible performance standards and then a good system for performance appraisal, and if the employee can't hack it, fire him or her. But to a symbolic manager a firing is a catastrophe. First, it should never happen. If the employee fits with the culture, lifetime employment should be secure. Second, when a firing is necessary, it should not be the end-result of poor performance, but of violations of cultural norms. Moreover, when such an event occurs, it demands the personal attention of the symbolic manager to make sure the cultural message of the firing is fully understood. For example, a senior financial manager at a strong culture company was fired for trying to institute systems that the symbolic manager (CEO) felt would bureaucratize the company. At the same company, the head of manufacturing was fired for covering up performance problems that occurred in one of his plants (not for the problems but for the coverup). In each case, the CEO was ready and willing to talk to anyone who argued about his rationale for the firings.

Making strategic decisions. The science of rational management says that a key responsibility of senior managers is to make the major strategic decisions that affect business. So very often, outside consultants are called in by senior managers to perform the definitive analyses required to frame these decisions in an appropriate fashion. The rapid growth of the management consulting industry in the past ten years gives mute testimony to how widespread this practice is.

However, the symbolic manager, more often than not, delegates these decisions to others in the culture; what the manager worries about is the *process* by which the decision is reached. In one instance, an excellent symbolic manager in a large multinational company was confronted with responsibility for deciding whether or not to shut down one of the original core businesses on which the company had been built. The business had fallen on hard times because of a worldwide slump in demand for its products, and for ten consecutive years before this manager took over, the business had operated at breakeven or slightly below. To make this decision, the manager established a steering committee of five highly respected, retired executives of the company (one of whom had turned around a similar business in the past). Then, he told the steering committee to use whatever resources it needed to develop a perspective on the problem.

Inevitably the committee told him to shut down the business. It was an obvious decision. The symbolic manager's real accomplishment was to signal the culture that this decision—to close down a core business—was not one he would take without the counsel of elders from the culture. He did not avoid the decision; rather, he fully grasped the event's cultural meaning.

Controlling costs. Everyone knows that cost-control is important in any business. Conventional wisdom says this can be achieved through good financial analysis, good cost-accounting systems and tough budgeting procedures. The image is one of the executive and a green-eye-shaded assistant huddling in an ivory tower and issuing cost-reduction edicts.

A symbolic manager would attack this problem differently. He would personally spend time in the functions where costs were going up to fully understood what these costs were. For example, one symbolic manager we know in a manufacturing-intensive business spent two hours each day in the factory. Every time he saw evidence of poor cost-control (like a forklift truck not being used) he would stroll back to his office and fire off a note to his vice president of manufacturing: "Why was forklift truck #27 sitting idle?" Obviously, he didn't care about the specific item in his note. What he was doing was acting as a continuing living reminder that attentiveness to cost was important.

The symbolic manager would delegate specific responsibility for cost-cutting and target-setting to those in the culture most likely to do it right; that is, those people right at the scene. In the words of Rene McPherson, when he was CEO of Dana Corporation, "Until we believe the expert in any job is the person performing it, we shall forever limit the potential of that person. Consider a manufacturing setting—within their twenty-five-square-foot area, nobody knows more about how to operate a machine, improve its quality, optimize the material flow, or keep it operating than the machine operators. Nobody."

How do symbolic managers become so adept at cultural management? They have a very good, very detailed understanding of the culture and their role in it. They know when it is crucially important to stay within the culture; they know equally as well when it is critical to step outside. Moreover, they know how to work with groups of people—cabals or subcultures—to make the overall culture stronger. Finally, they have the courage of their convictions—courage that leads them to take a direct hand in the shaping and refining of the culture. Let's look at each of these aspects of symbolic management in turn.

Living with the Culture

A problem arises, a normal run-of-the-mill business problem, the kind managers deal with day in, day out. Let's say the problem is that sales of an important new product are not meeting forecast expectations. How would a symbolic manager deal with such a problem?

Given our assumption that this is a normal problem, not one about to derail the company, the key action a symbolic manager must try is to tailor his response to the norms of the culture. In other words, in responding to a routine problem, a symbolic manager would be very conscious of reinforcing over and over and over again the message: "Our culture is A-OK; it can solve problems like this as easily as falling off a log."

Sounds simple so far. But the trick for a symbolic manager is to know his own culture well enough to be able to tailor the process by which the problem is addressed to fit the mainstream of the culture.

To illustrate, let's go back for a minute to the four generic types of corporate cultures. How would a symbolic manager tailor a culturally appropriate response in each cultural type?

Macho managers back the stars. In the tough-guy culture, the sales problem surfaces in a meeting on a totally different topic. Someone not related to the product or the marketing of it says, "This company would be just fine if it weren't for that dog of a product." What he means is: someone is screwing up and look how smart I am to catch it.

The meeting immediately erupts with five or six people jumping in with off-the-top-of-the-head solutions, "It's obvious that what we should do is . . ." The meeting breaks up and the incipient stars go off to solve the problem on their own. The symbolic manager will simply let them go—each in his own direction—to find a solution.

The fact that five people have rushed off independently to solve the problem can be a benefit if it is handled correctly. The manager hired risk-takers in the first place; by then encouraging them to take risks he or she reaffirms this culture. Chances are that five reasonably good solutions will come from this flurry of activity. The manager's job, then, is to force a consensus within the group. The sparks that will immediately fly as each player argues his or her case can create a good tension from which the best solution can emerge.

Often symbolic managers in these cultures will deliberately set up competing teams to solve problems. When everyone knows and accepts the values of this type of culture, they are more likely to accept defeat on one issue because they know they have a good chance of winning the next time. If the competition gets too fierce, then it's the manager's job to choose one of the solutions. In this case, the best approach is to unswervingly back the star in the group, or the person with the most star potential. This sends the cultural message loud and clear: "We're backing the winners because they have come through for us before. And in our culture, it's the stars who produce results."

Worker/player managers take advantage of the frenetic pace. In the work hard/play hard culture, no one will notice the problem for awhile. Although the sales manager sees daily reports, he doesn't use them to pinpoint problems. The problem will first get on the table when one of the top salespeople thinks to mention that sales seem to be slipping in his or her territory. A quick check confirms the fact throughout the country. A meeting is called to come up with a quick solution. The sales manager says, "We've got to go out there and get those sales." Unlike the macho culture, in the work/play culture, the meeting or some other form of group activity (such as a task force) would be used as the primary problem-solving mechanism. Deadlines, of course, would be tight, since energy is the engine of this kind of culture.

A good symbolic manager in this culture would be an active and relentless driver of the problem-solving group. He or she would ask many probing questions to make sure the right data are considered. The emphasis would be on lots of options to consider—all to make sure no stone is left unturned. Then, once a solution is decided upon, a good symbolic manager will back it wholeheartedly, personally kicking off the new campaign with a big ceremony. Again, the cultural message is clear: "It's our energy and togetherness that make this whole engine go."

Bettors make sure all the bases are covered. The bet-your-company culture has tracked this problem for six months now. At every regularly scheduled meeting, someone will report on the progress of the sales decline. Now the senior managers have decided that the problem is serious enough to warrant action. A task force is appointed; this group will include people from most divisions of the company, as well as those who have retired. The task force will be expected to meet regularly for the next several months to analyze the problem in detail and to present an interim report on "what the problem is." A later report will offer a detailed, step-by-step plan on how to fix it.

A good symbolic manager in this culture will orchestrate the problem-solving task-force approach to reinforce a sense of deliberateness in the decision-making process. First of all, the manager will make sure that the right people are on the task force. He or she may even institute a system of informal people polls—as input to the task force. The purpose here is to bring as much diverse expertise as possible to bear on the problem. Once the right people are involved, the symbolic manager will make sure that every issue is considered from every possible angle to ensure the best possible solution. To do this, he or she will spend lots of time in task-force review meetings; he or she will also ensure that the task force has all the time it needs to get its work done—unlike the tight time deadline tough guys face. Again, the cultural reinforcement message is clear: "We're going to get it right because we can't run the risk of an error."

Process managers manage through the process. In the process culture, there is a good chance that the problem won't be noticed at all. At a bank, for instance, it is often an achievement just to keep the records straight. It's difficult to notice if the bank is losing money or market share. As a result, it will take a major event just to bring the problem to the attention of employees. To counterbalance this tendency, a good manager in a process culture will cultivate lots of outside contacts to ensure that he or she becomes aware of a problem in adequate time to solve it.

Once the problem has been pinpointed, most symbolic managers in this culture allow the process to manage itself towards a solution. Often the solution chosen will be the design of a new process—for example, a new planning approach or an account-management system—where the right people from the culture are brought together in a structured environment to wrestle with the problem. The manager would show great patience while the new process worked itself out—signalling culturally that the right process will solve every problem.

The brief descriptions above are, of course, overdrawn because the framework that separates the world of corporate cultures into four neat boxes overstates the case. We hope, however, the distinctions are useful nevertheless. A symbolic manager who wanted to reinforce the culture would adopt different problem-solving approaches in each culture. When we consult with a client on a joint problem-solving effort, we can usually tell very early on what kind of a culture the company has just by paying attention to the problem-solving process used.

The more interesting question is: when should a symbolic manager step outside the culture?

Getting the Culture's Attention

A good symbolic manager will decide deliberately to step outside the culture when he recognizes that a weakness in the culture may get it into serious trouble. Again, let's look at the four generic cultural types for indications of when such behavior might be appropriate, that is, when each type is likely to get into trouble.

- Tough-guy cultures have a difficult time marshalling their forces. A manager should therefore be concerned in these cultures if a companywide threat emerges—for example, a fundamental change in industry economics.

- Work/play action cultures have their greatest weakness in the potential for superficiality. If a problem doesn't yield to a few quick-fix solutions, a manager ought to pay more attention to it.

- Bettor cultures have a hard time moving very quickly. If external events change, making a quick response necessary, (such as the entry of a major new competitor in the marketplace), a sensitive manager should stay with the matter until an appropriate response is found.

- Process cultures can be stymied by any major change in the external environment. (It is going to be fascinating to watch how banks react to the deregulation in the industry.) When such events occur, a manager in this culture must act.

Confronted with culture-threatening events such as these, a good symbolic manager will set as his or her objective a plan for getting the culture's attention focused on the event. To do so, he or she will deliberately attack the problem in a way that makes people in the culture sit up and say: "What in the world is going on here." The manager will, in other words, announce some startling reversal of normal cultural patterns. This might include, in a bettor culture, setting outrageously tight deadlines and launching competitive teams to work on solving a problem. In an action culture, it could involve slowing down the normal pace by, for instance, bringing in a consultant to do a careful assessment of the problem. In a macho culture, forcing collaboration is important, and this is best accomplished by setting up a task force and mandating consensus recommendations from the group. And in a process culture, it is useful to pull key players out of the normal process and put them full-time on a problem-solving assignment.

Our message is simple, but subtle: rational managers would solve the problem in any case; symbolic managers would focus on the process by which the problem gets solved and the messages thereby sent to the culture.

Working with Groups of People: Subcultures and Cabals

Although these are admittedly sketchy scenes, we hope they give some sense of how managers can react to problems in each of the four cultures. As long as the employees share common values, chances are that each culture can come up with an amicable—and effective—solution to the problem. But, of course, corporate life is never quite as simple and pat as that. Let's look at another meeting:

The problem is familiar—sales are down and market share needs to be recaptured. Joe is from sales. Mary represents research and development. Sam and George are managers of manufacturing. The chief executive officer attends—a signal that the meeting is important.

The company is typically work hard/play hard. Feedback is rapid and risk low. During the meeting, however, each manager displays differing signs of values and interests. The CEO wants sales volume increased, a view shared by the sales manager, who has been clamoring for a new product to conquer the market. R & D has been working for months on the prototypes, but hasn't moved into the practical world yet. Meanwhile, manufacturing already thinks that the new products will force a retooling of the whole division, a concern they repeatedly raise with R & D.

These groups do not speak the same language. Examples and stories raised by one group to support key points call up heroes and values that the others don't recognize. Even the pace and tempo of the meeting seems off—each representative has a different approach to the problem. The company is stuck in the quagmire of its subcultures.

All companies have subcultures, because functional differences—whether sales, R & D, or manufacturing—single out special aspects of the business environment. R & D encourages bet-your-company characteristics (high risks and slow feedback). Sales evokes the work/play culture (low risk and quick feedback). Accounting epitomizes the process outlook on life (low risk and no feedback). And the top echelon executives shine as the stars of the tough-guy culture (high risk with quick feedback).

Subcultures, however, are not just limited to functional differences. Gender is important—a man's cultural outlook is different from a woman's. Socio-economic and educational backgrounds also become the basis for subcultures. Each has its own relevant environment and world view; special heroes, rituals, ceremonies, language, and symbols communicate particular values. Subcultures can shape beliefs and determine behaviors in much the same way that cultures can.

In any company, subcultures tend to bump into each other. If the overall company culture is strong, then these clashes will promote healthy tension. But if not, these cultural wars can virtually bring productivity to a standstill. Let's look at one example in a major commercial bank in which operations (process culture) runs the bank while marketing (tough-guy, macho culture) makes the profits.

The introduction of new computer technology into this bank has forced a clash between the two groups. As banking procedures became automated, customers (and bank economics) demanded terminals in the local branches to ease the flow of information and to increase the speed of transactions for commercial customers. Because they were a strong sales advantage, marketing people were eager to install the terminals right away and start using them. But the implementation fell into the domain of operations.

A senior marketing official characterized the clash as a "dialogue of the deaf." Attempts at communication resulted in frustration and hostility. Operations would say, "We put in long hours. Our work is a lot more strenuous. Some of our people sit in front of those screens for days! We're tired of doing everything marketing wants at the drop of a hat."

Marketing replied, "The meetings we have with them are interrogatory, not participative. They say, 'Why do you need that?' They never want to understand. We have to put up with incredible pressure from the client. They want this. They want that. I can't go back to them and say, 'You can't get that because operations doesn't want to do it.' "

In a strong culture company, subgroups—like operations and marketing—do not cause problems since the overall values and beliefs are so strong. After all, differences are necessary to get things done.

However, subcultures can be very destructive in weak cultural environments. When the corporation's values are impossible to understand, a subculture can dictate behavior, and eventually cause a sort of cultural drift in the company. Sometimes this can turn out all right. A strong R & D department can clash with the larger company's work/play ideas but eventually provide innovations that allow the company to succeed where it now fails. But, on the other hand, a strong sales department can sway a bet-your-company culture into adopting short-term perspectives that can result in inferior products. Balancing the legitimate differences of subcultures with the corporate culture as a whole is one of the trickiest jobs for the symbolic manager. But it is also one of the most important ones.

One of the major jobs a symbolic manager faces is resolving and, in fact, reconciling differences among subgroups in a culture. Where a rational manager will seek to put both groups together and "get at the heart of the matter," a good symbolic manager will proceed in a more circuitous fashion. Specifically, he or she will:

Encourage each subculture to enrich its own cultural life.   Rather than be afraid of subcultures pulling apart, a symbolic manager will seek to strengthen each subculture as an effective cabal within the overall culture. Thus, he or she will often attend functions called to celebrate a particular subculture; participate in special awards for the heroes of the subculture; and generally endorse the subculture's existence and meaning within the larger culture.

Try to focus subcultures and cabals on understanding the problems of other subcultures and cabals.   A typical ploy of a symbolic manager confronted with an issue of possible cultural clash will be to assign teams—each drawn from one of the subcultures in conflict—to study the problems of the other and formulate recommendations. By setting each subculture tasks that force it to understand and cope with the problems of the other, the symbolic manager will benefit both by educating the members of each team to the problems of the other subculture and by the fresh perspectives that each team—conditioned by its own experience—will bring to the problems of the other subculture.

Point out how the overall culture is richer because of the strength of the subculture.   Once the learning and sharing of experience is complete, the symbolic manager will go out of his or her way to point out how each subculture brings unique strengths and values to the overall culture and *how the subcultures all add value.* Thus, the whole experience of subculture clash will be used as a forum for enriching the culture and bonding the groups together.

Companies with strong cultures are strong because they tolerate and encompass differences. Recognizing this, symbolic managers revel in opportunities to capture these differences in a truly productive marriage of mutual respect. In the process, all the people involved feel better about their own role in the culture and more strongly a part of the whole.

The Courage of a Symbolic Manager

We would like to comment further on something we have observed: good symbolic managers are courageous. They have the courage of their convictions. And they have the courage of their trust in the others around them.

The first impulse for most people is to fix a problem themselves. In particular, senior managers on their way up the ladder have probably had so much experience that few problems they encounter are new. They face the temptation of rolling up their sleeves and wading right into the problem.

Symbolic managers resist this temptation. They recognize that the longer-lasting solution is to rely on the culture to meander its way to a solution to the problem. They recognize that this means that they must wait for others to act. They recognize that they must trust that others will act. They do this because they are playing for longer-term stakes: the building of an institution that will stand the test of time. They content themselves therefore with playing their role as one of many actors in the daily cultural drama.

Consider the case we cited earlier of Jack Welch and his special phone line for purchasing agents. Welch could have attacked the problem of high costs in a number of ways. For example, he could have appointed a task force to study the problem and come up with solutions. Or, he could have hired consultants to do the same. Or, he could have reassigned his best managers to head up the purchasing function.

What he chose to do was install a telephone in his office. Suppose no one called? Suppose people called but the impact on purchasing costs was negligible? It took courage to pursue such an unconventional, culture-reinforcing approach to the problem—the courage to trust others in the culture to do the right thing.

It takes patience. And courage. But the long term payback is great for those who stay the course.

Being an effective manager of culture, a symbolic manager, is difficult. It requires courage and commitment to the values of the culture. The difficulty of managing culture pales, however, by comparison with the problems of changing culture, to which we turn now.

9

Change: Reshaping Cultures

The illusion of change has become the quick fix of the business world. Sales are down; reshuffle the marketing department. Operating expenses are too high; install a new budgeting procedure. Market share is slipping; call in the latest consultant to install the newest strategic-planning process. The rent is raised on New York headquarters; move the entire company to the Sun Belt. Change has become such a regular activity in the business world that companies suddenly become suspect if they stay the same.

Today's corporations are judged by outsiders on more than their product line and profit performance; they are judged all too often on appearance as well. Reputation, growth prospects, being in the right place (or market) at the right time, being up-to-date—change and the appearance of adaptation have become for many companies a dazzling show that keeps up the appearance of modernity and vitality. An organization's image begins to slip and a new CEO or major reorganization will signal new initiative and energy. Doubts about accountability or fiscal integrity can be dashed by installing computerized accounting procedures. Corporations not only change to keep pace with tangible shifts in technology or the business environment; today they change because they're expected to.

With all this activity going on, how much real change is occurring? And how much should be occurring given cultural barriers to change? Change always threatens a culture. People form strong attachments to heroes, legends, the rituals of daily life, the hoopla of extravaganzas and ceremonies—all the symbols and settings of the work place. Change strips down these relationships and leaves employees confused, insecure, and often angry. For example, the

157

simple installation of a computerized inventory system can dramatically alter work rituals and cause great anxiety. Because of these cultural barriers to change, effecting real and lasting change is time-consuming, costly, difficult, and risky—in short, not always a good idea.

Many times the hidden cultural barriers to change are overlooked. New CEOs may realign their organizations, but in the process may unknowingly topple heroes that people have revered since the companies began. A strategic review may launch a new business strategy or new acquisition, but may miss the fact that these new initiatives undermine important values that have guided a company for years and years. Unless something can be done to reduce such threats and provide support for transitions from the old to the new, the force of the old culture can neutralize and emasculate a proposed change.

Many managers underestimate the time it takes to achieve real and lasting change in an organization. It is always possible for a senior manager to "reorganize"—to shuffle the structural boxes in an organization. A manager may hire new people from the outside or transfer people from one part of the company to another. These actions are unarguably changes—but they are not the kind of long-term, all-encompassing behavioral and cultural changes we are talking about.

When we speak of organizational or cultural change we mean real changes in the behavior of people throughout the organization. In a technical sense we mean people in the organization identifying with new role-model heroes. We mean people telling different stories to one another to explain what is occurring around them. We mean people spending their time differently on a day-to-day basis—calling on different accounts, asking different questions, carrying out different work rituals. And we mean for this behavior to be pervasive—to involve virtually all the people in the organization. This kind of deep-seated cultural change is what we mean when we say that change takes a long time to achieve. Most meaningful change—for example, developing a "marketing orientation" or becoming more "cost effective"—involves just such cultural transformation.

Caveats about change aside, in a world moving as fast as ours is today, change is going to continue to be a fact of life. We would like to add to that fact a notion: changing culture is the difficult part of change. When managers get serious about change, they should recognize that to achieve change they will have to wrestle with their company's culture.

When Change Is Necessary

As individuals, we first became interested in the subject of culture when we found our clients were not often jumping up and down with eagerness to embrace the recommendations we made for how they should change. In fact, many times they would seem to embrace our recommendations wholeheartedly—but then nothing would happen. In time, we came to recognize that culture is *the* barrier to change. The stronger the culture, the harder it is to change. Culture causes organizational inertia; it's the brake that resists change because this is precisely what culture should do—protect the organization from willy-nilly responses to fads and short-term fluctuations. Recognizing this phenomenon, we think that in many cases change may not be as necessary as corporate image would have it.

Yet, changing circumstances can push even a strong culture into poor alignment with its environment. Change is often necessary for survival. How should a responsible manager determine when to take on the challenge of change and when to back off? Our experience suggests at least five situations in which top management should consider the reshaping of a culture as something close to its most important mission:

When the environment is undergoing fundamental change, and the company has always been highly value-driven. This is the case of AT&T which we discussed in Chapter 2. It is absolutely clear that traditional values will lead to serious decline, if not disaster. These values must be changed. Pan American Airlines is in a similar situation, as is the entire American auto industry. And with rising competition from our neighbors to the west—Japan—the computer industry should also be taking a good hard look at itself.

When the industry is highly competitive and the environment changes quickly. Why is Digital Equipment so successful as a company? Or Intel? Or Hewlett-Packard? One answer is that they are serving rapidly growing and highly profitable markets. But they also have been able to maintain a competitive edge by building a culture that pays extremely close attention to customers and believes in the ethic of adapting—changing—as customer needs evolve: in effect, a culture designed to cope with a changing environment. This openness to evolutionary change has become a belief in the value system of each company. Without it, the companies would collapse with every introduction of a new silicon chip by a competitor. Any other company in a field of technology or markets likely to undergo rapid change should also think hard about its culture. Building a responsive and adaptive culture may be the only way to institutionalize a real capability to adapt.

When the company is mediocre, or worse. Only a few years ago, when Frank Borman took over as chief executive, Eastern Airlines was on the ropes financially and beleaguered by its own discontented employees. Borman threw himself into the task of rebuilding a sense of shared commitment to the company's welfare, linked to an overriding orientation toward customer service. Today, Eastern—like most of the airline industry—is still in a difficult financial position, but it has succeeded in stabilizing its performance and is poised for an upswing. Other companies in similar straits should look hard at their cultures.

When the company is truly at the threshold of becoming a large corporation—a Fortune 1000-scale corporate giant. Corporate character, we believe, is forged relatively early. IBM, for example, had total sales of only about $100 million when Tom Watson, Sr., retired from management. The cultures of many of today's leading companies in electronics, consumer services, and retailing likewise seem to have taken shape long before these organizations attained their present size and competitive clout. This is not surprising; strong cultures tend to keep people moving in roughly the same direction even in a company's early days when formal policies and systems have yet to be developed. Later on, however, the process of bureaucratization begins to take hold. At this point, the original culture and the values that underpin it are often seriously threatened and may require retooling if they are to survive the transition to a large-company environment. Thus, most companies over the first entrepreneurial rush towards stability and success should pause to look hard at their cultures. They may not get another chance.

When companies are growing very rapidly. Especially in high-tech companies, growth sometimes comes very quickly. Prime Computer grew to over $500 million in sales in less than five years; Atari's sales have passed $1 billion in a similar time frame. Annual growth rates in excess of 25 or 30 percent per year imply massive annual infusions of new employees. These employees will not know what the company is all about unless they learn it quickly from the culture. Therefore, companies growing at such rates should worry a lot as to whether their culture is sound.

In most other situations, large-scale cultural change should simply not be undertaken.

The Money Side of Change

Once it becomes apparent that change is necessary, there are two other tough facts to face: change is time-consuming and very expensive. As with most things economic, a little quantification is helpful. To get some perspective on the hard economics of change, we identified ten consulting projects carried out over the past several years in which the desired end product was clearly and unequivocally organization and culture change. Then, we estimated the total cost of the change initiative as the sum of consultants' fees incurred plus the value of time spent in the change process by full-time employees of the client organization. Consulting fees make up a relatively small part of the true costs of change. To assess the value of employee time spent in the change process we valued each person-month at $3,000. We then interviewed people who were involved in the change initiatives to get their best judgments of the percentage of the change they attempted that was really accomplished in the organization.

The conclusions were startling even to us. To achieve even half of the change a company attempts, it must spend an amount equivalent to between 5 and 10 percent of its annual budget for the personnel whose behavior is supposed to be changed. Change was even more expensive to achieve than we had imagined! In other words, to get people in a culture to even begin to change, management has to capture 5 to 10 percent of their time for a year! This conclusion sparks several other observations about change:

- The argument for change that a manager advances to the organization must be credible, otherwise he or she will never convince anyone to change no matter how hard the manager works at it. Furthermore, the costs escalate dramatically the more capricious the desire for change.

- Many change efforts fail simply because not enough was invested in them—that is, those who attempted the change were naive about what it would take and put nowhere near enough effort into it.

- There may be quite a few instances where attempting to change something is simply uneconomical. While it goes against the grain to say so, the best economic answer in some cases may well be to let a moribund institution die.

- Even a simple-minded notion of the economics of change may be helpful in deciding which cultural problems to attack and which to walk away from—an exercise few of us take seriously enough.

All of the above points are notional at best. To try to make them a bit more real, consider a few real-world—if hypothetical—examples:

Case 1: Should Xerox spend the money required to enable it to compete against the Japanese in the copier market? Xerox has roughly 100,000 employees. Let us assume their average salary is around $30,000. The cost of a major cultural change such as adapting to low-cost Japanese competition is therefore likely to be $150 million to $300 million. Since Xerox earns more than twice this amount every year, it seems likely that this investment would be a wise one.

Case 2: How much should AT&T be spending to adapt to its newly deregulated environment? AT&T is roughly ten times the size of Xerox. Therefore, the price tag for a significant cultural shift in the Bell system is likely to be $1.5 billion to $3.0 billion. We wonder whether Bell is spending anywhere near this amount to help its organization adapt.

Case 3: How much is it going to cost the U.S. auto industry to become competitive with the Japanese? Again the answer per our rule of thumb is around $5 billion to $10 billion in organizational costs alone. We have heard figures like this bandied about in terms of capital investment required; nowhere have we seen such figures associated with operating costs to build a more cost-effective culture. Perhaps the red ink will continue to flow in Detroit for some years to come.

Obviously, effecting cultural change is a very expensive business—much more expensive than most people realize. It is so expensive, in fact, that the very expense itself is a significant barrier to change. The other barrier is the fact that reshaping a culture takes a considerable amount of time. It literally takes years to achieve fundamental change in an organization's culture.

What are some of the factors that influence the time necessary to achieve cultural change? Urgency is clearly one: in times of real crisis people understand the need, listen for suggestions, and adopt them more quickly. Change in times of crisis can occur quite rapidly, even in a six- to eighteen-month time-frame. Another factor influencing the speed at which change can occur is the attractiveness of the proposed change to individuals. Win/win proposals tend to be adopted more readily than proposals that involve losing for some. The third factor influencing the speed of change is the strength of the culture being changed. If the old culture has supported people well for years they will be reluctant to abandon it to embrace a new one. And change in this situation may take decades to achieve.

Before moving on to how-to mechanics, let us summarize the dismal economics of effecting real and lasting cultural change: it costs a fortune and takes forever. So managers be cautious. Take on these problems only if you are convinced the need is real.

Managing Change

Most managers we know worry a lot about change, but too few of their worries focus on the cultural issues of changing. As a result, many times the change they attempt does not happen; in its place instead is anger, employees who are emotional wrecks, and file cabinets full of ambitious plans gone for naught. The business of change is cultural transformation. The question is how to do it in the most effective way possible.

Let's be candid about this. We don't know this area any better than anyone else. Cultural change is still a black art as far as we are concerned. What we do have, however, are a few tips for the manager who takes on the challenge.

Recognize that peer group consensus will be the major influence on acceptance or willingness to change. Most people, most of the time, are not zealots or true believers. Nor are most people strong opponents. People are generally resistant to change of any kind only because it disrupts the ritual and order of their lives. However, one of the strongest influences on people is the influence of their personal ties with others. Sharing is a sign of belonging to a culture, and few individuals in any culture want to stand alone for long. As a result, consensus-building processes based on this natural peer-bonding relationship are a major way to induce change in organizations.

Convey and emphasize two-way trust in all matters (and especially communications) related to change. Communications are better in high-trust situations. Individuals who trust one another may not communicate accurately, but this doesn't need to be an impediment to getting something done! Because they trust, they *feel* that it is not absolutely necessary to figure out precisely what the other is trying to say. Openness and trust in the change process therefore influence whether and how change occurs.

Because of this issue of trust, change initiated by an insider often takes place much more quickly and penetrates more deeply in the organization than change urged on by an outsider. A case in point: Reginald Jones's experience at GE was in its financial sector. Before becoming CEO, Jones was instrumental in saving the company from a potentially disastrous involvement in three simultaneous new product ventures—computers, jet engines, and nuclear reactors—ventures that threatened the solvency of the company. When Jones took over, he focused on making his major contribution a tightening in the financial discipline of the company. During his tenure, the finance function grew stronger, and finance people grew more prominent, more powerful.

Jones was an insider—indeed a hero for his financial feats. As an insider, he was able to pull off what was a revolutionary change in a company that for decades had insisted on the values of tinkers and inventors. We doubt that an outsider could have accomplished as much.

However, on Jones's recent retirement, GE didn't elevate another financial figure to be CEO. The risk in doing so would have been to bureaucratize the company. Instead GE promoted the candidate perceived to have the most entrepreneurial flair—a deliberate attempt, we believe, to rekindle the importance of the original values upon which GE was built. To many, Jack Welch's promotion is a sign that GE is once again a company of engineers and entrepreneurs. Meanwhile, through Jones's influence, the company has established a strong financial discipline to protect it against unnecessary risks in the future.

Think of change as skill-building and concentrate on training as part of the change process. Even if people understand and accept a change, they often don't have the required skills and ability to carry out the new plan. This is a major impediment to successful change. Consider an example from a rapidly growing technology company. This company found out that fully half of its worldwide sales came from only forty companies. To protect its position vis-à-vis the key accounts, it established a major-account program. The theory was that the manager of major accounts should "take care of" these forty accounts by providing them special service as required, being responsive to their needs, and so on.

To fill this critical job, it promoted a star salesman from the field. He had never done an analysis; he had never thought hard about special services for an account. His success as a salesman came largely from an energetic personality and a willingness to do whatever a customer asked. Needless to say, he was not given special training before undertaking his new responsibilities.

One year later, the program was dismantled. Unit sales were up but revenue was actually down. The salesman, behaving the way he had before, called on each account, asked them what they each wanted, and used the power of his new office to get it for them. Unfortunately for the company, each of the key accounts wanted lower prices, and so the entire major-accounts program consisted of quantity discounts. Given the salesman's background this outcome was fairly predictable, but no one stopped to think about it in advance. This, unfortunately, is not an isolated example but rather one which recurs over and over again in organizations attempting to change. It is, one hopes, a sufficiently stark example to remind managers of the need to focus on skill-building and training the next time they set out to make a change.

Allow enough time for the change to take hold. We hate to harp on this point, but it takes people a lot of time to grow accustomed to any non-trivial change. There is no substitute for this time. A manager attempting cultural change must allow for it.

Encourage people to adapt the basic idea for the change to fit the real world around them. Our final tip is essentially to "hang loose." In our experience, the most successful cultural change is that which is modified and adapted in thousands of ways by the people in the culture to accommodate the unique circumstances that impinge on them day-to-day. Thus, a manager attempting change should do little more than (a) articulate a "change concept"—i.e., a general sense of where the change is heading—and (b) launch a change process that involves many people and gives them significant opportunities to make adaptations in the concept as they see fit. Overmanaging a process to effect cultural change is almost certain to make it unsuccessful.

There are likely thousands of other tips for how to make change take hold. These five—consensus, two-way trust, skill-building, patience, and flexibility—are the ones we have found most useful in our own attempts at solving this difficult problem.

Managers not only must understand the issues involved in cultural change; they also need to have a sense of how to go about reshaping old cultural patterns. How do they do this? In effect, we have given tips on the process of change; what are the ways to attack the substance?

To begin with, managers concerned about cultural change give it as much attention as they give any other truly top-priority task—

a lot. They put culture at the center of their agenda and consciousness, not in the "get to it as soon as possible" category. This is not mere exhortation; it is an empirical conclusion drawn from the careers of the two Tom Watsons, Alfred Sloan, and from our own observation of other chief executives who have been effective culture-shapers in industries as diverse as oil, electronics, scientific instruments, engineering services, and government.

Often the first step top managers take to shape a culture is to begin talking about the culture and its values with their closest colleagues. They explore with them the role that shared values can play in a company, the state of the company's current values, and the ways in which they need to be reinforced, interpreted, or revised. These conversations have two aims: to gain collective commitment to the idea that a strong set of shared values is to be a principal legacy of this particular top management team, and to forge a common understanding of the specific values to be inculcated. Top managers depend heavily on the managers around them to transmit their message on a day-to-day basis. So it is critical that top managers ensure that middle-level managers understand the cultural objectives. To do this, they must spend time with middle managers talking about culture; spending this time also tends to signal to others their own commitment to the changes.

Next, culture-shaping top managers look for ways to reach into their organizations to establish the importance of the culture and its chosen values. They tap into all parts of the cultural network. Almost invariably, they spend an unusually high proportion of their time "in the field," making contact with as many people as possible in the organization. In addition, many look for relatively structured devices for focusing attention on key values. For example, "kick-off meetings" for managerial programs aimed, perhaps, at serving a new group of customers better, reducing excess costs, or developing more strategically oriented middle managers; special contests and awards to give public recognition to those who have done something to serve a key value, and for stimulating others to do likewise; and specially appointed ad hoc working groups with responsibility for short-term projects related to key values.

Any short list of mechanisms like this runs the risk of trivializing the kinds of things a culture-shaping manager can and should undertake; suffice to say creative managers can find literally hundreds of ways to get their message across, of which these are only a few.

Special management initiatives such as these go a long way toward dramatizing the values that a management team aims at establishing or reinforcing, but they are not enough unless the day-to-day behavior of the top managers reflects their concern—indeed, frequently their near obsession—with the importance of key values. People are interested in what other people say they value, but they are only really convinced by what others do. What counts is rarely the single dramatic act (managerial life is seldom like that, nor should it be), but the consistency of a pattern of behavior over time.

In building a strong culture into an organization, a manager implicitly communicates key values and inculcates them in employees via day-to-day actions. Values determine what actions are taken, and when any of the key values inherently conflict, the manager forces the conflict to the surface and resolves it. This is what happens at a technology company that has a strong and very thoughtful culture.

A group of managers at this company was interested in producing a digital watch. By tradition the company has always specialized in top-of-the-line quality products and avoided cost-driven markets. But costs and cost curves would be the key to success in the watch market. This sparked a conflict between two major values; the company values individual entrepreneurship and encourages its people to experiment with new ideas, yet it also believes in pursuing the high end of product lines, avoiding the mass market. When the interest in producing watches arose, the majority of the staff vetoed the idea. However, the CEO overrode them in support of it. He encouraged the managers to enter the watch business, though it eventually withered out and cost the company quite an amount of money.

By this willingness to back committed people, the company gained much more than it lost financially by reinforcing key cultural values over the long term. A manager less concerned with culture and more concerned with the bottom line than the CEO here would have decided the case on its merits and, in the course of doing that, torpedoed people who wanted to try something different. Such an act would have communicated to the organization that only the people with the most profitable business plans are going to get ahead—not the people who are willing to stand up and be counted and say, "I want to do this."

Thus, in changing culture, managers must be continually alert to the cultural fallout from all of their routine actions. Many managers, for example, develop questioning routines grounded in important values. The questions that the managers ask when subordinates make proposals, give presentations, or talk about their work tell these subordinates—and others listening—what expectations must be met to secure the managers' approval. Culture-shaping managers also develop something close to a reward routine; that is, they actively seek ways to provide frequent and visible praise or other recognition for even modest contributions to the service of important values. They seek to use each contact with another member of the organization—a meeting, a phone call, a chance encounter in the hall, a memorandum in the in-box—to send a message that reinforces a value theme. In fact, they organize their calendars so that they will be seen as spending a lot of time on matters visibly related to the values they preach. Even in dealing with outsiders they neglect no opportunity to reinforce the theme. What is said to customers, to investors, or to journalists can often have a powerful impact on people inside the organization. It provides further evidence that management's commitment to the values is "for real."

Finally, managers interested in changing a culture are extremely conscious of their own role in shaping the rituals of the workplace. These managers always seek to set an appropriate example by their own behavior; they also do not shy away from telling others that their behavior has stepped across acceptable cultural boundaries. Whether they are deciding who to invite to a meeting, laying out a process for developing a strategic plan, or participating in a bull session around the water cooler, these managers will keep an eye on the symbolic impact of the unfolding ritual on the culture.

Change: The Case of the MSWD*

Changing the culture of an organization is a difficult, time-consuming, often gut-wrenching process. This is as true in public corporations as it is in the private domain. In fact, effecting such

---

*This case is based on a real consulting assignment carried out by the authors. Names, titles, and a few facts have been changed in the interest of respecting the confidential interests of the client.

change in a public institution is, if anything, more difficult because of the number of legitimate constituencies—the public, legislators, unions, employees, special-interest groups—that can raise barriers to change. But change can be accomplished if a sufficient level of commitment is applied to the process for a long enough time. One example will reveal all the expenditures—of time, money, and morale—that are involved.

Metropolitan Sewer & Water District (MSWD—a major public wholesaler of these essential services to a large American city) is a public-sector corporation. It employs 2,500 people, has an annual budget of $75 million and spends $200 million a year on capital improvements. MSWD is one of the oldest public agencies of its kind in the country.

Throughout the years, the MSWD carried out its mandate in fine fashion. Its accomplishments were not achieved without difficulty and controversy, however. At times in the history of MSWD, senior officials were charged and convicted of misuse of public funds.

A second problem MSWD faced both internally and in the eyes of the public was patronage. Over the years, administration after administration had found ways to plant favorite sons on MSWD's modest operating-budget payroll.

The third problem MSWD faced was one of rampant bureaucracy—a problem that organization theorist Henry Mintzberg suggests affects all older organizations. The average contract required seventy-two separate signatures and took close to nine months to wind its way through the bureaucracy before being let. Even a minor contract involved a foot-high pile of forms.

Despite the presence of a modern computer system, there were at least six separate manual personnel record systems operating in MSWD. And even with these systems, no one could say with certainty how many people were on the payroll at any time.

All business was conducted by memo, and usually in a prescribed official format rather than face-to-face. Everything was done by the book. If it wasn't on paper, it wouldn't get done. A classic case of the process culture gone awry.

Still, this bureaucracy would not have been a serious problem except for some issues that surfaced in the late 1970s. Water usage continued to rise and gradually began to exceed the design capacity of the system. Moreover, federal EPA regulations that were enacted required MSWD to upgrade its facilities. Confronted with these problems, the state secretary of the environment was determined to "bring the MSWD into the twentieth century." He recognized that it would be almost irresponsible to launch the MSWD into these major capital expenditures with the organization in its current state of apparent bureaucratic ineptitude. He knew, however, that revitalizing this moribund culture would be difficult and would have to be accomplished without major infusions of new management talent. Nevertheless, he and his new general manager, Ken Dillon (not his real name), were determined to take on the challenge.

Ken Dillon was a key figure in changing MSWD. Dillon was in his mid-fifties, semi-retired, and a successful entrepreneur when he took over the reins at MSWD. He was used to getting things done and making things happen. When he brought this attitude to the career-oriented bureaucratic environment of MSWD, it was like a breath of fresh air.

During the first several months in revitalizing MSWD, Dillon familiarized himself with the organization. What he found was not encouraging. The MSWD's extremely cumbersome superstructure made Dillon officially responsible for running the organization, but most major and many minor decisions were subject to the review of an advisory committee. Decisions required a majority vote of the committee although Dillon did have veto power.

Further crimping his style was the fact that this highly centralized organization reported to a chief operating officer—a career civil servant. Originally this post was intended to help insulate MSWD from self-serving initiatives by politically minded general managers. In practical terms, it meant that Dillon had little direct authority in the day-to-day management of MSWD, since everyone else reported to the chief operating officer who could, in turn, go over Dillon's head to the advisory committee.

In terms of the MSWD's people, there were grounds for encouragement and disappointment. The biggest problem was the average age of the staff: fifty-five or older. The people in the agency had, for the most part, joined right after the war and spent their whole careers with it. The threat of impending retirements and the accompanying loss of the knowledge and skills of those who retired was a serious long-term problem for Dillon to deal with. On the positive side, the loyalty and motivation of the vast majority of the staff was remarkable. Despite public perceptions of a patronage-ridden bureaucracy, these people were dedicated public servants who were sincerely interested in making the MSWD work as well as possible.

Dillon's objective in this change was nothing short of changing MSWD from a reactive, bureaucratic culture to the proactive can-do attitude he was familar with in his own company—a shift from a process culture to a work hard/play hard culture.

After six months of study, Dillon decided the time had come to act. To reshape the culture, he began by taking two major steps: he engaged consultants to supplement his staff in an aggressive change process, and he announced in a memo to MSWD's permanent complement of 2,500 employees that there would be no firings or layoffs as a result of the process he was launching. His objective, he said, was to work with the talented people of MSWD to improve its effectiveness. This second step turned out to be very significant later in the process since it helped buy time for some basic changes to take hold.

THE CHANGE PROCESS

The team of four consultants spent its first six weeks learning about MSWD. In a meeting at the end of this period, the first gesture in the change process was decided on—to set up three major task forces of MSWD employees to work with the consultants on three commonly agreed-upon problem areas. The three areas selected were:

- *Contracting.* Everyone generally agreed something should be done to speed up contract processing.

- *Operations and Maintenance (O & M).* Over the objections of the chief operating officer's functional managers, a second task force was assigned responsibility for O & M.

- *Personnel.* All managers in MSWD used personnel constraints as their argument for why things couldn't be done differently no matter what the issue. The chief operating officer, for example, was convinced this task force would prove that nothing could be done.

In all, twenty-five professionals and/or middle managers were assigned to these task forces full-time for their indeterminate duration—a gesture that in itself caused great consternation in the agency. Reservations aside, people in the MSWD were used to following orders, so all twenty-five members dutifully showed up for the initial group meeting that launched their efforts.

Meanwhile, Dillon initiated a weekly series of staff meetings with the chief operating officer, functional officer, functional managers, and their assistants. He specifically excluded these people from membership on the task forces; he would work with them himself.

During their first week of work, the task forces accomplished little. Members were not used to working in this fashion; many of them felt uncomfortable in this new role. By the second week the members began to open up in their meetings. For example, engineers on the contracting task force admitted disappointment when projects they had worked on were not received warmly by operations personnel. They were astonished to learn that the operations people were often distressed when the engineers didn't consult them about projects they were working on and when they delivered equipment that was hard to operate and maintain. Both sides agreed that better communications on projects between the two sides was definitely called for. In the other task forces, similar revelations were occurring—to everyone's amazement.

By the third week, all three task forces were hard at work trying to formulate recommendations to deal with the problems they had identified. Their recommendations—delivered during the seventh week—were reviewed by Dillon, senior management, and the advisory committee.

Awaiting management's response, the task forces had gone back to work on their recommendations. A half dozen more members were added to the task forces. Everyone seemed more and more committed to the change process as time went on.

Six weeks later, the task forces presented their final recommendations—essentially offering details on their original plans. Senior management raised some objections, and modifications were discussed. Then attention turned toward the consultants' recommendations for significant steamlining and decentralization of MSWD. They suggested (1) the elimination of the job of chief operating officer, (2) elimination of the jobs of the assistant functional managers, (3) establishment of a line-of-business (in other words, sewer and water structure), (4) a reassignment of the staffs of major functions such as engineering and environmental planning to create the nucleus of real engineering functions within both the sewer and water divisions, (5) creation of a new director of planning position to run the new planning system, and (6) creation of an office of contract administration to run the new project-management and contracting systems. After some review the package was finally endorsed.

THE IMPLEMENTATION OF CHANGE

With the endorsement in hand, Dillon moved quickly. True to his original pledge, no member of the organization was fired; all were slotted into new jobs. The reorganization was comprehensive enough that, in effect, a new management team was put in place.

Offices were moved on a Monday. On Tuesday, Dillon launched the new planning process that was designed to get the new management groups of each division working together as a team.

The planning process was designed to dovetail with the state budget process, thus creating very tight scheduling. However, despite weekend and late evening flurries, both divisions made it under the wire. The head of the sewer division, exhausted by the process, said to one of the consultants just after the advisory committee had approved his proposed budget: "This is the best thing that ever happened to the MSWD . . . and the most exhilarating experience I have ever had. We'll never go back to the old way again."

Six months later, no one could doubt that the MSWD was significantly different. There was still too much paper and too much conformance to the book, but there was also a clear set of agreed-upon priorities, a sense of real urgency in pursuing these priorities, and the beginnings of a "we can make it happen" mentality. Dillon believed that with one more year of operation in this new mode, the new culture would really take hold.

The secretary of the environment, the person who launched the whole process, claims it is the greatest organization turnaround he has witnessed in his twenty-five years as a public-sector manager.

The Ingredients of Successful Change

While MSWD is in the public sector, our experiences in other, private organizations have isolated many similar themes. To effect change successfully in modern corporations, several of the steps illustrated by the MSWD case should be followed:

Position a hero in charge of the process. Dillon was totally committed to the change. He brought with him his own legend and unswerving conviction that the changes were necessary; and his vision, tenacity, and self-sacrifice inspired belief in the change process among all MSWD personnel.

Recognize a real threat from outside. For significant cultural changes to get off the ground, you need more than a hero: you need a good reason for mounting change. People at the top are always expendable, and business history is full of CEOs who have tried to impose new cultures on existing corporations only to find the old cultures the victors and themselves the victims. Cultural change is only needed when a culture doesn't fit in its environment, and even then it's difficult. But the greater the threat, and the more widely it is known, the greater the likelihood that a culture can be successfully turned in another direction.

Make transition rituals the pivotal elements of change. Involving many people in the process of changing is a suggestion that managers hear frequently. The best way to do this is via the transition ritual. Within the process, people mourn old ways, renegotiate new values and relationships, and anoint heroes. This helps people understand, accept, and believe in the new order. In one sense, the process becomes a temporary culture, much like a mourning rite. It prevents people from returning to old patterns or rushing thoughtlessly into unfamiliar new terrain. The task forces played this role in the MSWD change process.

Provide transition training in new values and behavior patterns. Management systems played a critical role in the MSWD change. Planning, contracting, and project management touch many people in the organization on a daily basis. Work on management processes often provides the opportunities for training in new values, new behavior, and even language that permits people to shift from one culture to another.

Bring in outside shamans. Earlier we said that change driven by trusted insiders—Dillon in this case—is more successful than change attempted by outsiders. Outsiders, however, can play a useful role—as shamans for the process. In bridging the gap from one organizational culture to another, consultants from the outside bring their own magic. They help provide lightning rods to defuse conflict as the change enfolds, beacons for where the change is heading, and talismans that the change will really work. In MSWD, we were invited back one year later to survey the results. People spoke of the successful outcome, and then we were ignored. The message was clear: "We did it; since you may have helped, we wanted you to bless it. But it's ours—goodbye."

Build tangible symbols of the new directions. Dillon instituted structural changes to signal new directions. As symbols of his seriousness, they provided tangible messages about the agency's new directions. Like road signs, structural changes can help groping people find their way; they seldom make a change happen directly by themselves.

Insist on the importance of security in transition. To wonder about whether our jobs will disappear creates strong feelings in us all. An axed manager or worker can quickly become a martyr or hero of the old way. By offering people security, Dillon dispelled much of the resistance that might have developed if he had made the issue of job security ambiguous. Keeping people (or buying them off) may be an important ingredient of successful change.

Sometimes, change is necessary and not all bad, although it is almost always risky, expensive, and time-consuming. Indeed, the difficult part of change is changing the culture. But cultures can be changed if the managers who would change them are sensitive enough to the key cultural attributes—heroes, values, rituals—that must be affected if the change is to succeed.

10
Cultures of the Future: The Atomized Organization*

Throughout this book we've looked at the past triumphs and present necessities of corporate culture. And in the process we've argued for a reinvestment in the shared values, heroes, rites, and rituals that have made American business a success story around the world. But there's an even more compelling reason to begin fostering strong cultures in all types of organizations—the future.

We see a revolution on the horizon that holds far-reaching implications for the American corporation. A combination of forces—from the rapidly changing business environment to the new work force to astonishing advances in technology—is forging a breakdown of the large traditional, hierarchical organizations that have dominated in the past. We think that this dismantling will result in highly decentralized organizations in which the work of the corporation will be done in small, autonomous units linked to the mega-corporation by new telecommunications and computer technologies. This change can turn us all into entrepreneurs and in the process will transform the role of middle management. Motivation will come from the opportunity to accomplish complex tasks in an intimate, relatively simple work environment. We won't waste time and energy worrying about how to climb the corporate ladder because there won't be one. Most middle-management rungs will be replaced by mechanisms of social influence—by emphasis on culture. We see it as a no-boss business. We call it the *atomized* organization. For it to work, strong cultural ties and a new kind of symbolic management will be required.

*Much of the original thinking and research on the ideas in this chapter were done by Jerry Mechling of Brandeis University (assisted by Gerry Brehm) in conjunction with the authors.

Our prediction may sound like brave new world, but it's not. There are signs that the revolution may be underway. Many companies are right now limiting the size of their factories and divisions, and thus are emerging as leaders in the move to decentralization. Others exhibit the increasing trend of corporate divestitures to manager-owners—a trend getting buried nowadays in the publicity about mergers. But the most conspicuous sign of the coming trend is the franchising boom. McDonald's, Dunkin' Donuts, and the other 900 franchisers in the United States are sweeping the country with a no-boss organization style.

The reason? The world around corporations is changing rapidly. The biggest change is the increasing use of distributed processing as companies discover that networks of mini- and microcomputers better serve their informational and communications needs than large centralized computer installations. Many think this technology will foster more centralization. We see precisely the opposite happening. Here's why:

The environment is becoming more complex. A generation ago, production required the coordination of relatively few specialized or professionalized tasks. Complicated specialties are now the rule. Harvard University, for example, now offers majors in over forty disciplines; big-city newspapers solicit applications for many hundreds of job titles; and, of the thousands of professional research journals published internationally, fully half have emerged over the past fifteen years. By almost any measure we could choose, the increasing complexity of the world seems unarguable.

The rate of change is accelerating. The electronics revolution has radically shortened product life cycles and led to an increasingly dynamic marketplace. Shorter lead times are required for very complex electronics-based products—the development of a typical electromechanical product may take thirty months. Its electronic replacement could be developed in as few as twelve months because the software needed to create specific applications is easier to create and modify than hardware. As one indication of shortened product life cycles, a survey of computers in use in 1981 showed that 55 percent of the minicomputers and

80 percent of the general purpose computers in the market had been introduced in the last four years.

Competition is intensifying and becoming more global. In 1970, with government regulation in full force, there were about sixteen scheduled passenger carriers serving U.S. markets. Today, with deregulation not yet at its fullest, there are more than double this number. In 1960, automobile sales ads offered products from four major companies; today there are twenty-three competitors, with fully 20 percent of the U.S. market in the hands of overseas manufacturers. And even with the famous report by the surgeon general in 1967, there has since been a threefold increase in cigarette brands.

The range of competition for even minor consumer and industrial markets is staggering. The share of the American market supplied by foreign companies has nearly doubled from 1968 to 1978. Within this total, foreign manufacturers gained 12 percent of the apparel and textile market, 27 percent of leather and leather products, 11 percent of electrical and electronic equipment, and 12 percent of instruments and related products.

What does this mean for the future of the business environment? It means quicker response, less time lost in bureaucratic problems, more premium on interpreting data quickly and taking action, and more reliance on the minds and initiatives of the already burgeoning knowledge-work sector. But what is the key to effectiveness and productivity in this fast-moving environment dominated by knowledge workers? Organizational theorists propose an answer—small work units. People are most productive and able to respond most quickly working in small teams—mainly because the complexity of communications increases geometrically as the number of people in the unit expands.

The Work Force

While so much is taking place all around modern business, a great deal is happening inside the corporation. In the next twenty years the baby-boom work force will continue to have significant impact both on productivity and on the society at large. With continued aging in the 1990s will come a trend toward resisting autocratic authority. Douglas McGregor and others began writing in the 1950s about "Theory Y" personality needs and workers who were motivated much more by opportunities for self-actualization and recognition than by basic needs for economic security. Since then, the work force has continued to gravitate more and more in the "Theory Y" direction. In comparison with their predecessors, the new workers are:

Richer. The average family income in 1978 dollars—that is, the real income—has increased from $7,000 in 1950 to $19,000 in 1980. The average family is thus *twice* as well-off as it was thirty years ago.

Better educated. In 1950, the country produced 438,000 college graduates; by 1978 this number had become 1,341,000. Fully 50 percent of the work-age population has had some exposure to higher education, and this proportion is still growing.

White collar. Today, the bulk of employees is engaged by the "information sector," and since 1954 there have been more white-collar workers than blue-collar workers in the economy. Further, within the white-collar segment, the major financial investment is not in clerical activity ($200 billion) but in professional and managerial work ($600 billion).

More flexible and less job-dependent. Today's richer and better-educated workers are taking advantage of expanded opportunities in life styles. The trend is exemplified in the high-technology world of Route 128 in Massachusetts and Silicon Valley in California, where people are continually changing jobs, companies, and careers. An incredible number have formed their own companies, mainly because they want autonomy—to be their own bosses. Some, like Gene Amdahl, are now in their third generation of such moves—thus economic gain cannot realistically be the driving force. The real motivator is the pyschological drive for self-actualization. We believe that this drive—in less dramatic but no less equally real form—must be given central recognition in the design of future organizations.

Familiarity with electronics. In 1961, the average American spent two hours and seventeen minutes per day watching television. By 1978, viewing time increased to three hours and eight minutes. Behind this rise is an amazing willingness to absorb electronically relayed entertainment and information.

On a more significant note, consider the growth in the number of computer programmers and the increase in computer literacy. In 1960, there were a negligible number of programmers in the United States. By 1980, this number had increased to 270,000 and states such as Minnesota were routinely teaching programing as part of the elementary- and secondary-school curriculum. In educational institutions, the allocation of computer use to instructional purposes (as opposed to administration or research) has risen from 23 percent in 1975 to over 50 percent today.

What does this mean for the future work force? An increasing proportion of the work force, soon to be a majority, is much more conversant and comfortable with electronic gadgetry than workers have been before. Organization designers will no longer have to rely on middle management—with its natural tendency to shape communications to fit its view of the world—to link workers together. Instead, the organization designers of tomorrow can—for the first time in history—consider using the computer and communications technologies on a major scale. What will be available to them?

Changes in Technology

Change inside and outside of corporations is more than matched by recent technological advances. The "Third Wave" revolution has been written about extensively, but the implications for business are only beginning to be recognized. Consider the amazing progress in computer price performance. The $3,000 Apple computer of today is the processing equivalent of many millions of dollars of IBM equipment only fifteen to twenty years ago. As the computer industry is so fond of saying: if the productivity of cars had kept up with computers, you could now buy a Rolls Royce for $2.89 and it would get 2,000,000 miles to the gallon.

It is little wonder that the microcomputer applications are already so pervasive: in blood analyzers, copy machines, telephone switches, calculators, cameras, microwave ovens, television sets, watches, scales—virtually everywhere. Consequently shorter product life cycles have put a premium on competitive response. And the introduction of new products based on standardized chips and customized software has almost eliminated the economies of scale in many traditional industries.

Computers are becoming easier to use as well as cheaper. As a result, general-purpose computer applications have continued to grow exponentially. IBM's installed base is in fact expected to expand as much in the next two years as it did over the total of the past sixteen years.

But perhaps the key developments are in telecommunciations. For communication over 1,000 miles, the new satellite systems are now cheaper than the Bell System, and even Bell has reduced its costs so rapidly—42 percent since 1960—that a three-minute transcontinental call is now only $1.35. By comparison with first-class mail, electronic mail cuts transmission costs by two-thirds and reduces the total document preparation and distribution costs even more. Meanwhile, computer technology is converging with communications technology toward the integrated office of the future.

What we often forget is how fast things are happening: 1981 was a watershed year, and 1982 promises even more. All this has been described before as futurology, even as recently as 1975, but it is here today.

What does all this mean for the completely technologized office of the future? Changes in both the environment and workers are pushing organizations toward smaller units and greater adaptability. And sophisticated technology provides a communications capability that will pave the way toward smaller work settings without producing chaos.

In short, we are now in the early stages of a major shift that will influence the shape of society and its businesses for a long time to come.

The Organization of the Future

In the wake of this change, the organization of the future will consist of

- small, task-focused work units (ten to twenty persons maximum),

- each with economic and managerial control over its own destiny,

- interconnected with larger entities through benign computer and communications links,

- and bonded into larger companies through strong cultural bonds.

We call this structure the *atomized organization* to emphasize the small size and flexibility of its basic units in relation to their present counterparts. Still, the "atoms" here are not bouncing around in blind chaos but are linked through telecommunications capabilities and are bonded together like molecules into a strong corporate whole through the shared cultural ties that define what the company of the future is all about.

Smaller Units

What is the optimum sized group for productivity? Is it the ten to twenty people found in the ancient hunting band? Is it, as some managers believe, limited to a unit in which people can know each other on a first-name basis? If they are knowledge workers, is it limited to sixty to seventy-five people, as many researchers have come to believe? There is no definitive answer, but one thing is increasingly clear: dis-economies of scale—often referred to as bureaucratic behavior—become almost unbearable beyond a few hundred people.

Still, there are serious trade-offs to be made between technical and organizational factors. How many people are really required to build cars efficiently? In the future, with heavily robotized factories, very few will be needed. Technological trends lead us to surmise that the organizational units of the 1990s will be much smaller than they are today. We predict that by the year 2000, normative standards for organizational design—be they for factories, branches, divisions, or self-standing firms—will suggest units of no more than 100 people. The units may band together into larger entities called governments, corporations, institutes, and so on, but the banding will be of a new kind.

With the advantages of large scale rapidly eroding, and with smaller entities better able to tap the human capital of their employees, competition will squeeze out the larger units—much as, long ago, the rising population of smaller, quicker, and smarter mammals squeezed out the dinosaurs.

This new form of organization will be more effective for four reasons:

- Countless studies demonstrate that people are more effective when they are in control (or at least feel in control) of their own destinies. In the atomized organization, salespeople will have joined their work unit because they wanted to; their pay will be directly linked to their performance.

- Peer-group pressure is widely believed to be the single strongest motivating factor for individuals in this post-industrial era, and this is the primary mechanism of control in the small work unit.

- Strong cultures are more easily built in smaller units, and these units will behave more cohesively and achieve higher productivity and effectiveness.

- The computer and communications links that bond individual units into corporations will be far cheaper than the layers of middle management in today's organizations.

Small is beautiful—small and semi-autonomous—because it best serves not just the needs of business, but the people's needs.

Why People Need Atomization

The atomized organization will create welcome new opportunities for people who feel "locked in" by conventional corporate structures. How will this occur? Norman McCrae, an editor of *The Economist,* relates one scenario:

In the period of exciting experimental opportunities and probing ahead, rich countries should no longer rely on entrepreneurship only by people lucky enough to be able or willing to gamble on their families' security. Also, entrepreneurship should not be the province only of those who have the organizational patience and ability to set up from scratch every bit of the infrastructure that a new business needs. The aim should be to give ordinary people more scope for becoming tycoons than they have had since the industrial revolution was young.

The mechanism should be for the management in each progressive firm to define the module of work that it wants to be done, and then invite "bids" from parts of the staff who think they could achieve the module more efficiently and happily than under the existing corporate bureaucracy. Sometimes the bids will be made individually, sometimes by groups of friends within the company.

In "far-out" ventures the bidder will say how much of the corporation's existing services (production, marketing, etc.) he would wish to use; and how rights of decision eventually to sell off the venture, if successful, to an outsider should be shared. Some of these "far-out" bids would be from employees willing to take risk with their own security—in effect, working for bare maintenance if the project failed, or even involving a loan which would have to be paid back to the firm over the years. In "closer-in" ventures, more of the bids would be from group cooperatives or executives who were willing to take the job over while being paid something like their present salaries or wages, although smaller profit participation. (*The Economist,* December 25, 1976)

We believe that McCrae's notions of the entrepreneurial organization of the future are identical with our notions about the atomized organization of the future, with one exception. Although McCrae is a free-market devotee, he seems relatively easygoing about the economic ties between his entrepreneurial units and the parent entity. We are more hard-nosed. In the increasingly literate and educated work force of the future it will be impossible for an employer not to share with employees the fruits of their labor. Thus we believe that the economic tie between the parent and the work unit will be an equally shared contract based on contribution in the value-added of the work done by the unit. Franchising begins to get at this, but in our view the greatest institutional barrier to be overcome in implementing the atomized organization is in developing financial mechanisms to facilitate these kinds of arrangements. It is hardly desirable to have a set of capital markets and instruments that encourage and even facilitate the spin-off phenomenon around centers of technology such as Route 128. Far better would be a set of mechanisms that encourage longer-term affiliations of convenience, but in such a free and totally decentralized manner as to capitalize on the full-talent and energies of our untapped human capital and stimulate its entrepreneurship. These mechanisms will be discovered and refined by the instutitions that gradually lead us toward the atomized organization. Thus the atomized organization will liberate people to the degree of entrepreneurship they want and can handle. And the people's drive for self-control will fuel the movement. The benefit to the society at large will be in the unleashing of the creative talents and entrepreneurship of all those so liberated.

The atomized organization will embody a work force with significantly different needs and values than ever before, and a major step beyond the stifling organization man of the not too-distant past. To illustrate this, we have added a fourth column to psychologist Frederick Herzberg's chart depicting the needs and values of work forces in our recent past.

The Transformation of the Middle Manager

There is one sector of people whose role will change dramatically in the corporate culture of the future. Middle management exists today, in large part, to carry communications from the top management of a company to the workers. This is one of its main functions. It is a thankless job—you are damned from below by those you are trying to direct and damned from above for not getting the directions right. Middle management is a focal point for much of the dissatisfaction in today's organizational life. In trying to rationalize its own existence, it has created rituals and in pursuit of these often questionable rituals has perpetuated a mythology of rationality and modern management techniques even where it doesn't work. It is often a barrier to improving productivity since it acts as a filter of enthusiasm, ideas, and initiative from below. Middle management is a creation of twentieth-century organizational life; fortunately for all of us, it is an obsolete profession, at least in its present form.

Needs and Values of the Labor Force

"Organization Man" (1950s)	Internal Immigrants (1960s)	Confused Mixture (1970s)	Limited Entrepreneurial Person (1990s)
1. Created system	1. Lived in kitchens of the system	1. Captives of larger conglomerate and multinational "organization man" system	1. Create you own "no boss" system within larger corporate structure
2. Expanded on myths	2. Saw weaknesses in myths	2. Confused about myths	2. Return to company myths without losing personal identity
3. Models were appurtenances of offices	3. Models were ideologists	3. Confused about models	3. Find models in own small work group or in imitation of others
4. Gobbled up rights and privileges	4. Demanded stolen rights privileges	4. Feel cheated	4. Feel expansive about rights and privileges
5. Time at work taken up with "looking good"	5. Time taken up with protest	5. Time taken up with special interests	5. Balance of time between work and play
6. Work perceived as related to efficient	6. Work perceived as related to society organizations	6. Work perceived as indirectly related to technology, organizations, and society	6. Work perceived as related to individual meaning and adding value to society
7. Narrow occupational specialists	7. Deficient capabilities	7. Obsolete talents	7. Use talents to utmost
8. Required experience rotation	8. Required remedial help	8. Required continuing education	8. Balance between continuing education and on-the-job learning
9. Suffered social pain in bright satanic factories and offices	9. Suffered psychological pain at home and in all social institutions	9. Suffered existential pain from lost surroundings	9. Existential pain mediated by rituals and ceremonies of work that extend into one's personal life

Needs and Values of the Labor Force (Cont.)

"Organization Man" (1950s)	Internal Immigrants (1960s)	Confused Mixture (1970s)	Limited Entrepreneurial Person (1990s)
10. Central meaning of work: career	10. Central meaning of work: personal significance	10. Central meaning of work: security	10. Central meaning of work: a well-rounded life
11. Life values multi-other-directed no personal values)	11. Life values innovated attempt at clarification	11. Life values confused (externals of tradition)	11. Life values based on a tension between tradition, faith, and individual needs
12. Didn't preach	12. Preached collectivism but practiced individualism	12. Confused preaching	12. Sporadic preaching is important ritual and ceremony
13. Growth would take care of debt	13. Debt-oriented	13. Confusion-oriented	13. Meaning-oriented
14. Future-oriented	14. Now-oriented	14. Time disorientation	14. Present-oriented with anchor in past and future
15. No blame	15. Projected blame	15. Vacillating blame	15. Taking blame
16. Public expression of feelings: abstract	16. Public expression of feelings: concrete	16. Public expression of feelings: cynical	16. Realistically optimistic
17. Organizational morality confused with personal ethics	17. Morality distinguished from ethics	17. Morality confused with ethics	17. Morality derived from shared values
18. Believed in one-upmanship	18. Believed in automatic equality	18. Believed in injustice of equality	18. Believe in earned equality
19. Believed in open hierarchy of organization	19. Believed in participative organizations	19. Has lost trust in organizations	19. Have bounded trust in organizations generally—fierce loyalty to atomized organization
20. Believed in service to employer	20. Believed in service to social justice	20. Has lost belief in service	20. Believe in service to society—and to corporation

Managers of the future will be confronted with a new set of roles fitted to the realities of the atomized organization. First, they will structure and negotiate appropriate economic arrangements with workers banded into semi-autonomous units. Second, given the increased voice of these workers in day-to-day affairs, managers will serve as brokers—to balance the legitimate self-interests of both the workers and the company. Third, on behalf of the company, managers will work at making individual work units aware of—and proud of—being part of the larger whole. Thus, managers will be both the bearers of culture as well as its promoters. Without them playing this culture-bonding role the economic benefits of the atomized organization will be difficult to achieve.

The Role of New Technologies

Large organizations exist today because complex tasks require the coordination of many people. This will be achieved in the future with the assistance of computer and communications links that can be extended directly to the individual, allowing him or her to plug in from anywhere, at anytime. Broad-band technologies, including cable, will provide ample opportunities for the transmission of data, text, graphics, voice, and even video. These links will tie workers not only to each other but also to major external data bases and services.

The emerging system will be more efficient than paper-based systems of memos and forms, and even more effective than the human linkages so prevalent now where layers of middle management too often distort communications to fit the world as they like.

Consider the case of an instrument salesperson in the field. In today's world, this person works out of a branch and reports to a sales manager who reports to a branch manager who reports to a regional manager who reports to a national sales manager who reports to a marketing vice-president, and so on. All of these links in the middle-management chain are necessary to ensure two things: (1) that the salesperson does the job well—that is, calls on the right accounts, makes the right product pitch, wins the right orders, and so on, and (2) that strategic (for example, new products), tactical (for example, pricing), and operational (for example, inventory levels) decisions made on high are communicated as relevant. The chain is expensive, slow, and often inaccurate. For the organization to work well, elaborate bureaucratic procedures and relationships must be developed and followed. What a terrible way to get things done.

In the atomized organization, such salespeople will work in a little business—called a branch, perhaps—that is paid on the basis of the volume of product it moves per a pre-negotiated schedule of commissions. If they want details on a new product announcement, they will tune in to a videotape or cable-televised presentation of the new product that describes all its features. If they want to know when they can deliver an instrument to a customer, they will hook into an inventory system and capture their machine. If they want to understand the company's new policy about replacement parts, they can tune on-line into the televised proceedings of the corporate policy committee and listen to the new CEO—as Cronkite—expound on why a new policy is needed. These tasks will all be done routinely, of course, because the salespeople will have worked with computers and video since elementary school.

And what if the salespeople are dealing with a new product? Today it can easily take eighteen months to collect centrally, interpret, and then disseminate the market feedback needed to adjust and make final commitments to full-scale production. We believe that they will participate, along with other salespeople of the future, in an electronic dialogue that will record their market experience and will respond almost immediately with ideas and answers from those facing similar situations. Adjustments in marketing strategy could be formulated as much as twelve months earlier, obviously with major financial implications. The technology exists today.

A key problem, however, is to live up to the scope of this ambitious vision of tomorrow. We hear much talk of the "office of the future" and the "post-industrial society." Despite the enormous advances made in the last few years, many observers today remain justifiably skeptical about these futuristic notions—mainly because they've seen no effect of these technologies on their own work lives.

The freedom and autonomy to be gained from the atomized organization can only come about when networks and systems exist that help people do their work better. And studies have shown the greatest productivity gains are to be won among the ranks of managers and professionals by an overwhelming margin. For this to happen, systems developers must eschew their focus on clerical automation and apply their energies directly to creating computerized supports for managers and professionals.

The development of these networks and services is by no means a trivial problem. It will require a fundamental and operational understanding of what managers and professionals actually do. Serious researchers, such as Mintzberg, are already at work on the problem. But when computer professionals start paying attention to this research and focusing on the right applications, they may even find them easier to develop than the complex productivity-oriented tasks they set for themselves today.

Early Evidence of an Organizational Revolution

What evidence is there that this new organizational form is emerging? We see several clues, among them the phenomenal growth of franchising. Franchising as an approach to business is not new. The basic concept is simple: a retail-oriented business expands its coverage of the market by:

- Selling exclusive rights to a territory and/or location to individual entrepreneurs who own—both figuratively and literally—their franchise.

- Supporting the overall system of franchisees by the efficient provision of needed central services—such as advertising, procurement, quality control.

- In return for giving the franchisees both the basic right and required support, the central business is paid a fee. Typically, to ensure that all are working toward common goals, the fee structure is set as a percentage of sales. Thus the economic fate of the peripheral entrepreneurs (the franchisees) is entwined with that of the central business. If one falls down on the job, all suffer.

This simple concept was first put into practice by food retailers like Howard Johnson's, McDonald's, and Burger King.

The idea of franchising quickly expanded to other areas: Midas Mufflers, tire centers, Century 21 Real Estate. Franchising has become big business. There are currently 476,000 franchise operations in the United States and many more overseas. Approximately 900 companies are involved in setting up franchises—a fact suggesting that the trend will accelerate. Not yet touched but ripe for franchise development are the fields of financial services, travel agencies, software development, educational services, and even product development related to certain kinds of technology (such as instrumentation). There is clear evidence that franchising is a form of business that seems to fit some basic economic and social need in this society. And franchise operations are the epitomy of the culture of the future as embodied in the atomized organization.

While franchising provides the clearest evidence of the evolution toward a new organizational form, there is a second development to consider. If the 1960s were known as the decade of the conglomerate, the 1980s are likely to be known as the decade of divestiture. A recent article in *The New York Times* focused on the divestiture of the Winchester Arms Company by its parent Olin Corporation to a group of owner-managers and suggested that the number of such transactions was growing rapidly and already approaching one hundred. To us, divestitures constitute an incomplete form of the atomized organization—more forward-looking parent companies would retain shares in these divested entities and thus share in whatever economic success they achieve on their own.

Finally, a third bit of evidence—the spin-off phenomenon. In many areas of relatively modern technology—electronics, instrumentation, software, biotechnology—a handful of knowledgeable people with only modest financial backing are fully capable of conceiving and building new generation products. To capture the economic benefits of doing so—given the way capital markets work today—they leave the parent company where they acquired their knowledge and "spin off" to form a new high-technology firm. This phenomenon is rampant around Route 128 in Boston and in Silicon Valley in California. As one measure of its extent, in the new field of biotechnology, there are already 146 separate companies active in the United States.

These spin-offs, we believe, are yet another sign of the

atomized organization. Were today's capital markets not such that they forced entrepreneurs to spin off in order to get rich, these companies would retain ties to their parents. We believe the mechanisms of the atomized organization will enable such organizations to remain tied together economically—each deriving the benefits of continued association.

All around us, then, are signs that the atomized organization is upon the business world already. The signs will become clearer as time goes on, but nowhere are they as clear as in strong culture companies.

Culture in the Organization of the Future

In the dispersed, helter-skelter world of the radically decentralized atomized organization, some glue is absolutely essential to hold independent work units together. The role that culture plays will be even more critical than it is in today's corporate world. Without strong cultural bonds, atomized work units would fly off in a centrifugal plane. The winners in the business world of tomorrow will be the heroes who can forge the values and beliefs, the rituals and ceremonies, and a cultural network of storytellers and priests that can keep working productively in semi-autonomous units that identify with a corporate whole.

As managers look for exemplars, they will need to widen their scope. Because few examples or theories today provide the guidance needed to manage atomized organizations, we need new models. Three different examples immediately come to mind as intriguing possibilities.

The first model is to be found in the recognized king of the franchisees, McDonald's. McDonald's dominates fast-food franchising because of a very strong culture—almost a mystique—that bonds its far-flung franchisees together. The core beliefs of this culture revolve around Quality, Service, Convenience, and Value (QSCV)—a slogan repeatedly drummed into the heads of management and the work force. Franchisees are educated into this culture at Hamburger University, where, in a program more extensive than any other in the franchising industry, newcomers are indoctrinated into the culture that is McDonald's.

Once the franchisees are in the field, the McDonald's culture

is continually reinforced by inspectors and by contests to determine who best reaches the standards McDonald's sets for all its
franchises. Ceremonies honor the most successful franchisees,
and regional associations among the franchisees keep awareness
of the parent company's values up to snuff.

Atop this culture sits a highly visible hero—Ray Kroc. But
there are many other heroes as well: waitress of the month, franchisee of the year; the originator of Egg McMuffin—a franchisee.
An assembly of heroes keeps the culture alive and strong.

The second management model is the U.S. Forest Service. As
Herbert Kaufman described in his important if little-read book,
The Forest Ranger, the U.S. Forest Service is an anomaly. Its divisions are scattered all over the country—often in remote areas—
which makes formal supervision difficult. It's the perfect candidate for a fragmented organization, and yet it is probably more
well-knit—accomplished with less formal effort—than many
organizations or companies half its size. Rangers act independently but in accord with the service's mission. They are "beings
in their own domains" who handle most situations as precisely as
they would if the boss were looking over their shoulder. There
have rarely been any scandals or whistle blowers among the rangers even though the opportunities for both are readily available.
There are no problems of sabotage or catering to special-interest
groups in local areas. Why? For many of the same reasons that
McDonald's has been able to maintain a common spirit among its
franchisees: common values—service, decisions based on long-
term considerations for the environment; common symbols—the
uniform and badge, "Smokey the Bear"; education—a training
program that inculcates values and the mission of the service; and
work rituals—specified procedures for reporting and responding
to various problems. Although the reasons for the strong bonds in
the U.S. Forest Service are complex, we believe its culture is the
key factor.

The third management model derives from one of the oldest
and most stable institutions in the world—the Roman Catholic
church. While it has gone through ups and downs, the Catholic
church has maintained enormous cohesion among various countries and parishes throughout the world.

And how has the Roman Catholic church maintained its sway

for so many centuries? Not by strategic planning systems. Not by layers upon layers of middle managers. But through one of the strongest and most durable cultures ever created. It is a culture rich in rituals and ceremonies of all kinds: white smoke from the chimney in the Sistine Chapel; a pope's blessing from the small balcony; masses and other religious rituals that govern the behavior of millions around the world. It is a culture that is rich with heroes, stories, and mythologies; martyrs; missionaries; saints; a Polish freedom-fighting pope; heroes for people to identify with day-to-day. And finally, whether you agree with it or not, it is a culture founded on the bedrock of a set of meaningful (to its followers) beliefs and values.

The Catholic church has been very successful in managing its atomized organization of parishes through the centuries by strong reliance on cultural management levers. We believe that the most successful businesses of the future, just like the most successful businesses of the past, will do the same.

The Catholic church is an important model for another reason: not only has it built a culture that unites people and parishes, provides faith and meaning across countries, and offers something of value in return for one's efforts. But beyond this, the Catholic church has something in common with IBM, Mary Kay, McDonald's, the Polaris project, the U.S. Forest Service, and countless numbers of other successful organizations—all of them capture some of the same religious tone. These corporations are human institutions and capture many of the expressive aspects of living that have been seen as soft and fuzzy by modern managers: soul, spirit, magic, heart, ethos, mission, saga. These words crop up again and again in the biographies and theoretical literature that we read in the preparation of this book. We believe that these ideas provide an important direction for corporations to consider in responding to modern dilemmas like productivity, competition, or morale. Whether in regard to conventionally structured organizations or atomized hybrids, we think that building strong corporate cultures is one of the fundamental tasks of the next decade.

In sum, the future holds promise for strong culture companies. Strong cultures are not only able to respond to an environment, but they also adapt to diverse and changing circumstances.

When times are tough, these companies can reach deeply into their shared values and beliefs for the truth and courage to see them though. When new challenges arise, they can adjust. This is exactly what companies are going to have to do as we begin to experience a revolution in the structure of modern organizations.

Bibliography

Allison, Graham T. *Essence of Decision: Explaining the Cuban Missile Crisis.* Boston: Little-Brown, 1971.

Allport, Gordon W. and Leo Postman. *The Psychology of Rumor.* New York: Holt, 1947.

Allyn, S. C. *My Half Century at NCR,* New York: McGraw-Hill, 1967.

Argyris, Chris. *Interpersonal Competence and Organizational Effectiveness.* Homewood, Ill. The Dorsey Press, 1962.

Arnold, T. W. *The Folklore of Capitalism.* New Haven: Yale University Press, 1937.

Arnold, Thurman. *The Symbols of Government.* New York: Harcourt, Brace, & World, 1962.

Ash, Mary Kay. *Mary Kay.* New York: Harper & Row, 1981.

Baldridge, J. Victor and Terrence E. Deal. *Managing Change in Educational Organizations.* Berkeley: McCutcheon and Company, 1975.

Bardach, Eugene. *The Implementation Game.* Cambridge: MIT Press, 1977.

Barnard, Chester I. *The Functions of the Executive.* Cambridge: Harvard University Press, 1938.

Barnard, Chester I. *Organization and Management: Selected Papers.* Cambridge: Harvard University Press, 1962.

Bateson, Gregory. "A Theory of Play and Phantasy." In *Steps To An Ecology of Mind.* New York: Ballantine Books, 1972.

Belden, Thomas and Marva Belden. *The Life of Thomas J. Watson: The Lengthening Shadow.* Boston: Little-Brown, 1962.

Bell, Daniel. *The Coming of Post-Industrial Society: A Venture in Social Forecasting.* New York: Basic Books, 1976.

Bell, Daniel. In *Computer Age: A Twenty Year Retrospective.* Ed. Michael L. Dertouzos and Joel Moses. Cambridge: MIT Press, 1979.

Bender, Marylin. *At the Top.* New York: Doubleday, 1975.

Bendix, Reinhard. *Work and Authority in Industry: Ideologies of Management in the Course of Industrialization.* Berkeley: University of California Press, 1974.

Bennis, W. "A Funny Thing Happened to Me on the Way To the Future," *American Psychologist,* 25 (July 1970), pp. 595–608.

Bettleheim, Bruno. "A Pocketful of Magic." Chapter 1 in *The Uses of Enchantment.* New York: Vintage, 1977.

Blau, Peter and W. Richard Scott. *Formal Organizations.* San Francisco: Chandler, 1962.

Blum, Albert A. "Collective Bargaining—Ritual or Reality." *Harvard Business Review,* 39, No. 6 (November-December 1961), pp. 63–69.

Blumer, Herbert. *Symbolic Interaction: Perspective and Method.* Englewood Cliffs, N.J.: Prentice-Hall, 1969.

Boas, Max and Steve Chain. *Big Mac: Unauthorized Story of McDonalds.* New York: New American Library, 1977.

Boulding, Kenneth. "In Praise of Inefficiency," *AGB Reports,* 20, No. 1 (January 1978).

Boulton, David. *The Grease Machine.* New York: Harper & Row, 1978.

Bower, Marvin. *The Will To Manage.* New York: McGraw-Hill, 1966.

Bralove, Mary. "Ma Bell's Orphans." *The Wall Street Journal,* 26 January 1982.

Broderick, John. *Forty Years With GE.* New York: Fort Orange, 1929.

Brown, Wilfred. *Exploration in Management.* New York: Wiley, 1960.

Burke, Kenneth. *A Grammar of Motives.* New York: Prentice-Hall, 1945.

Burke, Kenneth. *Permanence and Change: An Anatomy of Purpose.* 2nd edition. Los Altos: Hermes, 1964.

Campbell, Joseph. *Hero With a Thousand Faces.* New York: Pantheon Books, 1949.

Campbell, Joseph. *Myths to Live By.* New York: Bantam Books, 1973.

Caulam, Robert F. *Illusions of Choice.* Princeton, N.J.: Princeton University Press, 1977.

Chandler, Alfred, Jr., and Stephen Salsbury. *Pierre S. duPont and the Making of the Modern Corporation.* New York: Harper & Row, 1971.

Chase, G. "Implementing a Human Services Program: How Hard Will It Be?" *Public Policy,* 27 (Fall 1979).

Clark, Burton. "The Organizational Saga in Higher Education." In J. Victor Baldridge and Terrence E. Deal, *Managing Change in Educational Organizations.* Berkeley: McCutcheon and Company, 1975.

Cleverly, Graham. *Managers and Magic.* London: Longman Group Limited, 1971.

Cohen, Michael D., James G. March and Johann P. Olsen. "A Garbage Can Model of Organizational Choice." *Administrative Science Quarterly,* 1972, pp. 1–25.

Cohen, Michael and James March. "Leadership in an Organized Anarchy." Chapter 9 in *Leadership and Ambiguity.* New York: McGraw-Hill, 1974.

Cohen, Michael D., James G. March and Johann P. Olsen. "People, Problems and the Ambiguity of Relevance." In *Ambiguity and Choice in Organization.* Oslo, Norway: Universitetsfonlaget, 1976.

Cohen, P. S. "Theories of Myth." *Man,* 14, No. 3 (1969), pp. 337–353.

Cole, M. and S. Schribner. *Culture and Thought.* New York: Wiley, 1974.

Collins, Liza. "The Entrepreneur as Manager." Interview with Lore Harp. *Harvard Business Review,* 59, No. 4 (July–August 1981).

Colvin, Geoffrey. "The De-Geneening of ITT." *Fortune,* 11 January 1982. p. 34.

Cooney, Joan Ganz. "A Woman in the Boardroom." *Harvard Business Review* 56, No. 1 (January–February 1978), pp. 77–86.

Cunningham, Frank. *Sky Master: The Story of Donald Douglas.* Philadelphia: Dorrance, 1943.

Dalton, Melville. *Men Who Manage.* New York: Wiley, 1959.

Dandridge, Thomas Charles. *Symbols At Work: The Types and Functions of Symbols in Selected Organizations.* UCLA Dissertation, 1976.

D'Aprix, Roger. *The Believable Corporation.* New York: Amacom, 1977.

Davidson, H. Justin. "The Top of the World is Flat." *Harvard Business Review,* 55, No. 2 (March–April 1977).

De Mare, George. *Corporate Lives.* New York: Van Nostrand, 1976.

Dearden, John. "MIS is a Mirage." *Harvard Business Review,* 50 (January–February 1972), pp. 90–99.

Dittmer, Lowell. "Political Culture—Political Symbolism: Toward a Theoretical Synthesis." *World Politics,* 29 (July 1977), pp. 552–583.

"Dr. Land Redesigns His Camera Company." *Business Week,* 15 April 1972, pp. 70–74.

Dowling, John, and Jeffrey Pfeffer. "Organizational Legitimacy: Social Values and Organizational Behavior." *Pacific Sociological Review,* 18, No. 1 (January 1975), pp. 122–136.

Drucker, Peter F. *Concept of Corporation.* New York: John Day, 1972, pp. 60–65.

Edelman, Murray. *The Symbolic Uses of Politics.* Champaign, Ill. University of Illinois Press, 1964.

Edelman, Murray. *Political Language: Words That Succeed and Policies That Fail.* New York: Academic Press, 1977.

Edelman, Murray. "Political Leadership." Chapter 4 in *The Symbolic Uses of Politics.* Champaign, Ill.: University of Illinois Press, 1977.

Edelman, Murray. *Politics As Symbolic Action.* Chicago: Markham, 1971.

Eliade, Mircea. *Myth and Reality.* New York: Harper & Row, 1963.

Eliade, Mircea. *Rites and Symbols of Initiation.* Trans. Willard R. Trask. New York: Harper & Brothers, 1958.

"Encore At 3M." *Financial World,* 20 October 1980.

Enderud, Harold. "The Perceptions of Power." *Ambiguity and Choice in Organization.* Oslo, Norway: Universitetsfonlaget, 1976.

Engel, P. H. "The Rubinstein Religion." *Across the Board* (Conference Board Newsletter), October 1977, pp. 79–82.

Etizioni, Amitai. *Modern Organizations.* New Jersey: Prentice-Hall, 1964.

Evans, Charles. *The Micromillenium.* New York: Viking, 1980.

Everett, Martin. "Ma Bell Goes National." *SEMM,* March 1979, pp. 37–38.

Feldman, Martha S. and James G. March. "Information in Organizations as Signal and Symbol." Unpublished paper, Stanford University, n.d.

Ford, Julian. *Paradigms and Fairy Tales.* Vol. I and II. London: Routledge & Kegan Paul, 1975.

Foy, N. *The Sun Never Sets on IBM.* New York: Morrow, 1975.

Freud, Sigmund. *Totem and Taboo.* Trans. A.A. Brill. New York: Random House, 1946.

Freund, James. *Anatomy of a Merger,* New York: Law Journal Press, 1975.

Floden, R. E. and S. S. Weiner. "Rationality to Ritual—Multiple Roles of Evaluation in Governmental Processes." *Policy Science,* 9, No. 1 (1978), pp. 9–18.

Friedman, J. and B. Hudson. "Knowledge and Action: A Guide to Planning Theory." *Journal of the American Institute of Planners,* 40, No. 1 (January 1974).

Geertz, Clifford. "Deep Play: Notes on the Balinese Cockfight." *Daedalus,* Winter 1972, pp. 1–37.

Ginzberg, Eli & Alice Yohalem. *Corporate Lib.* Baltimore: Johns Hopkins University Press, 1973.

Ginzberg, Eli and Ewing Reilley. *Effecting Change In Large Organizations.* New York: Columbia University Press, 1957.

Gluckman, Max. *The Rituals of Social Relations.* Manchester, England: Manchester University Press, 1962.

Goffman, Erving. *Interaction Ritual.* New York: Doubleday, 1967.

Goffman, Erving. "Keys and Keying." *Frame Analysis: An Essay on the Organization of Experience.* Cambridge: Harvard University Press, 1974.

Goffman, Erving. *Relations in Public.* New York: Basic Books, 1971.

Goffman, Erving. "The Arts of Impression Management." Chapter 6 in *The Presentation of Self in Everyday Life.* New York: Doubleday, 1975.

Goode, William J. *The Celebration of Heroes.* Berkeley: University of California Press, 1978.

Goodman P., and A. Friedman. "An Explanation of Adam's Theory of Inequality." *Administrative Science Quarterly,* 16 (1971), pp. 271-288.

Gordon, William J. J. "Play and Irrelevance." *Synectics.* New York: Harper, 1961.

Gray, Edward. *Chrome Colossus: GM and Its Times.* New York: McGraw-Hill, 1980.

Gustin, Lawrence R. *Billy Durant, Creator of General Motors.* Grand Rapids, Mich.: Eerdsman, 1973, pp. 67-96.

Hall, Edward T. *The Hidden Dimension.* New York: Doubleday, 1966.

Hall, Edward T. *The Silent Language.* New York: Anchor Books, 1973.

Hall, Edward T. *Beyond Culture.* New York: Anchor, 1976.

Hansot, Elizabeth. "Some Functions of Humor in Organizations." Unpublished paper, Kenyon College, n.d.

Hardy, Charles. *Understanding Organizations.* New York: Penguin Books, 1976.

Harrigan, Betty Lehan. *Games Mother Never Taught You.* New York: Rawson, 1977.

Harrison, Roger. "Understanding Your Organization's Character." *Harvard Business Review,* 50 (May–June 1972), pp. 119-128.

Hennig, Margaret & Anne Jardim. *The Managerial Woman.* New York: Doubleday, 1977.

Herzberg, Fred. "Leadership in a Period of Psychological Depression." *Industry Week,* 15 September 1980, pp. 54-58.

Hirsch, Paul M. "Organizational Effectiveness and the Institutional Environment." *Administrative Science Quarterly,* 20, No. 3 (1975).

Hirsch, P. "Ambushes, Shortouts, and Knights of the Round Table: The Language of Corporate Takeovers." Paper presented at the Academy of Management Meetings. Detroit, 1980.

Hirschman, Albert O. *Exit, Voice, and Loyalty.* Cambridge: Harvard University Press, 1970.

Hooker, Richard. *Aetna Life Insurance Co.: Its First Hundred Years.* Hartford: Aetna Life Ins. Co., 1956.

"An Interview with Dr. Edwin Land." *Forbes,* 1 June 1975, pp. 48-50.

Jay, Anthony. *Corporation Man.* New York: Random House, 1971.

Jessup, Claudia and Genie Chips. *Supergirls.* New York: Harper & Row, 1972.

Johnson, R. and R. Lynch. *The Sales Strategy of Patterson of NCR.* The Dartnell Corp. 1932.

Jung, Carl G. *Man and His Symbols.* New York: Dell Publishing Company, 1964.

Kaufman, Herbert. *The Forest Ranger: A Study in Administrative Behavior.* Baltimore: Johns Hopkins University Press, 1960.

Kearns, Doris. *Lyndon Johnson and the American Dream.* New York: Harper & Row, 1976, pp. 121–125, 241–242.

Kellogg, C. W. *Samuel Ferguson: The Man and His Works.* Hartford: Hartford Electric Light Company, 1951.

Kennedy, Allan A. "Ruminations on Change: The Incredible Value of Human Beings in Getting Things Done." *Exchange: The Organizational Behavior Teaching Journal,* Spring 1981.

Kennedy, Allan A. "One Perspective on the Consulting Process (or, Does Anyone Know What's Going On Out There)." *Exchange: The Organizational Behavior Teaching Journal,* Summer 1979.

Koestler, A. *The Act of Creation.* London: Pan Books, 1975.

Kraar, Louis, "General Electric's Very Personal Merger." *Fortune,* 55, No. 2 (August 1977), p. 190.

Kuhn, Thomas S. *The Structure of Scientific Revolutions.* 2nd Edition. Chicago: University of Chicago Press, 1970.

Lief, Alfred. *It Floats.* New York: Rinehart & Company, 1958.

Lawrence, Paul and Jay Lorsch. *Organizations and Environment.* Cambridge: Harvard University Press, 1967.

Leavitt, Harold. "Beyond the Analytical Manager: Part II." In *California Management Review,* Summer 1975.

Leifer, Richard. "The Social Construction of Reality and The Evolution of Mythology as Means for Understanding Organizational Control Processes." Unpublished manuscript, University of Massachusetts, n.d.

Lewis, David L. *The Public Image of Henry Ford.* Detroit: Wayne State University Press, 1976.

Lindblom, Charles. "Strategies for Decision Making," *Decision Making in a Democracy.* Champaign, Ill.: University of Illinois Bulletin, 1971, pp. 3–22.

Lipsky, M. *Street Level Bureaucracy: Dilemmas of the Individual In Public Services.* New York: Russell Sage Foundation, 1980.

Loth, David. *Swope of GE.* New York: Simon & Schuster, 1958.

Louis, Meryl Reis. "A Cultural Perspective on Organizations." Monthly unpublished paper. Naval Post Graduate School, 1980.

Louis, Meryl. "Organizations as Culture Bearing Milieux." *Organizational Symbolism.* Ed. Pondy, Louis, et al. Chicago: University of Chicago Press, 1980.

Louis, Meryl. "Surprise and Sense Making: What Newcomers Experience in Entering Unfamiliar Organizational Settings." *Administrative Science Quarterly,* 25 (June 1980), pp. 226–251.

Lynch, Edith. *The Executive Suite Feminine Style.* New York: Amacom, 1973.

McCleery, R. H. *Policy Change in Prison Management.* East Lansing: Michigan State University Press, 1957.

McDonald, John. *The Game of Business.* New York: Doubleday, 1975.

McGregor, Douglas. *The Human Side of Enterprise.* New York: McGraw-Hill, 1960.

McKenney, James L. and Peter G. W. Keen. "How Managers' Minds Work." *Harvard Business Review,* 52 (May–June 1974), pp. 79–90.

MacRae, Norman. "The Coming Entrepreneurial Revolution: A Survey." *Economist,* 261 (25 December 1976), pp. 41–44, 53–58, 60–65.

"Making Room for Some Free Spirits," *Fortune,* 86, No. 2 (August 1972), p. 33.

Manning, Peter K. "Metaphors of the Field: Varieties of Organizational Discourse." *Administrative Science Quarterly,* 24 (1979), pp. 660–671.

Manning, Peter K. *Police Work: The Social Organization of Policing.* Cambridge: MIT Press, 1979.

March, James G. and Johann P. Olsen. *Ambiguity and Choice in Organizations.* Oslo, Norway: Universitetsfonlaget, 1979.

March, James "Bounded Rationality, Ambiguity, and the Engineering of Choice." *Bell Journal of Economics.* 9 (1978), pp. 587–608.

March, James G. "Executive Decision-Making: Some Implications for Executive Compensation." Unpublished paper, Stanford University, 1980.

March, James G. "How We Talk and How We Act." Unpublished paper, Stanford University, 1980.

March, James G. and Johan P. Olsen. *Ambiguity and Choice in Organizations.* Bergen: Universitetsfornlaget, 1976.

March, James and J. Olsen. "The Technology of Foolishness." *Ambiguity and Choice.* Oslo, Norway: Universitetsfonlaget, 1976.

March, James and H. Simon. *Organizations.* New York: Wiley, 1958.

Margulies, Walter. "Make the Most of Your Corporate Identity." *Harvard Business Review,* 55 (July-August 1977), p. 184.

Martin, Jo Anne. "Stories and Scripts in Organizational Settings." Research Report 543, Stanford University School of Business, July 1980.

Martin, Jo Anne and Melanie E. Powers. "Truth or Corporate Propoganda—The Value of A Good War Story." Research paper 564, Stanford University School of Business.

Maslow, Abraham H. *Eupsychian Management: A Journal.* Homewood, Ill.: Irwin, 1965.

Mason, Richard O. and Ian I. Mitroff. A Program for Research on Management Information Systems. *Management Science,* 19, No. 5 (1973), pp. 475–487.

"Mastering Diversity at GE." *Dun's Review,* 112, No. 6 (December 1978), p. 30.

Mead, George Herbert. *Mind, Self, and Society.* Chicago: University of Chicago Press, 1962.

Merelman, Richard. "Learning and Legitimacy." *American Political Science Review,* 60 (September 1966), pp. 548–561.

Merton, Robert K. "The Unanticipated Consequences of Purposive Social Action." *American Sociological Review,* 1 (December 1936), pp. 894–904.

Meyer, Marshall, et. al. *Environments and Organizations.* San Francisco: Jossey-Bass, 1978.

Meyer, Marshall. "Organizational Structure as Signaling." *Pacific Sociological Review,* 22, No. 4 (January 1979), pp. 481–500.

Meyor, John and Brian Rowan. "Institutionalized Organizations—Formal Structure as Myth and Ceremony." *American Journal of Sociology,* 1977.

Meyor, John W., W. Richard Scott, and Terrence E. Deal. "Institutional and Technical Sources of Organizational Structure." In Herbert D. Stein, *Organizations and Human Services: Cross-Disciplinary Perspectives.* Philadelphia: Temple University Press, 1981.

Mintzberg, Henry. *The Nature of Managerial Work.* New York: Harper & Row, 1973.

Mintzberg, Henry. "Planning on the Left Side and Managing on the Right Side." *Harvard Business Review,* 54 (July–August 1976), p. 154.

Mintzberg, Henry. "The Managers Job: Folklore and Fact." *Harvard Business Review,* 53 (July–August, 1975), p. 187.

Mintzberg, Henry. "The Myth of MIS," *California Management Review.* 15 (1972), pp. 92–97.

Mintzberg, H. D., and Theoret A. Raisinghani. "The Structure of Unstructured Decision Process." *Administrative Science Quarterly,* 21 (June 1976), pp. 246–275.

Mintzberg, Henry. *The Structuring of Organizations: A Synthesis of the Research,* Englewood Cliffs, N.J.: Prentice-Hall, 1979.

Mitroff, Ian and Ralph H. Kilman. "Stories Managers Tell: A New Tool for Organizational Problem Solving." *Management Review,* July 1975, pp. 18–28.

Montgomery, M R. "The Marketing Magic of L. L. Bean." *Boston Globe Magazine,* 27 December 1981, p. 13.

Moore, Sally Falk and Barbara G. Myerhoff. *Secular Ritual.* Assen, Netherlands: Van Gorcun, 1977.

Moore, Wilbert, "Some Social Functions of Ignorance." *American Sociological Review* 14 (December 1949), pp. 787–795.

Morgan, Gareth. "Paradigms, Metaphors, and Puzzle-Solving in Organizational Theory." *Administrative Science Quarterly,* 25 (December 1980), pp. 605–622.

Morris, William T. "Intuition and Relevance." *Management Science, 2* (1967), B-157–165.

Moss, Mitchell L., ed. *Telecommunications and Productivity: Proceedings of a Conference.* Reading, Mass. Addison-Wesley, 1981.

Murphy, Jerome T. *Getting the Facts.* California: Goodyear Publishing Co., 1980.

Myerhoff, Barbara. "The Revolution as Trip: Symbol and Paradox." *Annals of the American Academy of Political and Social Sciences.* 395 (May 1971), pp. 105–116.

"Nemesis at ITT." *Management Today,* July 1981, pp. 46 ff.

Neustadt, Richard. *Presidential Power.* New York: Wiley, 1960.

Nevins, Allan and Frank Ernest Hill. *Ford: Decline and Rebirth 1933–1962.* New York: Scribner's, 1963.

"The New Sears." *Business Week,* 16 November 1981, pp. 140–146.

Nystrom, Paul C. "Rummaging Through Organizations' Garbage Cans." *Contemporary Psychology,* 22 (September 1977), pp. 643–645.

OAC Digest. Proceedings of the Office Automation Conferences. 23–25 March 1981. Houston, Texas: American Federation of Information Processing Societies, 1981.

Ogilvie, David. *Confessions of an Advertising Man.* New York: Atheneum, 1963.

Olsen, Johann. "Local Budgeting—Decision-Making or Ritual Act?" *Scandanavian Political Studies.* 5 (1970).

Olshaker, Mark. *The Instant Image.* Briarcliff Manor, N.Y.: Stein & Day, 1978.

O'Neill, Dennis. *A Whale of a Territory: The Story of Bill O'Neill.* New York: McGraw-Hill, 1966.

Ortony, A. *Metaphor and Thought.* Cambridge, England: Cambridge University Press, 1979.

Ortner, Sherry B. "Is Female to Male as Nature is to Culture?" In Rosoldo Michelle, et al. *Woman, Culture and Society.* Stanford, Calif.: Stanford University Press, 1974.

Ortner, Sherry. "On Key Symbols." *American Anthropologist,* 75 (October 1973), pp. 1338–1346.

Ouchi, William G. *Theory Z.* Reading, Mass.: Addison-Wesley, 1981.

Our Story So Far: Notes from the First 75 Years of 3M Company. St. Paul, Minn.: Public Relations Department, 3M Company, 1977.
"Out for a 'Helluva Good Time'." *Fortune,* 12 January 1981, p. 15.

Parisi, Anthony J. "Management: GE's Search for Synergy." *The New York Times.* 16 April 1978.

Pascale, Richard. *3 Chief Executives: How Style Affects Results.* Stanford, Calif.: Stanford University, 1977.

Perrow, Charles. "The Institutional School," *Complex Organizations.* New York: Scott, Foresman, 1979.

Peters, Thomas J. "Doing The Little Things Well." *Efficiencies, Effectiveness, Productivity,* September 1980.

Peters, Thomas J. "Leadership: Sad Facts and Silver Linings." *Harvard Business Review,* 57, No. 6 (November–December 1979).

Peters, Thomas J. "Management Systems: The Language of Organizational Character and Competence," *Organizational Dynamics,* Summer 1980.

Peters, Thomas J. "Putting Excellence Into Management." *Business Week,* 21 July 1980.

Peters, Thomas J. "Symbols, Patterns and Settings: An Optimistic Case for Getting Things Done." *Organizational Dynamics,* Autumn 1979 (first appeared as "Change Tools for Chief Executives" in *The McKinsey Quarterly,* (Autumn 1978).

Peterson, Richard A. and David G. Berger. "Entrepreneurship in Organizations." *Administrative Science Quarterly,* 16, No. 1 (March 1971).

Pettigrew, Andrew M. "On Studying Organizational Cultures," *Administrative Science Quarterly,* 22, No. 4 (December 1979).

Pettigrew, Andrew M. "The Creations of Organizational Cultures." Paper presented to the joint Eiasm-Dansk Management Center Research Seminar on Entrepreneurs and the Process of Institution Building, Copenhagen, 18–20 May, 1976.

Pettigrew, Andrew M. *The Politics of Organizational Decision Making.* London: Tavistock, 1973.

Pettigrew, Andrew M. "On Studying Organizational Culture." *Administrative Science Quarterly,* 24 (Decemberr 1979), pp. 570–581.

Pfeffer, Jeffrey and Gerald R. Salanich. "Organizational Decision Making as a Political Process." *Administrative Science Quaraterly,* 19 (1974), pp. 135–151.

"Polaroid: Turning Away from Land's One Product Strategy." *Business Week,* 2 March 1981, pp. 108–112.

Powell, Horace B. *W. Kellogg: A Biography.* Englewood Cliffs, N.J.: Prentice-Hall, 1956.

Powell, Horace B. *The Original Has This Signature—W. K. Kellogg.* Englewood Cliffs, N.J.: Prentice-Hall, 1956.

Purcell, Theodore V. "How GE Measures Managers in Fair Employment." *Harvard Business Review*, 51, No. 6 (November–December 1974).

Putman, John J. "Napoleon." *National Geographic*, February 1982, p. 161.

Ramson, Stewart, Bob Hinings and Royston Greenwood. "The Structuring of Organizational Structures." *Administrative Science Quarterly*, 25 (March 1980), pp. 1–17.

Rowe, A. J. "The Myth of the Rational Decision Maker." *International Management*, August 1974.

Roy, Robert. *The Cultures of Management*. Baltimore: Johns Hopkins University Press, 1970.

Sampson, Anthony. *The Arms Bazaar*. New York: Viking, 1977.

Sampson, Anthony. *The Sovereign State of ITT*. Briarcliff Manor, N.Y.: Stein & Day, 1980, pp. 95–97.

Sapolsky, Harvey M. "PERT and the Myth of Managerial Effectiveness." In *The Polaris Systems Development*. Cambridge: Harvard University Press, 1972.

Schatzman, L. and Anselm Strauss. *Field Research: Strategies For a Natural Sociology*. Englewood Cliffs, N.J.: Prentice-Hall, 1974.

Schein, E. "On Organizational Culture." Research paper, MIT Sloan School of Management, June 1981.

Schisgall, Oscar. *Eyes on Tomorrow*. New York: Doubleday/Ferguson, 1981.

Schon, Donald A. "Generative Metaphor & Social Policy." In *Metphaor and Thought*. Ed. A. Oroney. Cambridge, England: Cambridge University Press, 1979.

Schwartz, Howard & Davis, M. Stanley. "Matching Corporate Culture and Business Strategy." *Organizational Dynamics*, Summer 1981.

Selznick, Philip. *TVA and the Grass Roots*. Berkeley: University of California Press, 1949.

Selznick, Philip. "Conclusion." *Leadership in Administration*. New York: Harper & Row, 1957.

Shakin, Bernard. "Bet on People." *Barron's*, 14 August 1978, pp. 4–5.

Shea, James (as told to Charles Mercer). *It's All in the Game*. New York: Putnam, 1960.

Shlein, John. "Santa Claus: The Myth In America." *Etc: A Review of General Semantics*, 16, No. 4 (Summer 1959), pp. 389–400.

Shook, Robert L. *Ten Greatest Salespersons*, New York: Harper & Row, 1978.

Silverzweig, Stan and Robert F. Allen. "Changing the Corporate Culture." *Sloan Management Review*, 17, No. 3 (Spring 1976), pp. 33–49.

Sloan, Alfred. *My Years With GM*. New York: Doubleday, 1964.

Smith Lee. "The Lures and Limits." *Fortune,* 20 October 1980.

Spradley, James P. *Participant Observation.* New York: Holt, Rinehart and Winston, 1980.

Spradley, James P. and Brenda J. Mann. *The Cocktail Waitress: Woman's Work in a Man's World.* New York: Wiley, 1975.

Staw, Barry M. and Gerald M. Salancik, eds. *New Directions in Organizational Behavior.* Chicago: St. Clair Press, 1977.

Stead, Bette Ann. *Women in Management.* Englewood Cliffs, N.J.: Prentice-Hall, 1978.

Strassmann, Paul. "Managing the Costs of Information." *Harvard Business Review,* 54, No. 5 (September–October 1976), p. 133.

Swanson, E. Burton. "System Heroes." *General Systems.* 19 (1974).

Talese, Gay. *The Kingdom and the Power.* New York: World, 1969.

Taylor, Thayer C. "Can Ma Bell End It's Marketing Hang-up?" *SPMM,* May 1978, pp. 49–56.

Tannenbaum, Robert, I. K. Weschler and F. Massarik. *Leadership and Organization: A Behavioral Science Approach.* New York: McGraw-Hill, 1961.

Thompson, J. *Organizations in Action.* New York: McGraw-Hill, 1967.

Toffler, Alvin. *The Third Wave.* New York: Morrow, 1980.

Trice, Harrison, James Belasco and Joseph A. Lutto. "The Role of Ceremonials in Organizational Behavior." *Industrial and Labor Relations Review,* 23 (1969), pp. 40–51.

Tsaklang, A. A. "Organization Chart—Managerial Myth." *SAM Advanced Management Journal.* 38, No. 2 (1973), pp. 53–57.

"Tupperware Shares Updart." *Business Week,* 5 May 1975, p. 64.

Turner, Victor. *The Ritual Process: Structure and Anti Structure.* Ithaca, N.Y.: Cornell University Press, 1969.

Uhlig, Ronald P., David J. Farber and James H. Bair. *The Office of the Future: Communication and Computers.* Amsterdam, N.Y.: North-Holland, 1979.

Van Buren, Paul. *The Edges of Language.* New York: Macmillan, 1972.

Vancil, Richard F. *Decentralization: Ambiguity By Design.* Homewood, Ill.: Dow Jones-Irwin, 1978.

Warner, W. Lloyd. *The Living and the Dead: A Study of the Symbolic Life of Americans.* New Haven: Yale University Press, 1959.

Warwick, Donald P. *A Theory of Public Bureaucracy: Politics, Personality, and Organization in the State Department.* Cambridge: Harvard University Press, 1978.

Waterman, Robert H. Jr. et al. "Structure in Not Organization." *Business Horizons,* June 1980.

Webb, Eugene et. al. *Unobtrusive Measures: Non-Reactive Research in the Social Sciences.*

Weick, Karl. "Educational Organizations as Loosely Coupled Systems." *Administrative Science Quarterly,* 21 (March 1976).

Weick, Karl. "On Repunctuating the Problem of Organizational Effectiveness." Unpublished Manuscript, Cornell University, n.d.

Weick, Karl. "The Spines of Leadership." *Leadership: Where Else Do We Go?* Durham, N.C.: Duke University Press, 1978.

Weinshall, T. D. *Culture and Management.* London: Penguin, 1977.

Weissberg, Robert. "Political Efficacy and Political Illusion." *Journal of Politics,* 37, No. 2 (May 1975), pp. 469–487.

Welser, Max. *Theory of Social and Economic Organizations.* New York: Macmillan, 1947.

Westerland, Gunnar and Sven-Erick Sjostrand. *Organizational Myths.* New York: Harper & Row, 1978.

"What Makes Tandem Run." *Business Week,* 14 July 1980, p. 73.

Whitehead, Alfred North. *Symbolism: Its Meaning and Effect.* New York: Macmillan, 1927.

Wilkins, A. and J. Martin. *Organizational Legends.* Research paper. Graduate School of Business, Stanford University, 1979.

Wright, Patrick. *On A Clear Day You Can See General Motors.* Grosse Point, Mich.: Wright Enterprises, 1979.

Zald, Mayer N. and Patricia Denton. "From Evangelism to General Service: The Transformation of the YMCA." *Administrative Science Quarterly,* 8 (September 1963), pp. 214–234.

Zald, Mayer N. "Politics and Symbols: A Review Article." *Sociological Quarterly,* 7 (Winter 1966).

Chapter Notes

Chapter 1

1. For general background on organization cultures, refer to Andrew M. Pettigrew, "On Studying Organizational Cultures," *Administrative Science Quarterly,* December 1979; "The Creations of Organizational Cultures," paper presented to the joint Eiasm-Dansk Management Center Research Seminar on Entrepreneurs and the Process of Institution Building Copenhagen, 18–20 May 1976; "Understanding Organizational Cultures," *Administrative Science Quarterly,* December 1979; and Meryl Reis Louis, A Cultural Perspective on Organizations," unpublished paper, Naval Post Graduate School, 1980.

2. The NCR story was taken from S. C. Allyn, *My Half Century at NCR* (New York: McGraw-Hill, 1967).

3. Marvin Bower's definition of culture was taken, with some poetic license, from his book *The Will to Manage* (New York: McGraw-Hill 1966).

4. The primary source we have used for general input on the beliefs and values of many companies—IBM, GE, DuPont, P&G, etc.—are company publications and statements, particularly annual reports, quarterly statements, internal magazines, and speeches to analysts published in the *Wall Street Transcript.*

5. Our ideas originated in research on educational organizations, as well as in businesses. A major tributary to our work was the research of The Environment for Teaching program, Stanford's Educational Center for Research and Development in Teaching (now The Center for Research at

Stanford). A five-year, large-scale study of school districts found that organizational structures do not always serve their intended purposes. This opened the possibility of considering organizational phenomena as symbolic. Relevant articles include:

John Meyer and Brian Rowan, "Institutionalized Organizations—Formal Structures as Myth and Ceremony." *American Journal of Sociology,* 1977.

John Meyer, W. Richard Scott, and Terrence E. Deal, "Institutional and Technical Sources of Organizational Structure" in Herbert D. Stein, *Organization and Human Services: Cross-Disciplinary Perspectives.* Philadelphia: Temple University Press, 1981.

6. Edwin Land's ideas behind Polaroid's culture are described in Mark Olshaker, *The Instant Image* (Briarcliff Manor, N.Y.: Stein & Day, 1978).

7. For background on Steinmetz see *The Steinmetz Era,* a publication of the Elfin Society or John Broderick, *Forty Years at GE* (New York: Fort Orange, 1929).

8. The best work we have seen on the role of culture in organizational effectiveness is *Findings From the Excellent Companies,* an internal McKinsey paper by Thomas J. Peters and Robert H. Waterman, 1980.

9. Material on Tandem Inc. was taken from an unpublished paper based on an interview by Sue Lowe, Harvard Graduate School of Education.

10. National and regional cultural patterns undoubtedly have a strong influence on individual companies. Here we emphasize the functional aspects of the business environment paralleling the work of Paul Lawrence and Jay Lorsch, *Organization and Environment.* Cambridge, Mass.: Harvard University Press, 1967. But successful organizations also reflect other less rational characteristics of the environment. Readers may wish to consult:

Marshall Meyer and Associates, *Environments and Organizations.* San Francisco: Jossey-Bass, 1978.

Charles Perrow, *Complex Organizations* (2nd edition). Chicago: Scott Foresman and Company, 1979, (chapters 5 and 6 especially).

11. Herzberg's comments on today's alienated workforce were taken from "Leadership in a Period of Psychological Depression," *Industry Week,* 15 September 1980, pp. 54–58.

Chapter 2

1. The primary source we have used for general input on the beliefs and values of many companies—IBM, GE, DuPont, P&G, etc.—are company publications and statements, particularly annual reports, quarterly statements, internal magazines, and speeches to analysts published in the *Wall Street Transcript.*

2. For general background on the role of values in organizations, readers might refer to:

Burton Clark, "The Organizational Saga in Higher Education." In J. Victor Baldridge and Terrence Deal, *Managing Change in Educational Organizations* (Berkeley: McCutcheon and Company, 1975).

John Dowling and Jeffrey Pfeffer, "Organizational Legitimacy: Social Values and Organizational Behavior." *Pacific Sociological Review,* 18, No. 1 (January 1975), pp. 122–136.

Meryl Louis, "Organizations as Culture Bearing Milieux," *Organizational Symbolism,* Louis Pondy, et. al., eds. (Chicago: University of Chicago Press, 1980).

Gunnar Westerlund and Sven-Erick Sjostrand, *Organizational Myths* (New York: Harper and Row, 1978).

Allen, Wilkins, "Organizational Stories as Symbols Which Control the Organization," unpublished paper, Brigham Young University, June 1980.

3. The background on Joe Girard was taken from Robert L. Shook, *Ten Greatest Salespersons* (New York: Harper & Row, 1978).

4. Comments on Coke and Pepsi were taken from a piece in the 27 October 1980 edition of *Business Week,* p. 148.

5. Extensive background on the history and evolution of Procter & Gamble is available in two fine books: Oscar Schisgall, *Eyes on Tomorrow* (New York: Doubleday/Ferguson, 1981) and Alfred Lief, *It Floats,* (New York: Rinehart, 1958).

Chapter 3

1. Books on corporate heroes abound—although judging from withdrawal cards at the Baker Library of the Harvard Business School, few now read them. Since most of these books are written about famous figures, what the authors say must be taken with a grain of salt to discount

for the hero-worshipping tendency of the authors. With this caveat in mind some of the better source books are:

Tom Watson: Thomas and Marva Belden, *The Life of Thomas J. Watson: The Lengthening Shadow* (Boston: Little, Brown, 1962).

Will Kellogg: Horace Powell, *W. Kellogg: A Biography* (Englewood Cliffs, N.J.: Prentice-Hall, 1956).

Pierre duPont: Alfred Chandler, Jr., and Stephen Salsbury, *Pierre S. duPont and the Making of the Modern Corporation* (New York: Harper & Row, 1971).

Will Durant: Lawrence R. Gustin, *Billy Durant, Creator of General Motors* (Grand Rapids, Michigan: Eerdsman, 1973).

John Patterson: R. Johnson and R. Lynch, *The Sales Strategy of Patterson of NCR* (Chicago: The Dartnell Corp., 1932).

Henry Ford: Allan Nevins and Frank Ernest Hill, *Ford: Decline and Rebirth 1933–1962* (New York: Scribner's, 1963).

Edwin Land: Mark Olshaker, *The Instant Image* (Briarcliff Manor, N.Y.: Stein & Day, 1978).

Alfred Sloan: Alfred Sloan, *My Years with GM* (New York: Doubleday, 1964).

Mary Kay: Mary Kay Ash, *Mary Kay* (New York: Harper & Row, 1981).

2. The material on Ed Carlson was drawn from Richard Pascale, *3 Chief Executives: How Style Affects Results* (Stanford, Calif.: Stanford University, 1977).

3. General academic references on the role heroes play in organization cultures can be found in:

Joseph Campbell, *Hero With a Thousand Faces* (New York: Pantheon Books, 1949).

Michael Cohen and James March, "Leadership in an Organized Anarchy," chapter 9 in *Leadership and Ambiguity* (New York: McGraw-Hill, 1974).

Melville Dalton, *Men Who Manage* (New York: Wiley, 1959).

William J. Goode, *The Celebration of Heroes* (Berkeley: University of California Press, 1978).

Carl Jung, *Man and His Symbols* (New York: Dell Publishing Company, 1964).

Thomas J. Peters, "Leadership: Sad Facts and Silver Linings," *Harvard Business Review*, November–December 1979.

Philip Selznick, *Leadership in Administration* (New York: Harper & Row, 1957).

Karl Weick, "The Spines of Leadership," *Leadership: Where Else Do We Go?* (Durham, N.C.: Duke University Press, 1978).

4. The distinction between heroes and leaders is subtle but important. Helpful discussions can be found in:

Amitai Etizioni, *Mordern Organizations.* New Jersey: Prentice Hall, 1964.

R. H. McCleery, *Policy Change in Prison Management.* East Lansing: Michigan State University Press, 1957.

William J. Goode, *The Celebration of Heroes.* Berkeley: University of California Press, 1978.

5. The distinction between born heroes and hero-making is quite complicated. For a detailed discussion about the issue see:

David L. Lewis, *The Public Image of Henry Ford.* Detroit: Wayne State University Press, 1976.

6. Material on the *New York Times* was drawn from Gay Talese, *The Kingdom and the Power* (New York: World Publishing Co., 1969).

7. For background on ITT and Harold Geneen's unique management style, refer to: Anthony Sampson, *The Sovereign State of ITT* (Briarcliff Manor, N.Y.: Stein & Day, 1980).

8. For background on the 3M Company, refer to:

Our Story So Far: Notes from the First 75 Years of 3M Company (St. Paul, Minnesota: Public Relations Department, 3M Company 1977).

"Encore At 3M," *Financial World,* 1 August 1980.

Lee Smith, "The Lures and Limits," *Fortune,* 20 October 1980.

Bernard Shakin, "Bet on People," *Barron's,* 14 August 1978, pp. 4–5.

9. For background on L. L. Bean see the article by M. R. Montgomery, "The Marketing Magic of L. L. Bean," *Boston Globe Magazine,* 27 December 1981, p. 13.

Chapter 4

1. The best analysis we have seen of the ritualistic side of ordinary organization life is James P. Spradley and Brenda J. Mann, *The Cocktail Waitress: Woman's Work in a Man's World* (New York: Wiley, 1975).

2. For perspective on three corporations where ceremonies are used as a major aspect of organization life refer to:

Mary Kay Ash, *Mary Kay* (New York: Harper & Row, 1981).

Mark Olshaker, *The Instant Image* (Briarcliff Manor, N.Y.: Stein & Day, 1978).

Liza Collins, "The Entrepreneur as Manager," interview with Lore Harp, *Harvard Business Review*, July–August 1982.

3. Material on Visa International was taken from an unpublished paper of the Department of Organizational Behavior and Intervention, Administration, Planning and Social Policy, Harvard Graduate School of Education, Cambridge, Mass., 1981.

4. The academic literature on organizational rituals is very rich; selected references include:

Gregory Bateson, "A Theory of Play and Phantasy," *Steps to an Ecology of Mind* (New York: Ballantine Books, 1972), pp. 177–193.

Albert A. Blum, "Collective Bargaining—Ritual or Reality," *Harvard Business Review*, 39, No. 6 (November–December 1961), pp. 63–69.

Joseph Campbell, *Myths to Live By* (New York: Bantam Books, 1973).

Mircea Eliade, *Rites and Symbols of Initiation* (Willard R. Trask, Translator). (New York: Harper, 1958).

R. E. Floden and S. S. Weiner, "Rationality to Ritual—Multiple Roles of Evaluation In Governmental Processes," *Policy Sciences*, 9, No. 1 (1978), pp. 9–18.

Clifford Geertz, "Deep Play: Notes on the Balinese Cockfight," *Daedalus* Winter 1972, pp. 1–37.

Max Gluckman, *The Rituals of Social Relations* (Manchester, England: Manchester University Press, 1962).

Erving Goffman, *Interaction Ritual* (New York: Doubleday, 1967).

William Gordon, "Play and Irrelevance," *Synectics* (New York: Harper, 1961).

Elizabeth Hansot, "Some Functions of Humor in Organizations," unpublished paper, Kenyon College, n.d.

Peter Manning, *Police Work: The Social Organization of Policing* (Cambridge, Mass.: MIT Press, 1977).

James March, "The Technology of Foolishness" in James G. March and Johan Olsen, *Ambiguity and Choice in Organizations* (Bergen: Universitetsfonlaget, 1976).

Sally Falk Moore and Barbara G. Myerhoff, *Secular Ritual* (Assen, Netherlands: Van Gorcun, 1977).

Johann Olsen, "Local Budgeting—Decision Making or Ritual Act?" *Scandinavian Political Studies,* 5 (1970).

Harvey M. Sapolsky, "PERT and the Myth of Managerial Effectiveness," in *The Polaris Systems Development* (Cambridge, Mass.: Harvard University Press, 1979).

Harrison Trice, James Belasco and Joseph A. Lutto, "The Role of Ceremonials in Organizational Behavior," *Industrial and Labor Relations Review,* 23, No. 1 (October 1969), pp. 40–51.

Victor Turner, *The Ritual Process: Structure and Anti-Structure* (Ithaca, N.Y.: Cornell University Press, 1969).

5. Source material on Robert S. McNamara was drawn from:

David Halberstam, *The Best and the Brightest* (New York: Fawcett, 1972).

"The War," *Newsweek,* 14 December 1981, pp. 63.

"The Administration—Department of a Titan," *Time,* 8 December 1967, pp. 22.

Shirley Hobbs Scheibla, "McNamara's Band Tour," *Barron's,* 3 December 1979, pp. 9, 26–27.

Ann Hughey, "Is the World Biting Off More Than It Can Chew?, *Forbes* 26 May 1980, pp. 122–128.

Tom Alexander, "McNamara's Expensive Economy Plane," *Fortune,* 1 June 1967, pp. 89–187.

"The Story of Robert McNamara," *U.S. News and World Report,* 25 July 1966, pp. 32–45.

"A Plea For Aid to 800 Million on Margin of Life," interview, *U.S. News and World Report,* 22 December, 1980, pp. 39–41.

6. Background on Polaroid's 1977 annual meeting was drawn from an unpublished paper of the Department of Organizational Behavior and Intervention, Administration, Planning and Social Policy, Harvard Graduate School of Education, Cambridge, Mass., 1981.

7. Source material for the case on women and minorities in corporate cultures was drawn primarily from interviews with women and minority friends and associates. Specific literature used in addition included:

Joan Ganz Cooney, "A Woman in the Boardroom," *Harvard Business Review,* January–February, 1978, pp. 77–86.

Eli Ginzberg and Alice Yohalem, *Corporate Lib.* (Baltimore: Johns Hopkins University Press, 1973).

Erving Goffman, *Relations in Public* (New York: Basic Books, 1971).

Betty Lehan Harrigan, *Games Mother Never Taught You* (New York: Rawson, 1977).

Margaret Hennig and Anne Jardun, *The Managerial Woman* (New York: Doubleday, 1976).

Claudia Jessup and Genie Chips, *Supergirls* (New York: Harper & Row, 1972).

Bette Ann Stead, *Women in Management* (Englewood Cliffs, N.J.: Prentice-Hall, 1978).

Marcelle G. Williams, *The New Executive Woman: A Guide To Business Success* (Radnor, Pa.: Chilton, 1977).

8. The collective bargaining example is from Blum (see citation above).

Chapter 5

1. One of the best sources available on the importance of the cultural network and the leadership style of one who uses it is Richard Neustadt, *Presidential Power* (New York: Wiley, 1960).

2. The definitive treatise on managerial life is Henry Mintzberg, *The Nature of Managerial Work* (New York: Harper & Row, 1973). Mintzberg's work provides the basis for rationalizing why the cultural network is so important in day-to-day organizational life.

3. There is an extensive academic literature on the role stories and story-telling plays in academic life; selected references are:

Bruno Bettleheim, "A Pocketful of Magic," chapter 1 of *The Uses of Enchantment* (New York: Vintage, 1977).

Herbert Blumer, "Society as Symbolic Interaction," chapter 3 in *Symbolic Interaction—Perspective & Method* (Englewood Cliffs, N.J.: Prentice-Hall, 1969).

Joseph Campbell, *Myths To Live By* (New York: Viking, 1972).

Julian Ford, *Paradigms and Fairy Tales*, Vols I and II (London: Routledge & Kegan Paul, 1975).

Jo Anne Martin, "Stories and Scripts in Organizational Settings," Research paper 543, Stanford University School of Business, July 1980.

Jo Anne Martin and Melanie E. Powers, "Truth or Corporate Propaganda—The Value of A Good War Story," Research paper 564, Stanford University Business School.

Gunnar Westerland and Sven-Erick Sjostrand, *Organizational Myths* (New York: Harper & Row, 1978).

Allen Wilkins and J. Martin, *Organizational Legends,* Research paper 542, Stanford University Graduate School of Business, 1979.

Allen Wilkins, "Organizational Stories as an Expression of Management Philosophy: Some Implications for Social Control in Organizations," Stanford University dissertation.

Allen Wilkins, "Organizational Stories As Symbols Which Control the Organization," Unpublished paper, Brigham Young University, June 1980.

Chapter 6

1. For another perspective on variations between cultural types, interested readers might refer to Charles Hardy, *Understanding Organizations* (New York: Penguin, 1976), or Robert Roy, *The Cultures of Management* (Baltimore: Johns Hopkins University Press, 1970).

2. While the typology we use in this chapter overstates the differences between the four cultures in such a way that no real world corporation perfectly fits any one type, a reader interested in an example that nearly fits the model might refer to:

Work hard/play hard: Tracy Kidder, *Soul of a New Machine* (Boston: Little, Brown, 1981).

Tough guy: David Ogilvie, *Confessions of an Advertising Man* (New York: Atheneum, 1963).

Bet your company: James Freund, *Anatomy of a Merger* (New York: Law Journal Press, 1975), or David Loth, *Swope of GE* (New York: Simon & Schuster, 1958).

Process: Donald Warwick, *A Theory of Public Bureaucracy: Politics, Personality, and Organization in the State Department* (Cambridge: Harvard University Press, 1978) or *Aetna Life Insurance Company: Its First 100 Years* (Aetna Life Ins. Co., 1956) or Patrick Wright, *On a Clear Day You Can See GM* (Grosse Point, Mich.: Wright Enterprises, 1979).

3. Material on a major insurance company was taken from an unpublished paper of the Department of Organizational Behavior and Interven-

tion, Administration, Planning and Social Policy, Harvard Graduate School of Education, Cambridge, Massachusetts, 1981.

4. Other related reading includes Thomas and Marva Belden, *The Life of Thomas J. Watson: Lengthening Shadow* (Boston: Little, Brown, 1962) Mary Kay Ash, *Mary Kay* (New York: Harper & Row, 1981).

Chapter 7

1. There is not a great deal of explicit literature on the subject of diagnosing culture. Most of what is published is descriptive of an organizational activity—rather than analytic. Two references that may be helpful are:

Roger Harrison, "Understanding Your Organization's Character," *Harvard Business Review,* May–June 1972, pp. 119–128.

Meryl Louis, "Surprise and Sense Making: What Newcomers Experience in Entering Unfamiliar Organizational Settings," *Administrative Science Quarterly,* 25 (June 1980).

2. One of the most important rules of diagnosing cultures is to use multiple sources of information. Some helpful clues are provided in:

Jerome T. Murphy, *Getting the Facts* California: Goodyear Publishing Company, 1980.

L. Schatzman and Anselm Strauss, *Field Research: Strategies for a Natural Sociology* Englewood Cliffs, N.J.: Prentice-Hall, 1974.

James P. Spradley, *Participant Observation* New York: Holt, Rinehart, and Winston, 1980.

Eugene W. Webb, et. al., *Unobtrusive Measures: Non-Reactive Research in the Social Sciences* Chicago: Rand, McNally and Company, 1969.

3. Chris Argyris, in particular, has studied the differences in what people say—their espoused theories—and what they do—their theories in use. See:

Chris Argyris, *Interpersonal Competence and Organizational Effectiveness* Homewood, Illinois: The Dorsey Press, 1962.

For a different interpretation of the discrepency between managers' words and deeds see:

James G. March, "How We Talk and How We Act." Unpublished paper. Stanford University, 1980.

Chapter 8

1. There is not a great deal of explicit literature directly on the subject of managing a culture of an organization. The best sources we know of are:

Michael D. Cohen, James G. March, and Johann P. Olsen, "A Garbage Can Model of Organizational Choice," *Administrative Science Quarterly,* 1972, pp. 1–25.

Michael Cohen and James March, "Leadership in an Organized Anarchy," chapter 9 in *Leadership and Ambiguity* (New York: McGraw-Hill, 1974).

Michael D. Cohen, James G. March, and Johann P. Olsen, "People, Problems and the Ambiguity of Relevance," in *Ambiguity and Choice in Organization* (Oslo, Norway: Universitetsfonlaget, 1976).

Murray Edelman, *Political Language: Words That Succeed and Policies That Fail* (New York: Academic Press, 1977).

Murray Edelman, *The Symbolic Uses of Politics* (Champaign, Ill.: University of Illinois Press, 1964).

Murray Edelman, "Political Leadership," chapter 4 in *The Symbolic Uses of Politics* (Champaign, Ill.: University of Illinois Press, 1977).

Murry Edelman, *Politics as Symbolic Action* (Chicago: Markham, 1971).

Richard Neustadt, *Presidential Power* (New York: Wiley, 1960).

Thomas J. Peters, "Doing The Little Things Well," *Efficiencies, Effectiveness, Productivity,* September 1980.

Thomas J. Peters, "Leadership: Sad Facts and Silver Linings," *Harvard Business Review,* November–December 1979.

Thomas J. Peters, "Management Systems: The Language of Organizational Character and Competence," *Organizational Dynamics,* Summer 1980.

Thomas J. Peters, "Putting Excellence Into Management," *Business Week,* 21 July 1980.

Thomas J. Peters, "Symbols, Patterns and Settings: An Optimistic Case for Getting Things Done," *Organizational Dynamics,* Autumn 1979 (first appeared as "Change Tools for Chief Executives" in *The McKinsey Quarterly,* Autumn 1978).

A. Wilkins and J. Martin, *Organizational Legends,* Research paper 542, Graduate School of Business, Stanford University 1979.

Allen Wilkins, "Organizational Stories as an Expression of Management Philosophy: Some Implications for Social Control in Organizations," dissertation, Stanford University.

Allen Wilkins, "Organizational Stories As Symbols Which Control the Organization," unpublished paper, Brigham Young University, June 1980.

Chapter 9

1. The literature on organization change is surprisingly sparse given the importance of the topic. Selected references include:

J. Victor Baldridge and Terrence E. Deal, *Managing Change in Educational Organizations* (Berkeley: McCutcheon and Company, 1975).

Marvin Bower, *The Will to Manage* (New York: McGraw-Hill, 1966).

Eli Ginzberg and Ewing Reilley, *Effecting Change in Large Organizations* (New York: Columbia University Press, 1957).

Allan Kennedy, "One Perspective on the Consulting Process," *Exchange*, 4, No. 3 (Summer 1979).

Allan Kennedy, "Ruminations on Change" *Exchange*, 4, No. 1 (1981).

Stan Silverzweig and Robert F. Allen, "Changing the Corporate Culture," *Sloan Management Review*, Spring 1976.

Robert H. Waterman Jr., et. al. "Structure is Not Organization," *Business Horizons*, June 1980.

2. The material on the decision to enter the digital watch business is taken from William Ouchi, *Theory Z* (Reading, Mass.: Addison-Wesley, 1980).

3. The MSWD case is a description of an actual consulting assignment carried out by the authors; organizational and individual names have been changed to preserve client confidentiality.

Chapter 10

1. General statistics on trends affecting the workforce were taken from a variety of government publications including: The Statistical Abstract of the United States, U.S. Department of Commerce, Bureau of the Census; Statistics of Income, Internal Revenue Service; U.S. Census Reports.

2. Background on worker motivation was taken from:

Douglas McGregor, *The Human Side of Enterprise* (New York: McGraw-Hill, 1960).

Abraham H. Maslow, *Eupsychian Management: A Journal* (Homewood, Ill.: Irwin. 1965).

Fred Herzberg, "Leadership in a Period of Psychological Depression," *Industry Week,* 15 September 1980, pp. 54–58.

Henry Mintzberg, *The Structuring of Organizations: A Synthesis of the Research* (Englewood Cliffs, N.J.: Prentice-Hall, 1979).

3. The MacRae quotation was taken from a very thoughtful piece: Norman MacRae, "The Coming Entrepreneurial Revolution: A Survey," *Economist,* 261 (25 December 1976), pp. 41–44, 53–58, 60–65.

4. A variety of publications focus on the impact of computers and telecommunications on the economy, especially in the computerization of support for "knowledge" work. These include:

Daniel Bell, in *Computer Age: A Twenty Year Retrospective,* Michael L. Dertouzos and Joel Moses, eds., (Cambridge: MIT Press, 1979).

Daniel Bell, *The Coming of Post-Industrial Society: A Venture in Social Forecasting* (New York: Basic Books, 1976).

Alvin Toffler, *The Third Wave* (New York: Morrow, 1980).

Mitchell L. Moss, ed., *Telecommunications and Productivity: Proceedings of a Conference* (Reading, Massachusetts: Addison-Wesley, 1981).

OAC Digest. Proceedings of the Office Automation Conference. 23–25 March 1981. Houston, Texas: American Federation of Information Processing Societies, 1981.

Paul Strassmann, "Managing the Costs of Information," *Harvard Business Review,* September–October 1976, p. 133.

Ronald P. Uhlig, David J. Farber, and James H. Bair, *The Office of the Future: Communication and Computers* (Amsterdam, N.Y.: North-Holland, 1979).

Charles Evans, *The Micromillenium* (New York: Viking, 1980).

5. Shortly after we had completed the draft for this chapter, one of our colleagues brought to our attention the second edition of Charles B. Handy, *Understanding Organizations* (New York: Viking, 1981), in which Handy has added a new chapter on the future of organizations. There, Handy described his idea about the federal organization—which in many respects parallels our notion about the atomized organization of the future. This book is also interesting because one chapter describes a four-cell typology of organization cultures which, while differing in detail and logic, roughly parallels our own typology.

Index